WILLS AND TRUSTS

IN A NUTSHELL®

SIXTH EDITION

SHERRI L. BURR
Dickason Chair and Regents Professor of Law Emerita
University of New Mexico

WEST ACADEMIC PUBLISHING

860 Blue Gentian Road, Suite 350
Eagan, MN 55121
1-877-888-1330

Printed in the United States of America

ISBN: 978-1-68561-189-7

Sherri Burr dedicates the Sixth Edition of Wills and Trusts in a Nutshell to her friend, philanthropist Cecilia Dunne, who passed away in 2021, a few days shy of her 94th birthday.

PREFACE

This book is designed to help law students master Wills and Trusts law and pass examination questions. It does not teach how to draft wills, trusts, or other documents. Instead, it provides an overview of basic legal knowledge. Lawyers and the general public may find this book helpful as well.

Some subjects, such as nuncupative (oral) wills and exoneration of liens, are barely mentioned while others, like intestate succession, anti-lapse statutes, disclaimers, and pretermitted heirs, are given extensive coverage because of the difficulties they present when interacting with other doctrines.

A few references are made to cases found in the common casebooks, but footnotes[1] do not appear. The book is designed to be read easily so that the student can tie together classroom and casebook discussions.

Welcome to the law of sex, greed, and family animosity. Wills and trust cases can often be as entertaining as they are educational.

SHERRI L. BURR

Albuquerque, New Mexico
December, 2022

---

[1] My deceased previous co-author Bob Mennell (1934–2013) prided himself on creating the first and second edition of this book with one footnote, which he considered sufficient. This tradition continues in this edition.

ACKNOWLEDGMENTS

Sherri Burr expresses gratitude to proofreaders Judith Schiess Avila, Dr. Sue Brown, Cheryl Burbank and Emilie McVay-Ash.

OUTLINE

TABLE OF CASES

References are to Pages

WILLS AND TRUSTS
IN A NUTSHELL®

SIXTH EDITION

INTRODUCTION

We begin our conversation about Wills and Trust law with an overview of terminology that you will see throughout this book.

The *decedent* is the person who died. When Michael Jackson moon-walked onto that great concert stage in the heavens on June 25, 2009, he became a decedent. So did Prince Rogers Nelson ("Prince") when he perished in his Minnesota residence on April 21, 2016 and actor Sidney Poitier who died in 2022.

Ancestors are individuals, such as parents, grandparents, and great grandparents, who were born before the decedent. In Mr. Jackson's case, he left behind both parents, Katherine and Joe Jackson, as surviving ancestors.

Descendants are primarily those individuals who were born to the decedent. Having been divorced twice, Jackson was survived by three children—Michael Joseph Jr., Paris-Michael Katherine, and Prince Michael II. Descendants may also be grandchildren, great-grandchildren, and so forth.

Those descendants who survive the decedent are sometimes referred to as *issue*. They are the potentially unending stream of progeny of the decedent. When Anna Nicole Smith ascended to that Reality TV Show in the Sky on February 8, 2007, she left Dannielynn Stern as her only living issue. Smith's son Daniel had predeceased her without leaving issue of his own.

Think of *collateral* relatives as those to the side of the decedent, such as siblings, nieces and nephews, aunts and uncles, cousins, and great aunts and uncles. Collateral relatives are connected to the decedent through parents, grandparents, great-grandparents and so forth. Depending on the size of the family of origin, a decedent may have dozens, if not hundreds of collateral relatives. The Bush and Kennedy families have produced presidents, senators, and representatives with numerous collateral relatives. By contrast, singer Prince left behind six full and half siblings.

The intestacy law prefers spouses and descendants over ancestors and ancestors over collaterals. For a person who dies without a will, the law will first look to distribute the decedent's estate to a spouse and children before any gifts to ancestors and collaterals.

An *heir* is a person entitled to inherit by *intestate succession*; that is, when the person dies without a will. An heir may be a spouse, a descendant, an ancestor, or a collateral relative. The individual must be related to the decedent by either marriage or blood. Friends, business partners, charities, and passers-by in the decedent's life cannot inherit by intestate succession. They may only receive estate gifts under a valid will or trust document.

Heirship is determined at one point in time—the death of an intestate decedent. No one is an heir before that time because living people do not have heirs. The heir does not necessarily receive any property. For example, the decedent may leave no property to be disposed of at his death. Any person dispose of all their property using wills or will substitute provisions, such as joint tenancies, life insurance, gifts and trusts. Gifts may be given *inter vivos* (while living). Trusts may be either established while living or as testamentary trusts set up in a will.

Heirs apparent and *heirs presumptive* are not yet heirs. They have no interest in the property of their living predecessor. Their rights are *inchoate*, or mere expectancies, like possessing a ticket in a state lottery. Paris Hilton and her sister Nikki present examples of heirs apparent, although the media constantly refers to them as the Hilton heirs.

Heirs apparent and heirs *presumptive* must survive and remain in a relationship (spouse, child, etc.) with the deceased to qualify for the inheritance. Prince Charles, as a three year old, became heir apparent to his mother when she became Queen Elizabeth II after her father died suddenly in 1952. When Queen Elizabeth II passed on September 7, 2022, her eldest son immediately succeeded her and became Charles III under British law that "a new sovereign succeeds to the throne as soon as his or her predecessor dies." Had Charles predeceased his mother, then his interest in inheriting the Crown Estate, which includes Buckingham and other palaces as well as the Crown Jewels, would have vanished in favor of his son William. Queen Elizabeth's personal property included Balmoral Castle, where she took her final breath, and Sandringham House. She had authority to distribute these as private property, although most likely left these items of realty and most of her $5000 million personal estate to her son Charles, along with some personal gifts to other members of her family.

In an example within the United States, a widowed mother of an intestate decedent will be an heir only if her son had not married and left issue surviving him. Under many intestate statutes, only when no issue survive (and sometimes when there is also no surviving spouse) does a parent become an heir.

To be *disinherited* is to receive nothing. Disinheritance can be direct in a will, or indirect by operation of law. Any person can write a will stating that relatives will receive nothing at all. The law disinherits individuals who murdered the decedent. The murderer is treated is if he predeceased the decedent and the estate is divided without the murderer receiving a share.

The *Law of Primogeniture* refers to English rules that restricted inheritance to the eldest son, such as when Prince Charles succeeded to the English crown upon Queen Elizabeth II's passing in 2022. Second and subsequently born sons, as well as daughters, were out of luck under the Primogeniture laws. Thus, Queen Elizabeth could not designate her daughter Princess Anne, son The Duke of York, or grandson Prince Harry as her successor. The Law of Primogeniture permitted ownership of land and accompanying title to be passed down as a whole from one person (the father) to another (the eldest son). In cases where there were no sons, then a daughter could inherit, such as when Princess Elizabeth succeeded her father King George VI upon his death in 1952. She was the eldest of his two daughters.

The Primogeniture laws have often left the remaining family to depend on the kindness of the eldest son. The widow was granted "dower," the right during her lifetime to one-third of her husband's lands.

The opening scene of the 1995 film *Sense and Sensibility* depicts a death bed promise a son makes to his father. "You must help them," the father tells the son as he pleads for his second family. After the father passes away, the son discusses the matter with his wife. Within a couple of hours, his planned "help" declines from a sizable monetary gift to nothing. Oral deathbed promises depend on the good will of the survivor to be carried out. No one is legally bound.

If there is no eldest son by birth or the eldest son is no longer living at the time of his father's death, then the estate will descend to the next eldest male relative. Fans of the television series and feature films *Downton Abbey* will recall the estate was set to bypass the eldest daughter (Mary) in favor of a second cousin. All was set right when Mary married her second cousin Matthew Crawley and had a son who would then be added to the line to inherit the estate and title.

Further, even if a decedent died leaving property not disposed of during life, the intestate heir may not receive it if there is a valid and effective will or payable on death clauses disposing of the property.

Dead hand control indicates attempts by decedents to manage the lives of others from the grave. They do this by placing restrictions on *inter vivos* (while living) or *testamentary* (by will) gifts. For example, a mother may give her son a parcel of land on the condition that he does not marry someone who adheres to a religious faith that differs from hers. This limits the son's choices. So long as there are many individuals within the mother's faith for the son to marry, such limitations have been held valid. A son retains the option to forfeit the gift rather than abide by its terms.

Non-Parenting Event (NPE) or *Misattributed Parentage* refers to instances where a person grows up thinking a parent is their biological parent when the person is not. This misattributed parentage on a birth certificate or other official documents is often uncovered by a DNA test. When one man asked his mother why he lacked his late father's Italian ancestry, she responded "So I had an affair! . . . Whoever thought there'd be 23andMe, for chrissakes." [*New York Times Book Review*, July 17, 2022.] An estimated 10% of individuals discover through DNA tests that they have a parent whose identity was previously unknown to them. Often the misattributed parent is the male, but it could also be a female where a child has been led to believe a person is his mother when she is not.

Any decedent may die leaving behind *real*, *personal*, or *intellectual* property. *Real* property refers to land and the items attached and considered immovable, such as a house or barn. *Personal* property items are tangible and movable, such as cars and clothes. What separates *intellectual* property from real and personal property is that the rights are intangible or non-tactile.

Intellectual property rights are obtained from using imagination or intellect to create products such as books or technology. The person who buys an ice cream maker acquires personal property but the inventor retains the right to make or license others to make the invention. The person who buys a book receives the personal right to read and dispose of that particular copy, but the author retains the *intellectual* property right to make copies and sell the book, known as the copyright or right to copy.

For example, Dr. Martin Luther King, Jr. was known to copyright all his speeches, including his "I have a Dream" speech. After delivering that speech on August 28, 1963, he mailed in the copyright registration form. Following his assassination in 1968, King's estate was valued at $66,492.29. It is now worth several million dollars, primarily because of his *intellectual* property.

Intellectual property, like *real* and *personal* property, may be inherited by intestate succession or disposed of by a will or trust.

Using this basic terminology, we begin our analysis of intestate succession, followed by sections on the rights of spouses and issue. This book contains several chapters discussing wills and trusts.

CHAPTER 1

INTESTACY

What do President Abraham Lincoln, actor James Dean, musician Prince, and business mogul Howard Hughes share in common? If you guessed that they all died without wills, you would be correct. In any given year, approximately two-thirds of all deceased Americans expire *intestate*, or without wills.

Intestate succession represents the default plan for distributing property upon death. If the person does not write a valid will, or the will or payable on death clauses do not effectively dispose of all the estate, then the law will parcel out the person's property. This will be done in accordance with the appropriate intestacy law of each jurisdiction where the decedent died or where property is located.

A. INTESTATE STATUTES

Originally, the *heir* was the intestate taker of realty, or real estate, while the *next of kin* shared the personalty, or personal property. Each jurisdiction has its own statute(s) of descent (connoting realty) and distribution (connoting personalty). Generally, these distinctions between realty and personalty have been eliminated, but a few traces remain.

Intestate statutes prescribe a specific pattern by which persons have priority to the property based upon their relationship to the decedent. Unlike the elective share statutes that will be discussed later, the intestacy statutes usually make no distinction based upon the length of time of the relationship.

In most but not all jurisdictions, a newlywed spouse is treated the same as one who was married to the decedent for 50 years. Thus a wife, like the one portrayed by Goldie Hawn in the movie *Private Benjamin*, whose husband dies on their wedding night would still be entitled to an intestate share of her husband's estate.

Further, the degree of friendliness or animosity between the decedent and the statutory heir is not taken into account unless there was an issue of abandonment or desertion. Arguing spouses, such as those depicted in the film *The War of the Roses*, could inherit from each other if they died intestate and it was not proven in a court of law that one killed the other.

Different intestacy statutes may apply to the estate of the same decedent. Under conflict of law rules, the *situs* of realty determines the applicable law. Therefore, if an intestate decedent possessed realty in all 50 states at the time of his or her death, the law of each state would apply to the parcel of realty located within it.

Personal property is distributed according to the laws of the decedent's domicile. A few courts, however, might assert jurisdiction over large items of tangible personalty that the intestate person habitually kept in the jurisdiction even though it was not his or her state of domicile. When distribution is to be made among remote relatives, the historical source of the property may be relevant, particularly whether it was derived from an ancestral connection.

In community property states, different intestate schemes are provided in many cases for community (or quasi community) property and separate property.

B. MODERN INTESTACY SCHEMES

Uniform Probate Code (UPC) §§ 2–102 and 2–103 provides examples of statutes covering intestate succession. The UPC was substantively amended or revised in 2019, with additional technical amendments in 2021. All references to the Uniform Probate Code in this book are to this version. The intestate shares come only after certain benefits are paid to the surviving spouse and (usually minor or dependent) children. These rights supersede intestacy and will be discussed in Chapter 2.

1. SURVIVING SPOUSE'S SHARE

A surviving spouse always receives an intestate share, which is in addition to the superseding rights mentioned above. The surviving spouse's share is dependent on whether the decedent also left surviving parents or children.

a. The Entire Estate

There are two situations under which the Uniform Probate Code gives the entire estate to the surviving spouse. First, the surviving spouse will receive everything if either "no descendant or parent of the decedent survives the decedent." Second, the surviving spouse will also receive the decedent's entire assets when "all of the decedent's surviving descendants are also descendants of the surviving spouse." In the latter instance, neither the decedent nor the surviving spouse had children from another relationship. Under both scenarios, if the decedent left an estate valued at $600,000, the surviving spouse would take all $600,000.

b. Portion of the Estate

If either the decedent or the surviving spouse had children with another partner or the decedent left a surviving parent, then the 2019 revised Uniform Probate Code gives the surviving spouse the first $150,000 to $300,000 and a portion of the balance. All dollar figures may be adjusted for inflation in various jurisdictions. What remains will be shared with decedent's children or parents if there are no children.

i. Decedent Leaves a Parent

The surviving spouse receives the first $300,000 plus three-fourths of the balance if only a parent survives the decedent but descendants do not. For example, if the decedent left an estate valued at $600,000, the surviving spouse would receive $525,000 ($300,000 plus $225,000) and the parent(s) would take the balance of $75,000, which is one-eighth or 12.5% of the estate.

ii. Decedent Leaves Stepchildren

The surviving spouse receives the first $225,000 plus one-half of the balance if the surviving spouse has one or more children who are not descendants of the decedent. These are the decedent's stepchildren, and they may only inherit under certain circumstances. The surviving spouse may also share children with the decedent, and may have children from a prior relationship who became the decedent's stepchildren. If the decedent left an estate valued at $600,000, the surviving spouse would receive the first $225,000 plus an additional $187,500 for a total of $412,500. This would leave a total of $187,500 for the descendants of the decedent, which would be both his or her children before marriage to the surviving spouse and any children shared with the surviving spouse.

iii. Decedent Leaves Children from a Prior Relationship

If the decedent left one or more children who are not related to the surviving spouse, the surviving spouse receives the first $150,000 plus one-half the balance. With an estate valued at $600,000, the surviving spouse would receive only $375,000 ($150,000 plus half of $450,000) and the decedent's children would share $225,000. The purpose of the scheme is to recognize that the decedent's children who are not related to the surviving spouse could be eventually disinherited should a surviving spouse choose to favor his or her children by another partner. Think about the fairy tale *Cinderella*, where the stepmother turned the decedent's surviving child into a servant. This Uniform Probate Code provision is designed to avoid such outcomes where the decedent's surviving child becomes penniless.

2. DESCENDANTS

The descendants or the parents will share the balance of the estate after the surviving spouse receives his or her share. Surviving children usually take equal shares of the estate. Other descendants, such as grandchildren or great-grandchildren, take by right of representation. That is, they represent their deceased parent or grandparent. If there is only one descendant, he or she takes the entire portion. If there are no descendants living, then parents are favored to inherit the balance of the decedent's estate after the surviving spouse receives his or her share.

3. PARENTS

Parents will receive a share of the decedent's estate under certain circumstances. If the decedent perishes, leaving neither descendants nor spouse surviving, the parents (or their issue) will receive the entire estate. The parents share equally if both are alive. If only the father or mother survive, then that person will receive it all.

If the decedent leaves a surviving spouse but no descendants, then the parents will take one fourth of whatever remains after the surviving spouse receives the first $300,000. With a $600,000 estate, the parent(s) will receive $75,000, or one-fourth of the remaining $300,000. Thus the surviving spouse takes $525,000 because decedent's parents receive a share.

If the parents predecease the decedent but leave issue, then their children (the decedent's siblings) will represent their parents and receive a share of the estate.

4. GRANDPARENTS

If there is no person within the foregoing categories (surviving spouse, children, parents or their issue), then the search for heir(s) proceeds to the grandparents and their descendants under most systems. One-half will descend to the maternal grandparents or their issue and the other half to the paternal grandparents or their issue, such as the decedent's aunts, uncles, and cousins.

5. COLLATERAL RELATIVES

As discussed in the introduction, collateral kin are those relatives who are connected to the decedent through parents, grandparents, great-grandparents, and so forth.

a. First-Line Collaterals

First-line collaterals are directly related to the decedent through parents. They may be brothers, sisters, and their descendants. The children of the decedent's siblings are considered nieces and nephews, whereas the grandchildren of the decedent's siblings are called grandnephews and grandnieces.

Brothers and sisters may be either whole-blood or half-blood relatives. At common law, half-blood collaterals were excluded from inheriting. The UPC and the majority of the states treat half-blood brothers and sisters the same as whole-blood brothers and sisters.

A few states vary their statutes from this general rule. In Virginia, for example, "collaterals of the half blood shall inherit only half as much as those of the whole blood." [*See* Va. Code Ann. § 64.2–202(B) (2004)]. In *Esper v. Gray*, 1990 WL 751098 (1990), a decedent left one whole-blood sibling and two half-blood siblings. The court doubled the whole-blood sibling's shares to create four shares instead of three. It gave the whole blood siblings one-half of the estate and the half-blood sibling one-quarter each. Thus, if a decedent died while domiciled in Richmond with two surviving siblings, one whole-blood and one half-blood as heirs, the court would create an extra share and the whole-blood sibling would receive two-thirds of the estate and the half-blood only one-third of the estate.

In Mississippi, "There shall not be, in any case, a distinction between the kindred of the whole and half-blood, except that the kindred of the whole-blood, in equal degree, shall be preferred to the kindred of the half-blood in the same degree." [*See* Miss. Code Ann. § 91–1–5 (2004)]. In a scenario with a decedent leaving one whole-blood sibling and one half-blood sibling, the whole-blood relative of a decedent domiciled in Mississippi would take the entire estate leaving the half-blood sibling with nothing. In *Scott v. Terry*, 37 Miss. 65 (Err. & App. 1859), all whole-blood brothers and sisters had predeceased the decedent and the court awarded the estate to a whole-blood nephew to the exclusion of the decedent's half-blood brothers. Over 100 ye… in *Jones v. Stubbs*, 434 So.2d 1362 (Miss. … another Mississippi court reached a similar … when it awarded the decedent's estate to the children of his whole-blood brothers to the exclusion of his surviving half-blood sister. In both instances, nieces and nephews represented deceased whole-blood siblings and thus received the share that would have normally gone to their parents.

An Oklahoma Statute, 84 Okl.St.Ann. § 222 (2014), provides, "Kindred of the half-blood inherit equally with those of the whole blood in the same degree, unless the inheritance come to the intestate by descent, devise or gift of some one of his ancestors, in which case all those who are not of the blood of such ancestors must be excluded from such inheritance." Consider the scenario of a decedent domiciled in Oklahoma inherited land from his mother, and left only two siblings—a half-brother with the same mother (and different father) and a half-brother with a different mother (but same father). In this instance, only the sibling with the same mother would inherit. The half-brother with the different mother would be excluded from inheriting the land through intestate succession.

b. Second and Third-Line Collaterals

Second-line collaterals are related through grandparents. These are the decedent's aunts, uncles, and cousins. The children of first cousins are the decedent's first cousins once removed.

Third-line collaterals are connected through the great-grandparents. These are the decedent's great-aunts and great-uncles as well as first cousins once removed, second cousins, and so forth.

c. Next of Kin

Some states trace the family tree beyond the great-grandparent level to find any kin, no matter how remotely related, to inherit. Such individuals are sometimes referred to as laughing heirs because they have no emotional connection to the decedent and thus may burst into laughter upon hearing of their good fortune.

d. Stepchildren

If there are no blood takers, the 2008 UPC § 2–103(b) permits the descendants of a decedent's deceased spouse to inherit. If the decedent had more than one deceased spouse with descendants, then they would receive an equal share of estate, or inherit by right of representation.

e. Preferences

First-line collaterals are generally preferred to second-line collaterals. This means that brothers and sisters will take the decedent's estate before aunts and uncles.

Some jurisdictions follow a degree-of-relationship system and calculate degree of kinship. This is determined by counting up the family tree to find a common ancestor between the decedent and the heir and then counting down to find a surviving relative.

For example, with an aunt as the surviving heir, one would count up one step to the grandparent (common ancestral) level and then down two steps (past the parents) to the decedent. There are three people between the aunt and the decedent and therefore three degrees of kinship between the aunt and decedent. The degree-of relationship system would prefer the second-line collateral aunt (three degrees) to the first-line collateral grandnephew (four degrees) because she is closer kin.

6. THE STATE

If there is no person who is within the preceding categories, the Uniform Probate Code and several jurisdictions have the estate escheat, or pass to the state. As such, escheat makes the state the ultimate heir.

The state may also receive the estate if otherwise eligible heirs cannot take for some reason, such as a person disclaims his or her share or kills the decedent. In both these instances, the heir is treated as if he or she predeceased the decedent.

7. COMMUNITY PROPERTY INTESTACY STATUTES

Of the fifty states, forty are completely separate property jurisdictions where the spouses accumulate property in their individual names. The discussion above about modern intestacy statutes applies mostly in these states.

In community property jurisdictions, both spouses own an undivided half interest in each other's income and property acquired during marriage. Eight states (Arizona, California, Idaho, Louisiana, Nevada, New Mexico, Texas, and Washington) are known as community property jurisdictions, which treat marriage as a partnership. Wisconsin adopted the Uniform Marital Property Act in 1999, which arguably converted it into a community property jurisdiction. In 1998, Alaska, a separate property jurisdiction, enacted a statute that permits a husband and wife to elect to hold property as community property. These ten states that possess community property legislation account for approximately one-third of the United States population.

If a client resides in one of these ten jurisdictions, the lawyer must look up the state's specific intestacy statute to determine distribution. New Mexico, for example, divides the decedent's estate between community property (property acquired during marriage) and separate property (property acquired before marriage or by gift or inheritance during marriage). The decedent has the right to dispose of one-half of the community property and all of his or her separate property. If he or she dies without a will, New Mexico gives the decedent's one-half of the community property to the surviving spouse. The decedent's separate property is given one-quarter to the surviving spouse and three-quarters to parents or descendants. The surviving spouse may receive the entire separate property estate if there are no surviving blood relatives.

C. SIMULTANEOUS DEATH

At common law, a person needed only survive a decedent for an instant to inherit by intestate succession. Some disasters can lead to simultaneous death, such as when John F. Kennedy, Jr., and his wife Carolyn Bessette perished together in a plane crash in 1999 or the couples who died together in the World Trade Center on September 11, 2001. Such tragedies raise the question as to who can inherit from whom.

The common law rule led to some difficult results, particularly when modern technology was used to keep parties artificially alive. In the *Janus v. Tarasewicz* case, 482 N.E.2d 418 (Ill. App. 1985), the court resolved the dispute as to whether the wife or husband perished first after both accidentally ingested poison-laced Tylenol. The court determined that because the wife survived her husband by two days, her estate (and thus her father) received his $100,000 life insurance policy rather than his mother, who was the contingent beneficiary on the policy.

The Uniform Simultaneous Death Act (USDA), which has been incorporated into the UPC, changes the common law rule and requires survivorship by 120 hours. Had the court applied the USDA to the *Janus v. Tarasewicz* case, both parties would have been considered to have predeceased each other and the husband's mother would have received his life insurance policy.

Consider this potential scenario from the 2016 death of two prominent actresses. When Carrie Fisher (*Star Wars*) died on December 27th, her mother Debbie Reynolds (*Singing in the Rain*) made plans for her funeral. Reynolds then expired the next day on December 28th. At common law, Reynolds would be considered to have survived Fisher and could inherit from her daughter, but under the USDA she would be considered to have predeceased her since she did not survive her by 120 hours and thus could not inherit. These rules may vary by state.

D. DIVISION AMONG CO-TAKERS

If there is more than one heir, they share the estate either equally, unequally, or by right of representation, "classic per stirpes," or "per capita at each generation." If sharing equally, each taker receives the same size share. Unequal sharing may occur in situations that divide the estate between the surviving spouse and other heirs. For example, § 2–102 of the Uniform Probate Code provides a dollar amount to the surviving spouse before dividing the remaining estate in fractions between the spouse and other heirs. The other three methods are discussed in detail below.

1. BY RIGHT OF REPRESENTATION

The "by right of representation" method distributes the property among the descendants (issue) of a person who predeceased the decedent. The first generation of issue are the children of the named ancestor. Problems arise when there are deceased children who are "represented" by other descendants who survive the intestate ancestor.

"By right of representation" and its Latin form, *per stirpes,* is a method of distributing among multiple issue, usually in different generations. The concept of right of representation allows a deceased member of one generation who leaves descendants surviving until the time for distribution (usually the death of the intestate ancestor) to be "represented" by the living descendants. The gift is substitutional; that is, the share of a deceased ancestor is divided among his issue. Thus, in a prior example of Mississippi law preferring whole-blood to half-blood relatives, whole-blood nieces and nephews substituted for their parents and received the decedent's estate to the exclusion of the decedent's half-blood siblings. A living ancestor prevents his issue from taking a share even though they are in existence at the time of distribution. Thus, in the Mississippi example, if the whole-blood siblings of the decedent had been alive, they would have taken the decedent's estate to the exclusion of their issue. Remember that issue stand in the shoes of their ancestor, but only if the shoes are empty.

The following illustration shows both the similarities and the differences in various aspects of "by right of representation":

BY RIGHT OF REPRESENTATION ILLUSTRATION

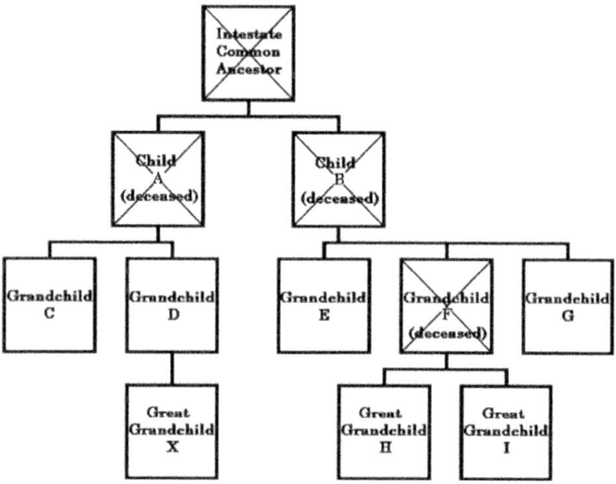

Assuming that children A and B and grandchild F predecease the intestate common ancestor and that each is survived as follows:

> A is represented by two issue, his children C and D, who are the grandchildren of the intestate common ancestor.
>
> B is represented by two children, E and G and two grandchildren, H and I, the children of a deceased child, F. Further, E and G, grandchildren of the intestate common ancestor represent, along with H and I who are great-grandchildren of the intestate common ancestor, their ancestor, B, in taking a share of the estate.

This hypothetical demonstrates why it is important to draft a family tree after someone dies to make inheritance rights visually clear to all concerned.

2. CLASSIC PER STIRPES

When all the children of the intestate common ancestor are dead, jurisdictions vary in approach and results. Classic *per stirpes* distributions start the process of representation at the highest possible level, i.e., at the A and B level of "children" even though all children are dead. This results in one-half of the estate being divided among the issue of A, i.e., one quarter each to C and D. (Note that X, having the linking ancestor still alive, cannot step into his or her shoes.)

This system was used in *Maud v. Catherwood*, 155 P.2d 111 (Cal. App. 1945). Under this system, E and G would each have one third of the one-half of B (i.e., one sixth each) and H and I would take one-half each of the one-third that F would have taken of the half that B would have taken.

The Uniform Probate Code has had two "representation" schemes. The original approach of Uniform Probate Code § 2–106, probably the majority approach in the United States, was to divide the stock at the highest generation at which there are living takers. Thus, in the Illustration, the division would be at the grandchildren level since there are no children surviving. Thus, C, D, E and G each receive one-fifth, and H and I share the fifth which F would have taken had F survived, or one-tenth each.

If there are any surviving children, the distribution is identical to the classic *per stirpes* scheme.

3. PER CAPITA AT EACH GENERATION

In 1990, the Uniform Probate Code § 2–106(b) substituted a concept called "per capita at each generation" wherein intestate shares of deceased persons are dropped down and divided equally among the representatives of the next generational level. In the Right of Representation Illustration, the Uniform Probate Code results are the same: the grandchildren C, D, E and G take equal one-fifth shares while H and I receive one-tenth each.

However, under the new "per capita at each generation" distribution scheme, the shares of H and I would change if D is dead in the Illustration, leaving X alive. Now the three great-grandchildren, X, H and I, would each receive two fifteenths (i.e., one third of the two-fifths pooled shares of the two deceased grandchildren, D and F).

E. NON-MARITAL, POSTHUMOUS, AND ADOPTED CHILDREN

Special legal issues may arise with genetic children who are born to unmarried parents, or who are born to a mother after the death of their father. Similarly, an adopted child may have to litigate to secure inheritance rights in some jurisdictions.

1. NON-MARITAL CHILDREN

At common law, the non-marital child was "the child of no one" and did not inherit from either his father or his mother. Only the child's spouse and descendants could inherit from the child. If such a person died intestate leaving neither a surviving spouse nor descendants, the estate went to the state. This could explain the urgency of the "shot gun wedding" in earlier centuries. Not only was honor at stake, but so were inheritance rights if a man failed to marry a woman after impregnating her.

Three trends have expanded the ability of a non-marital child to inherit: (a) narrower definitions of illegitimacy, (b) statutory trends toward allowing non-marital children to inherit (especially from their mothers), and (c) changing constitutional rights.

a. Expanding the Definition of Legitimacy

In a strict sense, only the parentage is illegitimate since it is the mother and father who failed to or chose not to legitimate their relationship through marriage. Nevertheless, a stigma has traditionally been cast upon the child conceived out of wedlock. Increasingly, statutes declare children legitimate when the parents marry prior to (and in some cases after) the birth of the child. In most jurisdictions, a child can be legitimated by acknowledgment (or other acts short of marrying the mother) by the father.

DNA testing can be used to prove paternity as well. Many athletes and other celebrities, such as former tennis star Boris Becker, have been sued after allegedly fathering children with women not their wives. DNA testing has conclusively proven the parent-child connection in some instances, and forced the father to support his child. Becker paid over a million dollars to support a child born to him by a Russian model after a one-time liaison in a broom closet in a posh London restaurant. Becker spent an additional $14.4 million to settle his divorce from his wife Barbara who was able to convince a court to set aside their pre-nuptial agreement.

Once the father dies, some states may grant a court order to exhume the father's body to test for DNA compatibility. A California statute, however, prohibits such DNA testing unless the father could not hold out the child as his own; e.g., he died without ever knowing that he fathered a child.

b. Statutory Trends Permitting Non-Marital Children to Inherit

All states currently have statutes or case law that recognizes the rights of non-marital children to inherit from their mothers. These laws also permit inheritance through the mother, meaning that non-marital children may represent the mother should she predecease an ancestor.

The Uniform Parentage Act, which was last amended in 2017, has been adopted in twenty-one states as of 2022. It recognizes a parent/child relationship regardless of the marital status of the parents. A father/child relationship, for example, is presumed under the Uniform Parentage Act if the father receives the child into his home and openly holds out the child as his natural child during the child's minority or acknowledges his paternity in a writing filed by an appropriate court or administrative agency. The father could, for example, sign the birth certificate when the child is born or another legal document that acknowledges parentage.

c. Constitutional Rights of Non-Marital Children to Inherit

The United States Supreme Court declared unconstitutional the Illinois statute denying non-marital children the right to inherit from their fathers in *Trimble v. Gordon*, 430 U.S. 762 (1977). North Dakota found its statute restricting the inheritance rights of non-marital children to be unconstitutional on both state and federal grounds. Thus it is now the law of the land that all non-marital children possess inheritance rights from both parents.

Consider the situation of Joseph Baena who was born to Mildred Baena and Christopher Schwarzenegger who was born to Maria Shriver, allegedly five days apart. Both Joseph (sometimes referred to as Tanner) and Christopher are the sons of Arnold Schwarzenegger who was married to Maria but not Mildred. Once a father has legitimated a child during his minority by holding out the child to be his in public, then the non-marital child is entitled to the same inheritance rights as his siblings that were born during marriage. Thus, if Arnold Schwarzenegger were to die intestate, then his non-marital and marital children would share his estate equally.

d. Disinheritance of Non-Marital Children by Will

A parent can disinherit both illegitimate and legitimate children by writing a will. Elvis Presley, for example, left the bulk of his estate in a residuary trust for his "lawful children." He also directed his trustee to pay maintenance and support for his daughter "Lisa Marie Presley, and any other lawful issue I might have." When Deborah Delaine Presley came forward in 1989 claiming to be Presley's illegitimate child, the court held in *Presley v. Hanks*, 782 S.W.2d 482 (Ten. Ct. App. 1989), that Elvis Presley's will expressly excluded her because she was not born during Presley's marriage to her mother. Indeed, he never married her mother.

2. POSTHUMOUS CHILDREN

This phrase refers to children born after the death of a parent. Children traditionally have been treated as in existence from time of conception if born alive. The normal period of gestation is 280 days or 10 lunar months. Section 204 of the Uniform Parentage Act presumes a child born within 300 days to be the husband's child after a marriage is terminated, whether by death, divorce, annulment, declaration of invalidity, or decree of separation. This is a rebuttable presumption and may be challenged by an individual with a vested interest in the outcome, such as another child who would inherit a larger share if proven to be the only child of the father. In *Hecht v. Superior Court*, 16 Cal.App.4th 836 (1993), the children of the decedent sought unsuccessfully to have 15 vials of their father's sperm destroyed to keep his girlfriend from conceiving another heir. The Court held that their father could legally devise his sperm deposited in a sperm bank to the girlfriend.

Reproductive technology that permits children to be conceived many years after the death of either the father or mother may challenge traditional notions of posthumous children. Because the gametic reproductive material of both men and women can be harvested for future implantation, children may be born years, if not decades, after the death of a parent. In at least one instance, a daughter was conceived through in-vitro fertilization twenty-two years after her father froze his sperm before being treated for leukemia. Sometimes this kind of conception delay can give rise to legal issues.

In *Woodward v. Commissioner of Social Security*, 760 N.E.2d 257 (Mass. 2002), a mother gave birth to twin girls two years after her husband died. She sought Social Security survivor's benefits for the girls. The Massachusetts court held that under certain conditions a child resulting from posthumous reproduction may enjoy the inheritance rights of "issue" under the Massachusetts' intestacy statute. The mother must show that the father consented to the use of his sperm and agreed to support the child.

In *Astrue v. Capato*, 566 U.S. 41 (2012), the United States Supreme Court clarified that there is no uniform federal rule on this matter by holding that posthumous children must be eligible to inherit from their decedent parent under state intestacy law before they can qualify for Social Security survivor benefits. Karen Capato gave birth to twins conceived from her husband Robert's frozen sperm.

He died nine months before the twins' conception and 18 months before their birth. When Karen sought Social Security survivor benefits for the twins, her request was denied because Florida law required posthumous children be conceived during the decedent's lifetime.

DNA testing also has the potential to permit children to establish paternity even after the death of their parent. Since paternity can now be proved with virtual certainty with tests readily available for purchase, some states have adopted laws to permit individuals to prove their parental connection even after the death of the decedent. In *In re Estate of Dicksion,* 286 P.3d 283 (Okla. 2012), a male was permitted to prove that he was the son of the decedent through DNA testing and was awarded a share of his deceased father's estate. The Oklahoma court said that "posthumous paternity testing is expressly authorized by statute."

In a DNA paternity test seeking to prove one of two twin brother was the father of the child, K.A.A., the court in *State v. Miller*, 218 S.W.3d 2 (Mo. App. 2007), considered additional information. The mother testified that she had sex with both brothers on the same day, but one had used a condom and the other did not. Both the trial and appeals court found the mother's testimony to be dispositive of which of the twins had conceived her child, the one who had not used the condom.

3. ADOPTIONS

Adoptions may be traditional, virtual, or motivated by inheritance.

a. Traditional Adoptions

The process of adoption results in the complete grafting of the branch from one family tree onto another tree. In other words, the child severs legal ties to biological parents and obtains legal ties to adopted parents.

Statutes may be incomplete in specifying that the adopted child shall be treated as if born into the new family for all aspects of inheritance, including by, from and through the new family and not by, from or through the old family. The following four questions may come up: (1) Does the adopted child inherit from the adopting parent?; (2) Does the adopted child inherit through the adopting parent from the adopting parent's family?; (3) Does the adopting family inherit from the adopted child?; and (4) Does the adopting family inherit through the adopted child, e.g., will the adopting father inherit from his grandchild traced through the adopted, but now deceased, intervening generation?

Most statutes resolve the answers to questions #1 and #3 with an affirmative yes. If a statute is incomplete, it is usually because it fails to specify the inheritance *through* the relationship (i.e., where the intestate or the potential heir was not directly involved in the adoption) or indicate that the rights of the old family are terminated.

In *Hall v. Vallandingham*, 540 A.2d 1162 (MD Ct. Special Appeals 1988), a Maryland court considered whether adopted children could represent their deceased birth father and inherit *through* their birth father from his brother's estate. The court answered negatively, stating that "[w]hat may not be done directly most assuredly may not be done indirectly."

Uniform Probate Code § 2–119 would have changed the outcome of *Hall v. Vallandingham* since the children in that case were adopted by the spouse of their mother. Section 2–119(b)(2) provides, "A parent-child relationship exists between an individual who is adopted by the spouse of either genetic parent and . . . the other genetic parent, but only for the purpose of the right of the adoptee or a descendant of the adoptee to inherit from or through the other genetic parent." This statute recognizes that with step-parent adoptions, children tend to maintain relationships with their biological families.

b. Virtual and Equitable Adoptions

Virtual adoptions are sometimes referred to as equitable adoptions in that the law will construe done what ought to have been done. For example, if there was an agreement to adopt and the child fulfilled her portion by making herself available to be adopted but the parent did not legalize the relationship, then a court sitting in equity may permit the child to inherit from the parent. Equity essentially enforces a contract between the child and parent by decreeing that the child is entitled to the fruits of a simulated legal adoption.

This form of adoption must be litigated to be effective for the child. Sometimes, as in *O'Neal v. Wilkes*, 439 S.E.2d 490 (Ga. 1994), the court may reject the claim of equitable adoption because the child's relatives lacked the legal authority to enter into the contract for adoption. Nevertheless, the parent is not permitted to inherit from the child because it was the parent who failed to legalize the relationship.

c. Inheritance-Motivated Adoptions

The technique of adopting a person to qualify as "issue" of the adoptor, usually for the purpose of an already established irrevocable trust, meets with varied judicial reaction. In a strict sense, the adopted person qualifies as a child. As a practical matter, the adoption is often a sham which has little substance of the traditional adoption.

In *Minary v. Citizens Fidelity Bank & Trust Co.*, 419 S.W.2d 340 (Ky. 1967), a Kentucky Court reversed a trial court declaration that Myra Galvin Minary was an heir of Amelia S. Minary. Myra married Amelia's son Alfred in 1934. To qualify Myra to inherit from his mother's trust, Alfred divorced Myra and adopted her in 1959. When he died in 1963, the trust terminated and the question became whether Myra qualified as an heir of Amelia. The Kentucky Court of Appeals distinguished its 1957 holding in *Bedinger v. Graybill's Executor* by stating the reference was to the man's heirs in *Bedinger* as opposed to the mother's heirs in *Minery*. The court concluded that Myra did not qualify as an heir of Amelia, and thus could not inherit from her estate.

Similarly, when partners in homosexual relationships adopt each other to guarantee inheritance, the law may frown. A sexual relationship is considered incompatible with a parent-child bond.

Further, the partners may break-up and sever their sexual relationship but their adoption ties remain until legally voided. This problem arose in 2007 when Patricia Ann Spado, the lesbian former partner and adopted daughter of Olive Watson, sued to be considered a grandchild of her former partner's mother in hopes of receiving a share of her estate. Although at the time of the adoption Olive was 43 and Patricia was 44 (only one year older than her adopted child), age is of little consequence with adult adoptions. Olive Watson's mother (a descendant of Thomas J. Watson Sr., the founder of I.B.M.) died in 2004, leaving multimillion-dollar trusts to be divided among her grandchildren.

In the case of *In re Adoption of Spado*, 912 A.2d 578 (Me. 2007), Patricia Spado successfully sought to vacate a default judgment that had been entered in favor of the estate's trust lawyers who had previously filed to annul the adoption as a violation of public policy and a fraud. In *In re Adoption of Patricia S.*, 976 A.2d 966 (Me. 2009), the Supreme Judicial Court of Maine declared that annulment of the adoption decree was not justified based on an alleged public policy of prohibiting adoptions between same-sex couples. The Court noted, "There are a multitude of valid legal reasons why one adult would choose to adopt another adult. Historically, adult adoptions have been recognized as a means to convey inheritance rights, to formalize an already existing parent-child relationship, or to provide perpetual care to a disabled adult adoptee."

For the trustees to succeed in their efforts to annul the 18-year-old adoption decree, they would have needed to prove fraud by clear and convincing evidence. The Court found that the trustees failed to establish sufficient facts to support their fraud claim.

As homosexuals have gained the right to marry and form civil unions, they also attained inheritance rights equivalent to heterosexual couples. This should eliminate the need to resort to adoption to guarantee such rights.

F. BARS TO SUCCESSION

Several actions by potential heirs could bar them from receiving a share of a decedent's estate. The most common are disclaiming or renouncing any claims to the estate, divorcing the decedent, committing bigamy, or murdering the decedent.

1. DISCLAIMER

Under the Uniform Probate Code § 2–1105 and § 2–1106, a person disclaiming property is treated as having predeceased the decedent. Some heirs disclaim their share of the estate to avoid tax consequences, to prohibit their creditors from receiving the estate, or to redistribute the property to other beneficiaries.

In *Drye v. United States*, 528 U.S. 49 (1999), the Supreme Court held that a disclaimer is not effective to avoid a federal tax lien. In *Troy v. Hart*, 697 A.2d 113 (Md. App. 1997), a Maryland court held that disclaimed property remained subject to a government claim for reimbursement of Medicare benefits.

2. DIVORCE AND BIGAMY

Once two individuals divorce, neither can be treated as the other's surviving spouse for intestate succession purposes. Former spouses do not take under the Uniform Probate Code or other intestacy statutes.

Similarly, spouses in bigamous relationships (those married to two or more people) may also be prohibited from inheriting. Simultaneous multiple marriages are illegal. In *Doherty v. Traxler*, 66 So.2d 274 (Fla. 1953) and *Harrison v. G. & K. Inv. Co.*, 115 So.2d 918 (Miss. 1959), the Florida and Mississippi Supreme Courts both prohibited bigamous husbands from inheriting from their wives' estates. In *Blount v. Dean*, 1 S.E.2d 653 (Ga. 1939), the Georgia Supreme Court held the husband's second marriage to be void so that he could inherit from his first wife.

More recently, after soul singer James Brown ascended to do splits in that concert hall in the sky on Christmas Day 2006, his burial was delayed for several months while claims were asserted to his estate by his alleged surviving spouse. When Brown married the woman, however, she was still married to her former husband. While they planned to remarry, they did not do so before Brown's death. Once these facts surfaced in the press, the woman then refocused her efforts on proving that Brown fathered her child so that the child could inherit along with Brown's other surviving children.

3. MURDER OR MANSLAUGHTER

If a wife kills her husband by whacking him over the head with a cast iron pot because she has grown tired of listening to the same old story (as in a scene from the TV show *Six Feet Under*), she also eliminates her chances to inherit from him. Murdering the decedent bars heirs from inheriting by intestate succession. Some states distinguish between voluntary and involuntary manslaughter and sometimes permit inheritance in the latter instance but not the former.

In *In re Mahoney's Estate*, 220 A.2d 475 (Vt. 1966), after shooting and killing her husband Howard, Charlotte Mahoney sought to inherit from his estate. She emphasized that she was convicted of manslaughter, and not murder. The Vermont Supreme Court overturned a probate court ruling that distributed Howard's estate to his parents. It remanded for a determination of whether Charlotte was convicted of voluntary or involuntary manslaughter, implying that the former would prevent her from inheriting but not the latter.

When children murder their parents, like the Menendez brothers did in 1989, they also foreclose their right to inherit. Not only did they not receive the money they were seeking, they ended up in prison. In 2015, the Supreme Court of Mississippi made an exception for a mentally ill son who killed his mother in *Armstrong v. Terry L. Armstrong*, 170 So.3d 510 (2015). The mother's other children sought to prevent their sibling from inheriting under their mother's will. The Mississippi Court held that the slayer statute did not apply in cases where the killer was determined to be insane at the time of killing, and remanded for a determination of whether the mentally ill son had acted willfully when he killed his mother.

Nevertheless, courts in Illinois, Virginia and Washington have disagreed with Mississippi's exception. They held that the slayer rule applies even if the killer was insane at the time of the murder. In *Dougherty v. Cole,* 401 Ill. App.3d 341,343, 934 NE.2d 16, 22 (Ill.App.Ct. 2010), an Illinois Appellate Court held the slayer statute applied to prevent a son from inheriting after he killed his mother and she died intestate leaving him and his sister as her sole heirs. In 2013, the Supreme Court of Virginia held in *Osman v. Osman*, 285 Va. 384, 737 S.E.2d 876, 879 (2013), that a son who had been diagnosed as suffering from paranoid schizophrenia could not inherit after murdering his mother, as proven by a preponderance of the evidence. The Supreme Court of Washington concurred with these courts when it held in *In re Estate of Kissinger*, 166 Wash. 2d 120, 122, 206 P.3d 665, 666, 671 (2009), that a son found not guilty of murdering his mother by reason of insanity in a criminal proceeding could still be prohibited from inheriting from his mother under the slayer statute.

Thus in most states slayer statutes prohibit the mentally insane who murder from profiting from their wrongdoing.

CHAPTER 2

RIGHTS OF THE SPOUSE AND CHILDREN

A. SUMMARY OF SPOUSAL RIGHTS

Certain rights have been granted to the surviving spouse (and sometimes minor or other dependent children) in the strongest possible terms: Those rights supersede both intestacy and any will that could be written. Spouses include all those involved in a legitimate marriage. In 2015, the Supreme Court decided *Obergefell v. Hodges,* 576 U.S. 644, which granted homosexuals the same right to marry as heterosexuals. The rights of same-sex couples to marry are protected under the Fourteenth Amendment to the United States Constitution. For all married couples, the probate estate available for distribution by will or intestacy is that which is left after certain determining rights. These can be quarantine, homestead, exempt property, family allowance, small estate procedures, dower, curtesy, or statutory substitutes. These rights are discussed below.

1. QUARANTINE

At common law, the widow was not an heir of realty, but was "next of kin" for her spouse's person property. She was allowed to remain as occupant of the principal house of the deceased husband for forty days after his death. The film *Sense and Sensibility* depicts the widow and her daughters packing to leave the estate of her dead husband which was to pass to his son from his first mother. She was able to keep personal property but had to abandon the real property within a certain period of time.

2. HOMESTEAD AND EXEMPT PROPERTY

While the meaning of the term "homestead" may vary among jurisdictions, it basically means the principal dwelling and adjoining land occupied by a family. Most states exempt from execution and other judicial process the principal dwelling house and certain amounts of personal property, usually clothing, furniture and equipment used to earn a living. Often special statutory provisions permit a "probate homestead" to be set aside to the surviving spouse (and sometimes to minor or other dependent children).

3. FAMILY MAINTENANCE ALLOWANCE

In addition to the other rights of the spouse and dependent children, most jurisdictions authorize relatively liberal periodic payments of cash to the surviving spouse, dependent children or both. These payments, often characterized as extensions of the duty of support of the decedent, are given priority over almost all other debts and expenses of the decedent and his or her estate.

Among the matters that prompt litigation (or need to be covered by a statutory provision) are the following: Is the amount flexible according to a "station in life" test or fixed? Must the estate be (and remain) solvent? Can the allowance be granted retroactively? Does the court consider the other assets and sources of income of the person applying for the family allowance? Are children and other issue entitled? If so, must they have been minors or dependent upon the decedent for support? The family allowance is designed as a shield to keep the family maintained immediately after the death of a spouse. It is sometimes used offensively to enlarge the share of the surviving spouse at the expense of other beneficiaries.

4. SMALL ESTATE LEGISLATION

Statutory provisions permitting persons to obtain possession of assets or take small estates without full probate proceedings are additional procedures available to the surviving spouse (and, often, the children and other close relatives). These techniques are extremely practical. In the United Kingdom, a small estate is considered under 5,000 pounds. In some states within the United States, a small state may be as much as $500,000. New Mexico, for example, permits inheritors to skip probate when a married couple owns real property as community property valued at less than $500,000 for tax purposes, or the entire estate is valued at less than $50,000.

5. DOWER, CURTESY, OR STATUTORY EQUIVALENTS

Almost every jurisdiction has some provision permitting the surviving spouse to claim a portion of the estate of a decedent despite a valid will attempting to dispose of it to others. The same right does not exist for children or other relatives except for the Louisiana *legitime* for legitimate children.

Dower is the common law right of the widow to a life estate in one-third of the realty of which the husband was seised, or in possession of, at any time during their marriage. Curtesy was the corresponding right of the husband to a one-half interest in fee simple to his wife's lands when children had been born of the marriage.

Dower and curtesy, being rights in the probate estate, only became effective when one spouse died. Most states have varied the dower provisions. The fraction of the estate has often been increased from one-third to one-half. The property affected has been expanded from only real property to both real and personal property. The time of ownership has tended to be changed from "seised during marriage" to "owned at death" with extensions to certain lifetime dispositions which are considered to be will substitutes, e.g., joint tenancy, life insurance, gifts, revocable trusts, and so forth. The type of interest given to the surviving spouse has been expanded from a life estate to a fee in most cases. The statutes usually make identical provisions for widows and widowers.

Table 2-1 compares dower, statutory substitutes and community property. For review, a life estate means the person occupies the estate only for his or her life. A fee simple estate gives the person full ownership of the property. The person can dispose of a fee simple estate as desired.

Table 2-1
Comparison of Surviving Spouse Rights

ASPECT	DOWER OR CURTESY	STATUTORY SUBSTITUTE	COMMUNITY PROPERTY
Length	Life Estate	Fee Simple	Fee Simple
Fraction	One-Third	One-Third to One-Half	One-Half
Property	Realty Only	Realty & Personalty	Realty & Personalty
Time Owned to Qualify	During Marriage	At Death and Some Will Substitutes	Acquired During Marriage & Domicile in CP Jurisdiction

As discussed in Chapter One, community property refers only to property acquired during marriage while domiciled in a community property jurisdiction. Ten states are either officially community property jurisdictions or permit couples to hold property as belonging to the community.

Two different approaches extend the resources available to the surviving spouse beyond the probate estate. First, Uniform Probate Code § 2–203 defines the composition of the augmented estate to include property otherwise disposed of by certain will substitutes. This permits the surviving spouse to elect against a broader range of property, including the decedent's net probate estate, the decedent's nonprobate transfers to others, the decedent's nonprobate transfers to the surviving spouse, and the surviving spouse's property and probate transfers to others. As indicated by Table 2-2, the surviving spouse is granted a percentage of the augmented estate based on the number of married years.

Table 2-2
Percentage of Property Subjected to Elective Share Based on Years of Marriage

0–1 years = 3%	5–6 years = 30%	10–11 years = 60%
1–2 years = 6%	6–7 years = 36%	11–12 years = 68%
2–3 years = 12%	7–8 years = 42%	12–13 years = 76%
3–4 years = 18%	8–9 years = 48%	13–14 years = 84%
4–5 years = 24%	9–10 years = 54%	14–15 years = 92%
		15+ years = 100%

Second, the concept of an illusory transfer is applied in some states, following the lead of *Newman v. Dore*, 9 N.E.2d 966 (N.Y. 1937) in which the surviving spouse was granted her forced share not only from the probate estate, but also from a revocable trust.

B. WHO IS A WIDOW OR WIDOWER?

Traditionally, a widow or widower was a person who had entered into a valid marriage that had not been terminated by divorce prior to the death of the decedent. This concept has undergone some stretching and may see further changes concerning unconventional "marriages."

Until a divorce is "final" under the applicable domiciliary law, a couple remains married for the purposes of probate law. Although affinity traditionally initiates the marital status, it is not required to continue it. In jurisdictions which employ the concept of the interlocutory divorce, the divorce is not final until a final decree is entered and it may be impossible to enter the decree after the death of one of the parties.

Normally, certain marriages are voidable while others (usually incestuous and bigamous) are void. The "putative" spouse is one who innocently enters a marriage that is void because of a prior unterminated marriage of the other spouse. In the example mentioned in Chapter One, soul singer James Brown was the putative spouse of a woman asserting herself as his surviving spouse, although records revealed that when they married, she was still married to her former husband.

In *Estate of Butler*, 444 So.2d 477 (Fla. App.2 Dist. 1984), the first wife filed a petition to administer the decedent's estate, but the second wife objected. The first wife had entered into a second marriage knowing her first husband was still alive. She claimed that he told her he had "bought" a divorce and she believed him before marrying her second husband. After the first husband's death, the first wife could not claim the rights of a widow because the court found she abandoned her marriage when she married her second husband. In this case, the court found the "second" wife to be more deserving to be called a widow since she had lived with the decedent continuously as husband and wife until his death. They had one child and adopted one child, whereas the first marriage produced no children.

The unmarried couple living together, whether of the same gender or not, generally does not have a sufficient marriage upon which surviving spousal rights can be granted. Jurisdictions that permit civil unions may, by statute, give unmarried couples similar inheritance rights as married couples.

C. PRE-MARITAL WILLS

The marital share (statutory substitute for dower and curtesy), usually is not a full intestate share. In one situation, however, most jurisdictions permit the surviving spouse to take his or her intestate share as if there were no will.

When a person writes a will, and subsequently marries without changing the will to provide for (or express the intention to exclude) the new spouse and then dies, the post-will spouse is usually permitted to take his or her intestate share of the decedent's estate. This permits revocation of the will to the extent necessary to satisfy the share of the post-will spouse. Uniform Probate Code § 2–301 provides some protection for stepchildren by preserving testamentary provisions for children born before the marriage and who are not the children of the surviving spouse.

D. PRETERMISSION (OMITTED CHILDREN)

Pretermission occurs when a will fails to provide for or show intention to exclude a protected descendant, such as a minor child. Individuals have the right to disinherit their adult children. Louisiana provides a small loophole in that it protects children up to the age of 23, or who are mentally infirm or disabled. La. Civ. Code Ann. § 1621(A) (2008) provides, however, that a parent can disinherit a child for just cause if the child has struck a parent, been guilty of cruel treatment or committed a crime toward the parent, married as a minor without the consent of the parent, or fails to communicate with a parent for a period of two years without just cause.

Usually the protected descendants are only the first generation, i.e., children of the decedent. Most of the pretermission statutes limit themselves to children born or adopted after the execution of the will. These statutes operate on the assumption that the testator would have wanted to provide for the child, but inadvertently neglected to do so.

For example, Anna Nicole Smith had written in her will that "Except as otherwise provided in this Will, I have intentionally omitted to provide for my spouse and other heirs, including future spouses and children and other descendants now living and those hereafter born or adopted, as well as existing future stepchildren and foster children." At the time she executed this document, Anna Nicole Smith had one child, Daniel Wayne Smith. She gave birth to a daughter, Dannielynn Hope on September 7, 2006. Three days later, her son Daniel passed away. Anna Nicole Smith followed him to the heavens five months thereafter. Her sole descendant survivor was Dannielynn Hope, but Anna Nicole Smith's will disinherited her. It took a lawsuit to determine Dannielynn Hope's right to inherit from her mother's estate.

The rights of the post-will spouse and the rights of pretermitted children generally operate only against a will (giving what is usually the intestate share) if the will does not provide to the contrary. In other words, they are the presumed intent of the decedent.

Uniform Probate Code § 2–302(c) gives an omitted child's share of the estate to a child living at the time that the will was executed, but whom the testator believed to be dead.

Uniform Probate Code § 2–302

(a) Except as provided in subsection (b), if a testator fails to provide in his [or her] will for any of his [or her] children born or adopted after the execution of the will, the omitted after-born or after-adopted child receives a share in the estate as follows:

(1) If the testator had no child living when he [or she] executed the will, an omitted after-born or

after-adopted child receives a share in the estate equal in value to that which the child would have received had the testator died intestate, unless the will devised all or substantially all of the estate to the other parent of the omitted child and that other parent survives the testator and is entitled to take under the will.

(2) If the testator had one or more children living when he [or she] executed the will, and the will devised property or an interest in property to one or more of the then-living children, an omitted after-born or after-adopted child is entitled to share in the testator's estate as follows:

(A) The portion of the testator's estate in which the omitted after-born or after-adopted child is entitled to share is limited to devises made to the testator's then-living children under the will.

(B) The omitted after-born or after-adopted child is entitled to receive the share of the testator's estate, as limited in subparagraph (A), that the child would have received had the testator included all omitted after-born and after-adopted children with the children to whom devises were made under the will and had given an equal share of the estate to each child.

(C) To the extent feasible, the interest granted an omitted after-born or after-adopted child under this section must be of the same character, whether equitable or legal, present or future, as that devised to the testator's then-living children under the will.

(D) In satisfying a share provided by this paragraph, devises to the testator's children who were living when the will was executed abate ratably. In abating the devises of the then-living children, the court shall preserve to the maximum extent possible the character of the testamentary plan adopted by the testator.

(b) Neither subsection (a)(1) nor subsection (a)(2), applies if:

(1) it appears from the will that the omission was intentional; or

(2) the testator provided for the omitted after-born or after-adopted child by transfer outside the will and the intent that the transfer be in lieu of a testamentary provision is shown by the testator's statements or is reasonably inferred from the amount of the transfer or other evidence.

(c) If at the time of execution of the will the testator fails to provide in his [or her] will for a living child solely because he [or she] believes the child to be dead, the child is entitled to share in the estate as if the child were an omitted after-born or after-adopted child.

(d) In satisfying a share provided by subsection (a)(1), devises made by the will abate under Section 3–902.

Pretermission is a doctrine that applies to wills in probate estates. Although pretermission may be affected by a transfer made during the testator's life (e.g., an advancement or a settlement will prevent pretermission), the doctrine of pretermission is not applied to will substitutes such as trusts, gifts, life insurance or joint tenancies.

Adopted children pose the additional dual problems of whether they are covered by the pretermission statutes and whether the effective date in relation to the will is the date of birth of the child or the date of adoption. Is a child born before, but adopted after, the date of the will covered by the statute? The answer varies according to the jurisdiction.

CHAPTER 3

THE STATUTE OF WILLS

A. INTRODUCTION

Each jurisdiction has enacted its own version of the Statute of Wills. Naturally there are conflicts in the terms and constructions of the various statutes. A preliminary issue therefore is *which* Statute of Wills applies to the estate of a particular decedent.

The validity of a will and the administration of a decedent's estate are governed by the law of the location of "immovables" (such as land and attached structures) and by the law of the decedent's domicile as to "movables" (such as personal property) Unfortunately, the jurisdictions are not uniform in determining what is a "movable" and what is not.

There is a trend spearheaded by the Restatement, Second, Conflict of Laws § 269, which temporarily suspends a party's obligation to perform during the period of impracticality or frustration, but typically does not discharge the obligation altogether, to stress variables other than movables and immovables. However, the fact remains that the nature of the decedent's property (real, personal, or intellectual) is the main test for jurisdiction. Thus, a decedent possessing realty in 50 states of the United States could require 50 separate probate proceedings, of which one would be the "domiciliary" administration and 49 would be "ancillary" administrations.

Finally, even if the involved jurisdictions can agree on what is a movable and what law, such as the law of the decedent's domicile, should apply, there may be an unresolvable conflict about which state is the decedent's domicile. The states agree that a person may have only one domicile at a time and that the domicile at the time of death generally determines the validity of the disposition of the personalty (or at least those parts of the personalty classified as "movables"), but different states may reach differing conclusions as to where the decedent was domiciled at the time of his death.

Once a court has determined itself to be the appropriate jurisdiction, the Statute of Wills of that jurisdiction must be examined. The state will generally permit one, two or three types of wills Nuncupative (oral), Formal (witnessed) and Holographic (handwritten). Louisiana offers a few additional variations that are discussed in this chapter.

The nuncupative will is declared orally. The terms and conditions under which oral wills are permitted vary greatly from state to state, sometimes limited to a mortally wounded soldier or sailor. Only a low value amount of personal property can be involved, and it cannot apply to real property.

The focus herein is on the formal will (which every state permits) and the holographic will (which are permitted in approximately half the states). Nevertheless, holographic wills may be validated in other states because of Conflict of Laws rules concerning execution of wills. Uniform Probate Code § 2–506, for example, provides "A written will is valid if executed in compliance with Section 2–502 or 2–

503 or if its execution complies with the law at the time of execution of the place where the will is executed, or of the law of the place where at the time of execution or at the time of death the testator is domiciled, has a place of abode, or is a national."

B. FORMAL WILLS

Statutes specifying the requirements for a formal will range from the relatively simple Uniform Probate Code § 2–502 through New York Estates, Powers & Trusts Law § 3–2.1. The two statutes are set forth below.

1. NEW YORK ESTATES, POWERS AND TRUSTS LAW § 3–2.1

This law provides that except for oral nuncupative and handwritten holographic wills, every will must be in writing, and executed and attested in the following manner: "(1) It shall be signed at the end thereof by the testator . . ." and "(2) The signature of the testator shall be affixed to the will in the presence of each of the attesting witnesses or shall be acknowledged by the testator to each of them to have been affixed by him or by his direction. The testator may either sign in the presence of, or acknowledge his signature to each attesting witness separately."

Under subsection (3), the "testator shall, at some time during the ceremony or ceremonies of execution and attestation, declare to each of the attesting witnesses that the instrument to which his signature has been affixed is his will." Subsection (4) requires that there "shall be at least two attesting witnesses, who shall, within one thirty day period, both attest the testator's signature, as affixed or acknowledged in their presence, and at the request of the testator, sign their names and affix their residence addresses at the end of the will. There shall be a rebuttable presumption that the thirty day requirement of the preceding sentence has been fulfilled." Further, subsection (4) makes clear that the "failure of a witness to affix his address shall not affect the validity of the will."

2. UNIFORM PROBATE CODE § 2–502

UPC § 2–502(a) requires a will to be (1) in writing; (2) signed by the testator or in the testator's name by some other individual in the testator's conscious presence and by the testator's direction; and (3) signed by at least two individuals, each of whom signed within a reasonable time after he or she witnessed either the signing of the will or the testator's acknowledgment of that signature or acknowledgment of the will.

Further, under subsection (b), "a will that does not comply with subsection (a) is valid as a holographic will, whether or not witnessed, if the signature and material portions of the document are in the testator's handwriting."

In both the formal will and the holographic will, the testator must intend that the document constitute the testator's will. Under UPC § 2–502, testator's intent can be established "by extrinsic evidence, including, for holographic wills, portions of the document that are not in the testator's handwriting."

3. ANALYSIS OF REQUIREMENTS

The requirements listed above have led to will contests throughout the centuries. While the Uniform Probate Code requirements are unlikely to diminish the number of will contests, it may reduce the number of wills defeated by the statutory requirements as the number of statutory formalities are condensed.

Uniform Probate Code § 2–503 introduced the concept of "harmless error" to save some wills that did not strictly comply with the requirements. Under this section, "the document or writing is treated as if it had been executed in compliance with [Section 2–502] if the proponent of the document or writing establishes by clear and convincing evidence that the decedent intended the document or writing to constitute: (1) the decedent's will, (2) a partial or complete revocation of the will, (3) an addition to or an alteration of the will, or (4) a partial or complete revival of his [or her] formerly revoked will or of a formerly revoked portion of the will." As of the year 2020, only seven states (Colorado, Hawaii, Michigan, Montana, New Jersey, South Dakota and Utah) have adopted this rule.

Despite the fact that contests concerning improper execution are seldom motivated by an impartial desire to improve the symmetry of the law, courts have been notoriously quick to penalize the decedent by denying admission to a will executed without the full statutory pomp. They protect the decedent into intestacy.

a. Wills Must Be in Writing

This is the basic rule, stemming from the 1677 Statute of Frauds (not the original Statute of Wills in 1540). The requirement excludes non-written wills, but does not answer the questions of what is a writing and in what language must it be written.

The written document apparently can be in any language, so long as there is someone who can translate it. The most extreme example in this area was a private code used by the decedent and explained only by his sons, the beneficiaries of the will, in an 1856 English case. In that case, there was intent to make a gift shown in English, so the amount, written in a jeweler's code, was more a matter of ambiguity than translation.

Writing materials are as varied as the imaginations and needs of testators. The written document must be affixed to a permanent surface. Letters have been held to constitute a valid will and there have been instances where courts have admitted handwriting on a nurse's petticoat, walls, desks, envelopes, egg shells, and even a tractor fender as valid wills. Hiring a plane to write a will in the sky exemplifies impermanence and cannot be probated.

b. Exceptions to the Written Requirement

A few jurisdictions, like New York, permit oral or nuncupative wills. Its Section 3–2.2(a)(1) provides, "A will is nuncupative when it is unwritten, and the making thereof by the testator and its provisions are clearly established by at least two witnesses." This will is limited to three types of individuals: (1) A member of the armed forces of the United States while in actual military or naval service during a war; (2) A person who serves with or accompanies an armed force engaged in actual military or naval service during such war or other armed conflict; and (3) A mariner while at sea. This section recognizes that where a person faces impending death, an oral may be his or her only option to put forth testamentary wishes.

Typically, such statements apply to small amounts of a property and must be made during the last sickness or in anticipation of death. In a few other jurisdictions, three people must hear the oral will and must reduce it to writing soon thereafter.

c. Subscribed and Signed at the End

The words and phrases "subscribed," and "signed at the end," is a requirement imposed upon the testator, the witnesses or both, has created problems for many wills and therefore is excluded from the Uniform Probate Code. Signature, which can be almost any act intended as a signature (i.e., act, combined with intent), is still required of the testator. A court must decide whether the name is signed wherever it is written, for example, "Will of Anna

England" or "I, Lovina Bauman" at the beginning of the will or "Bonds belonging to Helene I. Bloch" in the body of the document.

What is "the end" of the will? A literal interpretation would require the signature to be the final entry (which is often true of the witnesses' signatures, but not the testator's). The "spatial end" test mechanically searches for the signature at such a spot. The "logical end" test, on the other hand, reads the text of the will and finds the end to be at the conclusion of the testamentary provisions. (Testamentary provisions include not only the dispositive provisions, but also the revocation of prior wills and the nomination of executors.) This approach saves many wills in which the decedents exercised frugality in the use of paper by signing in margins, on reverse sides of the page, or at the bottom of a cover page to which attachments were made.

Generally, a purported will which fails the statutory test of "subscribed" is not a valid will. However, courts can ignore any language that follows the signature. The New York Estates, Powers & Trusts Law § 3-2.1(a)(1) requires the following:

> (A) The presence of any matter following the testator's signature, appearing on the will at the time of its execution, shall not invalidate such matter preceding the signature as appeared on the will at the time of its execution, except that such matter preceding the signature shall not be given effect, in the discretion of the surrogate, if it is so incomplete as not to be readily comprehensible without the aid of matter which

> follows the signature, or if to give effect to such matter preceding the signature would subvert the testator's general plan for the disposition and administration of his estate.
>
> (B) No effect shall be given to any matter, other than the attestation clause, which follows the signature of the testator, or to any matter preceding such signature which was added subsequently to the execution of the will.

Some laws thus permit courts to indulge in a presumption that material after the testator's signature was added after the signature and witnessing of the will.

d. Signature by Another for the Testator

In view of the infirmities of those who are close to death, an alternative for signature by the testator is provided by most jurisdictions including the Uniform Probate Code and New York. The procedure for signature by another is often in addition to provisions for signature by "X" (which is a "signature" by the testator); both procedures have detailed requirements which tend to be strictly enforced. The portion of New York Estates, Powers & Trusts Law § 3–2.1(a)(1) states:

> (1) It shall be signed at the end thereof by the testator or, in the name of the testator, by another person in his presence and by his direction, subject to the following:

* * *

(C) Any person who signs the testator's name to the will, as provided in subparagraph (1), shall sign his own name and affix his residence address to the will but shall not be counted as one of the necessary attesting witnesses to the will. A will lacking the signature of the person signing the testator's name shall not be given effect; provided, however, the failure of the person signing the testator's name to affix his address shall not affect the validity of the will.

These additional requirements of "presence" and "request of the testator" and the signing of his own name by a person who is not also a necessary witness to the will make this provision particularly difficult to comply with.

e. Presence of the Testator

Signing or acknowledging in the *presence* of the testator, when required, as it is in New York and many states, has led to prolonged debate about whether the presence is a strict "line of sight" test in which each person must be in view of the others or a liberal "conscious presence" test in which persons in the next room qualify as being in the presence if they are able to "hear" the testator (or the other witness, if required by statute) sign.

More difficult problems arise when the parties are connected by telephone or videophone or remote two-way television. The Uniform Probate Code eliminates this troublesome requirement except for the person who is signing the testator's name for him in lieu of an "X" or more complete signature.

f. Signing or Acknowledging

The testator normally would *sign* in the presence of both witnesses. Alternatively, the testator can *acknowledge* that a signature already made is his or her signature on the will. Some jurisdictions require that both witnesses follow the same alternative; i.e., either both see the testator sign or both hear him or her acknowledge that it is his or her will. The requirement that both witnesses observe either the signature or the acknowledgment (but not one doing each) is often found in statutory language that the witnesses observe the signing or acknowledgment "at the same time."

New York and the Uniform Probate Code both permit a liberal mixing of the two techniques to permit the additional possibility of one witness seeing the testator sign and the other hearing the testator acknowledge that it is his or her will. What must be acknowledged by the testator: Is it the testator's *signature* or is it the testator's *will*? New York says "signature"; the Uniform Code permits either. Jurisdictions vary on this matter.

g. At the Same Time

Normally, the formalities of execution are considered as one ceremony to be completed "at the same time." Some courts have extended the time to some extent under the concept that the signings are a "continuous transaction." New York is unusual in admitting that the various signings and other acts required of a formal will are "ceremonies" rather than "a ceremony." Further, New York allows an extended time (up to 30 days) to complete all the ceremonies.

h. Number of Witnesses

All United States jurisdictions require at least two witnesses for a formal will. Testator may elect to have more than two witnesses. Virginia requires three witnesses.

i. Request by the Testator

The requirement that the testator "request" the witnesses to witness his signature to his will has been carried to extremes. In *In re Hale's Will*, 121 A.2d 511 (N.J. 1956), the client in a lawyer's office to sign his will failed to ask legal secretaries to witness his signature to the attorney-prepared and secretary-presented will. The New Jersey Supreme Court set aside probate of William Hale's will, resulting in increasing the share of his estate going to his second wife of twenty years at the expense of that left to his two grown sons from his previous marriage.

j. Sign "His" Name

The extent to which the unexpected can defeat a will is shown by one case in which a will was held invalid because the statute required that the witness "sign his name" (as New York presently does) and the witness signed the *testator's* last name instead of his own. The Uniform Probate Code's appropriate response to that type of interpretation was to delete the requirement as to whose name the witness should sign, although a court could still so interpret the requirement of a signature.

k. Addresses for Witnesses

The non-essentiality of the witnesses' addresses is a sharp contrast to the mandatory language of the balance of the statute; it serves as support for the position that the remaining provisions are essential to the validity of the will.

C. WITNESSES TO A FORMAL WILL

Witnesses are required for formal wills. In jurisdictions which do not recognize holographic or noncupative wills (and in all jurisdictions as to wills which do not satisfy those requirements), the only possibility of a will with fewer than two witnesses being valid is if it qualifies as an international will or other foreign will which was valid under the laws of a jurisdiction which has sufficient connection with the will (e.g., domicile of testator, location of realty or place of execution).

The requirements to be a witness (other than being "disinterested") are not different from the requirements of a witness generally. The witness should be able to observe, understand, remember and relate the events which happened at the signing of the will. There is no minimum age for being a witness to a will, although it is common to require the testator to be an adult in order to create a valid will.

The witness's role becomes most important on two occasions: at the time the will is signed and after the testator's death at the time the will is to be proved. Generally, the focus is upon the time that the will was signed. Thus, a will is generally not invalid even though both of the witnesses are deceased or unable to testify as to the events of the execution. Some jurisdictions have a "self-proving" provision as in Uniform Probate Code § 2–504 and the International Will, Uniform Probate Code § 2–1005. In those jurisdictions, the time of the execution should properly be the only appropriate time for consideration. The timing may be a material factor in the case of a witness who is "interested" at one time, but not at another, e.g., a bequest to a class such as "my employees" which class includes the witness at the time of execution, but not at the time for proving the will.

D. THE "INTERESTED" WITNESS

There are three approaches to dealing with the problem of a will in which a necessary witness is an interested party. Older common law (and statutory posture) invalidated the entire will if a bequest was made to a person who served as a witness to it. An extreme case is *Crowell v. Tuttle*, 105 N.E. 980 (Mass. 1914) in which the court nullified a will witnessed by someone with a direct pecuniary interest in the subject-matter of a bequest. Although the interest was small, the court noted that "such an interest, however minute, will disqualify a witness." This approach caused the entire will to fail.

A second posture is found in statutes such as in Illinois which specifically state (or imply) that the will is externally valid, but invalidate the bequest to the interested witness in order to validate the will. For example, Illinois requires that

> "If any beneficial legacy or interest is given in a will to a person attesting its execution or to his spouse, the legacy or interest is void as to that beneficiary and all persons claiming under him, unless the will is otherwise duly attested by a sufficient number of witnesses . . . exclusive of that person . . . but the beneficiary is entitled to receive so much of the legacy or interest given to him by the will as does not exceed the value of the share of the testator's estate to which he would be entitled were the will not established. . . ." IL ST CH 110 1/2 ¶ 4–6.

Typically a statute of this type makes the bequest to the "necessary" interested witness void unless one of three exceptions applies.

The first exception occurs when the "interested" witness is not "necessary," i.e., he or she is a "supernumerary." An example of this occurs when a will is witnessed by three persons, one of whom is "interested", in a jurisdiction requiring only two witnesses. In that case, the "interested" witness is not "necessary" and is permitted to take his or her bequest (usually without regard to the order of signing of the will).

A more difficult question arises when two or more of the witnesses are interested. For example, suppose that T, whose heir is H, writes an otherwise valid will in which his estate is given to A, B and C, who are the only witnesses to the will. Although each of A, B and C could maintain that there are two "disinterested" witnesses as to the bequest to him or her, it is probably the better view that there are no disinterested witnesses because of the possibility of collusive action.

A second exception occurs when the bequest is unnecessary in the sense that the bequest to the interested witness does not exceed what the witness would otherwise have received. The better phrasing of the alternative is "as if the will were not established," or "if there were no will." The difference between the two phrasings is seen if the interested witness has participated in the execution of a second or subsequent will or is an heir (intestate taker).

The third exception to the statutory rule arises in jurisdictions which permit holographic wills. If the will is otherwise valid as a holograph, the witnesses' signatures may be ignored as surplus. This is really a variation upon the "necessary" witness theme.

The final approach can be found in the Uniform Probate Code, which has no specific provision to invalidate either the will or the bequest of interested witnesses. Rather, the Uniform Probate Code considers the interest of a necessary witness to the will to be a factor to be considered in determining whether undue influence (or fraud) has been exerted upon the testator.

E. HOLOGRAPHIC WILLS

Approximately half the states permit as an alternative to the formal, witnessed will a holographic will. Louisiana, having removed the "H" out of the name, refers to it as "olographic." The key requirement is that the will be in the "handwriting" of the decedent. The most lenient phrasing of the requirements is that contained in Uniform Probate Code § 2–502(b): "A will that does not comply with subsection (a) [dealing with formal wills] is valid as a holographic will, whether or not witnessed, if the signature and material portions of the document are in the testator's handwriting."

Holographic wills must be written on a permanent surface. They have been probated as letters, on a handbag, bottom of a chest of drawers, eggshell, plaster on wall, and a tractor fender. The Montana Supreme Court upheld a letter that television personality Charles Kuralt wrote to his mistress as a holograph codicil to Kuralt's formal will. [*In re Estate of Kuralt*, 303 Mont. 331, 15 P.3d 931 (Mont. 2000).]

A wheat farmer used a knife to scratch a will on a tractor finder after he was inadvertently pinned underneath and subsequently died. A Surrogate Court in Saskatchewan admitted the tractor fender into probate. [Sitkoff & Dukeminier, *Wills, Trusts, and Estates,* 210 (Wolters Kluwer: 11th Ed. 2022).]

The key requirements are that the will be in the handwriting of and signed by the decedent. Other statutes impose greater restrictions by stating that the will be "entirely" in the handwriting of the decedent and a few states require that the will be dated.

1. "HANDWRITING"

Script handwriting in reasonably durable form poses few problems. Block printing, especially if that is the style of writing commonly used by the decedent, is generally acceptable. Although most types of writing require the use of some instrument other than the "hand" itself (e.g., pen or pencil) courts have generally declined to admit documents as holographic wills when they were typed, even if that was the customary method of writing used by the decedent.

In *Estate of Hand*, 295 N.J.Super. 33 (1996), the court considered whether hand-printed, as opposed to cursive writing, satisfied the requirement that the document be entirely in the decedent's handwriting. The court noted that handwriting is required by statute for three reasons: (1) to decrease the opportunity for fraud; (2) to ensure that a testator is aware that he or she is making testamentary dispositions; and (3) to make more certain that the testator expressed only and exactly what he or she intended. Since the authenticity of printing can be tested as well as cursive writing, the court found that both printing and cursive "address the goals of reassuring that the testator's state of mind was one of knowing that he or she was doing and of guaranteeing that the testator was expressing what he or she intended." The court concluded that hand printing or block lettering satisfied the definition of handwriting and ordered the holographic will probated.

2. "ENTIRELY"

In jurisdictions which use the term "entirely in the handwriting of the decedent" the court is often faced with the question of whether portions not in the handwriting (e.g., printed letterheads or the signature of one or more witnesses or printed text or caption of a stationer's form "Will") can be ignored. A mechanical approach would allow the trimming of upper or lower edges in order to validate an otherwise valid holographic will.

It is more difficult to ignore non-handwritten material in the body of the will, such as machine-printed clauses on a form. The most extreme case is *In re Thorn's Estate*, 192 P. 19 (Cal. 1920) in which a single word, not necessary to the meaning of the will, was stamped by rubber stamp into the body of the will; the will was denied probate because it was not "entirely" in the decedent's handwriting.

3. "SIGNED"

A signature identifies the testator and authenticates the document as belonging to the testator. Almost any act performed with the intention that it be a "signature" will suffice as a signature. Indeed, the signature does not have to be in cursive, legible, or even the full or formal name of the decedent. In *Estate of Hand*, 295 N.J.Super. 33 (1996), the court clarified that a signature can be hand-printed and still validate the will. However, when one of the issues was that the signature did not contain the decedent's customary middle initial, the court remanded it for factual determination.

Problems of what is intended as a signature may also arise when the decedent has written his or her name in a spot where it may not have been intended as a "signature," e.g., at the top in a space starting "Will of ______" or in the beginning as "I, ______, hereby make my will." This problem of deciding when the writing of one's name is intended as a "signature" gave rise to the requirement that the testator "sign at the end" or "subscribe" in the formal will requirements. As we have seen, that requirement raised additional problems of defining what is "the end." Many otherwise valid wills were denied probate because of the misplacement of the signature. However, some jurisdictions will admit the will under the doctrine of substantial compliance.

4. "DATED"

The "dated" requirement can also cause problems for would-be testators. California and Louisiana invalidated countless wills by strict adherence to the requirement that holographic wills be "dated." The date must be complete—month, day and year—and can be expressed in numbers. Louisiana until 1975 did not permit extrinsic evidence to establish the exact date when a numbered date contained a day numbered "12" or less and therefore was capable of being confused with the number for the month. The date does not have to be correct, but is usually rebuttably presumed to be correct. In *Estate of Hand*,

295 N.J.Super. 33 (1996), for example, the decedent wrote the date as 9/17/96, when he actually signed the will on 9/17/95. The court applied the general rule that an error in the dating will not vitiate a holographic will.

Note that the Uniform Probate Code tends to eliminate the major "trouble" spots of statutory wills requirements. For the formal will, the "subscribed" and "both present at the same time" requirements and for the holographic will the "entirely" and "dated" requirements. The UPC has adopted the doctrine of substantial compliance permitting some mistakes to be excused if the testator substantially complied with the rules.

In jurisdictions that do not have as permissive a statute, an astonishing number of otherwise-valid wills are denied probate for failure to comply with the exact requirements of the statute. Everyone concerned may concede they were intended as wills by persons not suffering from any undue influence, fraud, duress, mistake or lack of capacity. Although courts will occasionally twist to fit within a term (e.g., ignoring as surplusage the signature of a single witness to a holographic will or accepting initials as a signature), failure to satisfy the precise statutory requirements causes the purported will to be denied probate; it is a nullity.

F. STRICT VS. LIBERAL INTERPRETATION

It is easy to divide court attitudes toward wills into two camps—strict and liberal. It is not so easy to determine in advance which attitude will control a particular situation.

The ambivalent attitude of the courts toward the preparation and validity of wills has existed as long as wills themselves. The purposes of the Statute of Wills—to eliminate fraud and undue influence and to allow people to provide in a clear, inexpensive, easy and certain manner for the post-death ownership of their property—are themselves divisible into "strict" and "liberal" purposes.

Strictness and tolerance are not matters of "majority" or "minority" jurisdictions, although the trend is clearly in favor of liberalization of the formalities for will execution. Differing attitudes are often found within the same jurisdiction, although the flexibility within a particular jurisdiction is often limited by the terms of the applicable statute of wills itself and the judicial doctrine of *stare decisis*.

G. TESTAMENTARY INTENT

Every legal act is a combination of some type of act and some type of intent. Wills require testamentary intent, the intention to make a will (*animus testandi*), and the act of making a will. While the formalities are almost always set out in a statute, the description of *animus testandi* is left for common law development. The essence of testamentary intent is that the transaction be effective at (and not before) death with no interest vested before that time.

Testamentary intent is involved in two different equations. First, we are concerned about those dispositions during life intended to take effect at death in which the formalities of the statute of wills are not satisfied. Second, we focus on those written documents that satisfy the requirements of the statute of wills but which may not have been intended to be a will. In summary, since both act and intent are required, the problems usually arise when there is intent without the act or act without the intent.

The preceding portion of this chapter dealt with situations in which the testamentary formalities did not exist. In those cases, it was irrelevant whether testamentary intent was present since there was no valid will. Now we examine situations in which the formalities exist, but intent is questionable: Letter wills, conditional wills, mock wills and sham wills.

1. LETTER WILLS

In jurisdictions which permit holographic wills, the issue arises whether certain writings were intended as wills. For example, in *Kimmel's Estate*, 123 A. 405 (Pa. 1924), a father wrote a letter to his sons in which he told them:

> I have some very valuable papers I want you to keep fore me so if enny thing happens all the sock money in the 3 Bank liberty lones Post Office stamps and my home on Horner St goes to George Darl & Irvin Kepp this letter lock it up it may help you out.

The Pennsylvania Supreme court ruled that the letter was a valid holographic will because it was testamentary in character. The words "if enny thing happens," conditioned the gift and thus made the letter a will, according to the court.

Similar language can indicate testamentary intent include. For example, "keep this it may be of use to you some day your Father" [In re Morrison's Estate, 65 A.2d 384 (Pa. 1949).] Another example inked at the bottom of a letter was, " "P.S. You can have my entire estate. s/ Harry J. Blake (SAVE THIS)" " [Blake's Estate v. Benza, 587 P.2d 271 (Ariz. App. 1978)]. The *Blake* court opined, "We disagree with the contention that the letter, on its face, demonstrates a lack of testamentary intent. Unlike the letter in the cases cited by the contestants, the one in this case is definite in its terms that Benza is to have the decedent's estate."

In *Matter of Olschansky*, 735 P.2d 927 (Colo. App. 1987), the Colorado Court of Appeals declined to admit a 1983 letter into probate in a situation where the decedent had also written a 1980 holographic will. The court held that the subsequent letter lacked testamentary intent, and that the decedent did not intend for the letter to operate as her will. The decedent had written her daughter, "Whatever is left after I'm gone is all yours." The court found that nothing in these words indicated the decedent intended the letter to be an important document to have immediate significance, unlike the letter in *In re Kimmel's Estate*, 278 Pa. 435, 123 A. 405 (1924).

With suicide notes and letters of instructions to attorneys, "this very paper" test is traditionally applied to admit documents which are deemed to have been dispositive or appointive rather than contemplating that a further document will be written. Thus a letter to an attorney stating "Please draft a will which states . . ." is not itself a will. On the other hand, a letter which states "This is my desire; it'll do until I put it in more formal style" does demonstrate testamentary intent.

In *Breeden v. Stone*, 992 P.2d 1167 (Colo. 2000), the Colorado Supreme Court upheld the probate of a handwritten will executed by Spicer Breeden right before he committed suicide. Although the Petitioners presented evidence that Breeden had engaged in a chronic use of alcohol and drugs before he wrote the note, this was not sufficient to invalidate the will on grounds that he lacked testamentary capacity.

In a subsequent Colorado case, the court in *Estate of Romero*, 126 P.3d 228 (Colo. App. 2005), noted that the testator did not need a perfect memory to have testamentary capacity, nor was his capacity restricted because he was a protected person under a Veterans Administration guardianship over his financial affairs. The Veterans Administration guardianship meant "the decedent was incompetent only as to the handling of his VA disability funds and did not mean he was incapacitated as to other matters." The Colorado Court of Appeals found the decedent had capacity to execute a will that left nominal amounts to two children with whom he had limited interaction and the bulk of his estate to his mother and sister, or the survivor of the two, from whom he had received years of love and support.

2. CONDITIONAL WILLS

There may be circumstances that cause a testator to make either a bequest or the entire will conditional upon the happening of some event. (Of course, all wills are conditional upon the death of the testator.) This ability to limit by condition is often in sharp contrast to the ability to create a will which is revoked under certain conditions. Thus, the phrasing of the determinative event as a condition which must exist for the will to arise will generally be given effect while the same event may not be acceptable as a condition upon which the will is automatically revoked.

The issue of whether a will is truly conditional often arises in the context of a self-drawn will in which the testator makes psychologically explainable rationalizations as to why he or she is writing the will: "In case I fail to return from the trip to Idaho which I am making, this is my will." The testator completes the journey successfully, retains the will and then dies.

Was the preamble a true condition or simply an explanation of why the will was being written? If the former, the condition has not been fulfilled and there is no will because of a lack of intention that the document be his or her will. If the latter, the dispositive provisions will be carried out. Courts have tended to be reasonable in determining that most supposed "conditions" are not such when the will has been retained and it appears to do more justice to admit rather than deny probate to the will.

3. MOCK WILLS AND SHAM WILLS

There are some occasions when a will, satisfactory in form and apparent intent, is not truly intended as a will. Law professors may demonstrate a sample will on a black or white board or in a PowerPoint presentation. Sometimes, individuals attempt to impress or induce action by another person by drafting a written document purporting to be a will.

In *Fleming v. Morrison*, 72 N.E. 499 (Mass. 1904), Francis M. Butterfield left a will leaving the residue of his estate to Mary Fleming and naming her as his administrator. The will was properly witnessed, including by Sidney Goodridge, Butterfield's attorney. After Goodridge signed the will, but before they parted, Butterfield told Goodridge that the document was a 'fake' will, made for a purpose. Butterfield's goal was to make Mary Fleming think that he had made a will in her favor to induce her to let him sleep with her. The court decided that since Butterfield lacked *animus testandi* when he executed the will (his true goal being to seduce Mary Fleming), the will was not valid.

The lack of testamentary intent is also the cornerstone for will contests which are based upon the equitable concept that one must intend to do a legal act as a matter of capable decision without compulsion or fraud.

H. WILL CONTESTS: INCAPACITY, FRAUD, UNDUE INFLUENCE

There are many phrasings for the factors which prevent the testator from being able to form the intention to make a will. Incapacity, fraud and undue influence are almost always included in any such list. Other terms such as duress or menace may also be used. You will note that these factors are "equitable overrides" in the sense that the courts of equity would negate an otherwise valid transaction (be it a purported will, contract, trust or other arrangement).

Among the implications that flow from the nature of these grounds of will contest are the following:

- Each case must be determined on a case-by-case approach, dependent upon its particular facts.
- The grounds are predominantly decisional, rather than statutory. Although a statute may state the name of the ground (e.g., "lack of capacity"), the development of what is capacity and incapacity has been left to the courts.
- Because there is no authoritative statement of the exact terms (cf. a statute), the definition of a particular ground will vary within a jurisdiction as it is stated and restated by its courts.
- While there is great variation within a single jurisdiction, the decisional nature of this area of the law tends to create a greater uniformity

among various jurisdictions as the decisions from one are used in the others. For example, almost identical definitions of incapacity may exist although statutes use such differing terms as "Sound Mind," "Sound and Disposing Mind and Memory" or "Capacity."

- Results are more unpredictable because of the case-by-case approach. Certainty of result is sacrificed for "fair" results.

- Common sense, tempered by the application of certain legal realities (such as the fact that persons who make wills are often ill or close to death), will generally lead to acceptable results.

- The grounds of contest dealt with here are involved only in the attorney function of will contest and not in the attorney function of will preparation. There is no language that can, or should, be inserted into a will to avoid challenges for incapacity, fraud or undue influence.

- Examinations in this area are particularly unrealistic because the number of factual details given is finite and not capable of being enlarged. In practice an attorney would continue to investigate and might discover additional facts or variations on the facts as they originally appeared.

- Discussion in an examination answer would be lengthier because of the need to examine each relevant fact with no particular fact being immediately determinative.

1. INCAPACITY

Mental derangement sufficient to invalidate a will is generally said to consist of one of two forms: First, insanity of such broad character as to establish mental incompetency generally, or, second, some specific and narrower form of insanity under which the testator is the victim of some hallucination or delusion.

In the delusion situation, the evidence must establish that the will itself was the creature or product of such delusion, that the delusion bore directly upon and influenced the creation and terms of the will and that the testator devised his property in a way which, except for the existence of such delusion, he or she would not have done. In *In re Strittmater's Estate*, 53 A.2d 205 (N.J.Err. & App. 1947), the New Jersey Court of Errors and Appeals affirmed the setting aside of a will gift to the National Women's Party. The Court determined that it was Ms. Strittmater's "insane delusions about the male . . . that led her to leave her estate to the National Women's Party." Four years after her father's death, Ms. Strittmater had written, "My father was a corrupt, vicious, and unintelligent savage, a typical specimen of the majority of his sex. Blast his wormstinking carcass and his whole damn breed."

One has testamentary capacity if he is able to understand and carry in mind the nature and extent of his property and his relationships to his relatives and those around him, with clear remembrance as to those in whom and those things in which he has been mostly interested, capable of understanding the act he is doing and the relation in which he stands to the objects of his bounty. This is often divided into the following sub-abilities:

a. Ability to know the nature and extent of his own property, although a perfect knowledge is not required.

b. Ability to know the persons who "have claims upon his bounty."

c. Ability to dispose of his property to his beneficiaries in a rational manner, although authorities differ as to the extent to which the testamentary plan itself should serve as the basis from which capacity may be deduced.

d. Ability to relate the previous three abilities to each other, i.e., to form a rational plan for the disposition of one's property to the objects of one's bounty.

The tests for general mental capacity are relatively easy to satisfy. More rigid tests would invalidate many wills because of the common tendency to postpone making a will until one is weaker and in contemplation of impending death through old age, sickness or injury. Isolated instances of unusual behavior, especially when not related to the testamentary process of disposing of property to people, probably will not invalidate a will.

A weakened state of mind may be relevant for other grounds of will contest. For example, if the issue is undue influence, the fact that the testator is of weakened mental condition tends to show the relative ease of overpowering that mental condition and imposing another person's desires in place of the testator's.

2. FRAUD

Fraud consists of willfully false material statements of fact made by the heir or will beneficiary with the intention of deceiving the decedent, which do deceive the decedent and which cause the decedent to write or change (or refrain from writing or changing) a will in reliance upon such statements.

Although fraud is essentially an equitable ground (which suggests that it should be broadly interpreted), in Wills law the fraud ground is given a narrower interpretation. The foregoing description is held to be required in all of its parts so that the will is not denied probate if a person making a false statement believes the statement to be true, or makes it for a purpose other than to deceive the decedent or if the decedent is not thereby "caused" to write his will.

The most common phrasing of the causation test asks whether the bequest would have been made "but for" this fraud. A second phrasing asks if the fraud was the "sole motive" for the gift. Partial invalidity is also possible due to undue influence and possibly because of a delusion, but generally the entire will fails for improper execution, lack of intent or a generalized mental (or age) incapacity.

Fraud is a ground to prevent the probate of a will that has been duly executed. Another application of fraud, but not involving a "will contest," is the equitable action to impose a constructive trust to avoid unjust enrichment. Thus, where beneficiaries of a purported will that was to be executed alleged that the beneficiary of a prior will murdered the testatrix in order to prevent the execution of a new will, a constructive trust for the purported new will beneficiaries was the proper remedy, not the denial of probate of the earlier will, *Latham v. Father Divine*, 85 N.E.2d 168 (N.Y. 1949).

Purportedly fraudulent wills are sometimes divided into two types: Fraud in the execution cases involve a spurious will which is signed by the testator after he is told that it is another type of document. These are generally easy cases because there is no intention to write a will. The other type of fraud, fraud in the inducement, is more difficult. In fraud in the inducement cases, there is a generalized intention to create a valid will. The rigid "but for" causation test will be applied. But for the inducement by another person, courts ask whether the testator would have signed this document.

It is also possible that the erroneous belief of the testator was the product of mistake, rather than fraud. Courts give short shrift to claims that the testator made a mistake in executing his will. For example, in *Gifford v. Dyer*, 2 R.I. 99 (1852), the testatrix believed her son to be dead and expressed to the will draftsman her intention to exclude him even if living. The court stated in dictum that the mistake must appear on the face of the will and that this would have been the will of the testatrix but for the mistake must also appear. This position sharply contrasts with claims that the testator made a mistake *in revoking* his will, a situation which calls for the application of the doctrine of dependent relative revocation to revive the mistakenly revoked will. Without strong proof, the court is reluctant to nullify the formally stated words of the decedent in order to give credit to claims by the living of what they believed the testator wanted. Similarly, mistakes in the execution of a will, e.g., the signing of a will prepared for one's spouse, are seldom rectified by the court.

Between the two points—the unremediable mistake and the fraud which voids the will—is the innocent beneficiary of another's fraud. Is his or her gift more in the nature of a mistake which will be left uncorrected or is it so tainted by the fraud that it must be set aside? Courts differ. In a non-probate action for fraud, it may depend upon whether the relief sought is equitable (constructive trust) or legal (a tort action for deceit).

3. UNDUE INFLUENCE

Undue Influence is the kind of influence that destroys the testator's free agency and substitutes another person's will for his own. Mere general influence, however strong or controlling, that does not bear on the testamentary act is not enough. It must be influence used directly to procure the will and must amount to coercion destroying free agency on the part of the testator.

The evidence of undue influence is usually a combination of factors. For example, where one who unduly profits from a will maintains a confidential relationship to the testator and is active in procuring the execution of the will, the burden is usually shifted to the proponent to show that the will was not induced by undue influence. Similarly, there are indicia of undue influence when the following factors are present:

(a) The relationship between the proponent and the decedent afforded the proponent an opportunity to control the testamentary act. (Confidential Relationship);

(b) The decedent's condition was such as to permit a subversion of his free will (Weak Condition). It is in the weakened condition of the testator that there is an overlap between undue influence and incapacity;

(c) The proponent was active in procuring the instrument to be executed (Participation); and

(d) The proponent "unduly profited" as beneficiary under the challenged will (Undue Profit). The relative nature of "undue" is elaborated on a case-by-case basis. Equally vague is the concept of "natural objects of bounty," but the exclusion of such an "object" is often balanced by "undue profit" to another person.

These factors permit several inferences to be drawn from the same facts. For example, a statement that "We were like sisters" both indicates a confidential relationship and tends to indicate that the profit was not undue; i.e., the evidence could be used by either side in the will contest. In some cases, the courts have deduced a confidential relationship from the act of requesting the person to assist in the preparation of the will, but this seems to be an unwarranted blending of the elements.

A more difficult area is the attribution of the action of a participant to another who is the beneficiary, e.g., a father influences testatrix to devise her estate to his son, or a wife induces the bequest by her mother-in-law to her son. Generally, the courts have been reluctant to attribute to a beneficiary the exertion of undue influence by a non-beneficiary. A possible exception is action by members (including clergymen) of a church to induce devises to the church.

A few states, such as Florida, still have Mortmain statutes that restrict bequests to charities to a certain percent of the estate or if the will is made at a time close to death. This is an ancient doctrine to alleviate potential undue influence by charities. To stop the Catholic Church from inheriting certain lands, King Edward I enacted "The Statutes of Mortmain" in 1279 and 1290. These enactments stated that "No land shall be given nor used in Mortmain" and made it illegal for the Catholic

Church to own gifted property and illegal for English landowners to give their property to the Catholic Church. Most states follow the Uniform Probate Code practice of having no specific provision that limits gifts to charities, although attorneys can still allege undue influence with specific facts.

CHAPTER 4
REVOKING AND CHANGING WILLS

A. REVOCABILITY

The essential characteristics of a will are that a will is secret, ambulatory and revocable during the testator's life time. The testator is free to keep the contents to himself or herself during his or her life, and can continue to acquire property long after the will is executed. A will can convey property in several jurisdictions. It can also be revoked or its contents changed at any point up until the testator's death or loss of testamentary capacity.

Revocation must happen in accordance with the statutes to be legal. All states permit revocation by either (1) a subsequent writing; or (2) a physical act such as destroying, obliterating, or burning the will. The Uniform Probate Code § 2–507 requires that any act performed by the testator be accompanied with intent. If the testator accidentally shreds her will in a pile of other papers, then she has not revoked her will. The contents can be proven with extrinsic evidence such as a copy kept in her lawyer's office.

In Elvis Presley's will dated 3 March 1977, the first paragraph states:

> I, Elvis A. Presley, a resident and citizen of Shelby County, Tennessee, being of sound mind and disposing memory, do hereby make, publish and declare this instrument to be my last will and testament, hereby revoking any and all wills and codicils by me at any time heretofore made.

This clause is a typical first clause in a Last Will and Testament. It makes clear that this document is not an attempt to supplement or add to a previous document or documents, but rather to revoke all previous documents.

You cannot set up a provision in a will to revoke it conditioned upon the occurring of some event. This may be treated as a nullity because it is an attempt to revoke the will in a manner not specified in the applicable statute. Similarly, even though a testator contractually promises not to revoke his or her will, he or she still has the power to revoke the will. Such a revocation can make the testator liable for a breach of the contract and a constructive trust might be imposed upon the takers of the estate to satisfy the contractual terms.

B. INTENTIONAL REVOCATIONS

Revocations are either intentional or by operation of law. All intentional revocations require that there be *animus revocandi*. In order to form this intention, there must be the same capacity and freedom from undue influence and fraud as is necessary to execute a will.

The acts which comprise a valid revocation are typically set out in a statute such as the following:

Uniform Probate Code § 2–507

(a) A will or any part thereof is revoked:

(1) by executing a subsequent will that revokes the previous will or part expressly or by inconsistency; or

(2) by performing a revocatory act on the will, if the testator performed the act with the intent and for the purpose of revoking the will or part or if another individual performed the act in the testator's conscious presence and by the testator's direction. For purposes of this paragraph, "revocatory act on the will" includes burning, tearing, canceling, obliterating, or destroying the will or any part of it. A burning, tearing, or canceling is a "revocatory act on the will," whether or not the burn, tear, or cancellation touched any of the words on the will.

(b) If a subsequent will does not expressly revoke a previous will, the execution of the subsequent will wholly revokes the previous will by inconsistency if the testator intended the subsequent will to replace rather than supplement the previous will.

(c) The testator is presumed to have intended a subsequent will to replace rather than supplement a previous will if the subsequent will makes a complete disposition of the testator's estate. If this presumption arises and is not rebutted by clear and convincing evidence, the previous will is revoked; only the subsequent will is operative on the testator's death.

(d) The testator is presumed to have intended a subsequent will to supplement rather than replace a previous will if the subsequent will does not make a complete disposition of the testator's estate. If this presumption arises and is not rebutted by clear and convincing evidence, the subsequent will revokes the previous will only to the extent the subsequent will is inconsistent with the previous will; each will is fully operative on the testator's death to the extent they are not inconsistent.

The code section therefore provides two alternate categories of revocation: writing and revocatory act. Within each category there are sub-categories: Written revocations can be express or implied. The first paragraph in Elvis' will is an example of an express revocation. Revocatory acts include burning, tearing, canceling, obliterating or destroying.

C. REVOCATION BY WRITING: EXPRESS AND IMPLIED

The statute concerning revocation may require interpretation as to what type of "writing" is sufficient as a revocation. If the statute permitted *any* type of writing, the testamentary formalities need not be complied with. If a "will" is required the question arises whether a codicil, or supplement, is included. The Uniform Probate Code answers the problem by defining "will" in § 1–201(57) to include codicils "and any testamentary instrument that merely appoints an executor, revokes or revises another will, nominates a guardian, or expressly excludes or limits the rights of an individual or class to succeed to property of the decedent passing by intestate succession."

Express revocations seldom present difficulties unless they are ambiguous or encounter the doctrine of dependent relative revocation. The revocation could be hopelessly ambiguous, such as writing that "I revoke some, but not all, of my prior will." The revocation may be ambiguous to the point where it resolves nothing, such as writing, "To the extent this disposition is inconsistent with my earlier disposition, the earlier disposition is revoked."

Implied revocations are involved only when there is no express written revocation. As a practical matter, wills drafted by attorneys traditionally include an express revocation of prior wills, such as in Elvis Presley's will, but such a clause only states what would occur in any case because of the inconsistency in the dispositions.

Without an express revocation clause in a subsequent testamentary document, the prior will is not wholly revoked, and thus usually becomes a codicil to the prior will. Only if the subsequent testamentary document is wholly inconsistent with the old will does it become the single new will. Thus, the reference to the "Last" will is the first to be examined to determine if indeed the document does revoke all prior dispositions by implication.

When is a subsequent disposition "inconsistent"? Some cases are easy, such as disposition of the same unique personal or real property to different persons or different dispositions of the residue of the estate. Other cases are difficult. For example, A's first will makes a bequest of $5,000 to B. Subsequently, another testamentary document (obviously containing no express revocation clause) makes a bequest of $10,000 to B without mentioning the prior bequest. Is the second bequest "inconsistent" with the first? Does B receive $10,000 or $15,000? Is the second bequest "substitutional" or "supplementary"? Obviously, the intent of the testator is controlling, so no absolute answer is possible, but what presumption should prevail in the absence of evidence to the contrary? Jurisdictions differ.

More as a matter of semantics than practical value is the distinction between an equitable inconsistency. For example, a testator may gift Blackacre to A in document #1 and Blackacre to B in document #2, which creates a formal inconsistency. In the formal inconsistency case, the second document is probably a "will" totally replacing the prior document even though it is the same disposition. This inconsistency leads to the gift to A being replaced in favor B who becomes the substitute taker.

D. REVOCATION BY ACT

The requirements for a revocation by act involve rigid interpretations of the statute and precise adherence to its language to produce many results which offend common sense. For example, if Testator crumples her will and throws it into the wastebasket where the will is subsequently dumped into the trash and taken to a landfill, the will is not revoked unless her conduct was accompanied with intent to revoke and it can be proven that the act done did fall within the precise language of the statute. The attorney may have a tough time demonstrating that this action can be considered as testator having "burned, torn, canceled, obliterated or destroyed" the document.

In another example, a Testator can telephone his lawyer and say "Rip up that will of mine; I want to revoke it." If the lawyer hangs up the telephone and complies, the will is not revoked because the act for a testator by another person must be "in his presence." Query whether maintaining the telephone connection would consist of being "in his presence."

In a third example, Testator tells his nephew, the will beneficiary, "Burn that will." Nephew removes the will from inside the envelope and burns the envelope in the next room. The revocation was not effective since it did not take place in the testator's presence.

In a fourth example, Testator writes in the margin of his will "I hereby cancel this will." Is it canceled? No, according to the prevailing view (and contrary to the UPC position), because a "cancellation" much touch the face of the writing. Here the writing of the will did not touch the face of the writing. What effect does the writing have? None, legally. It showed intention, but the act was missing. Can it be a revocation by writing? No, because not signed by the testator and not witnessed in jurisdictions which do not permit holographic wills.

As the foregoing examples demonstrate, a precise knowledge of and adherence to the statutory requirements for revocation is demanded. Despite this strictness, there is a situation in which the courts operate by "presumption." In the situation where the will is in the "secure possession" of the decedent and the will is either not found or found in an altered condition, courts may presume that the testator did the act of changing or destruction and that the testator intended it to be a change or revocation of the will. In summary, the court presumes all that the statute requires in such a situation.

E. PARTIAL REVOCATION BY ACT

The Uniform Probate Code specifically permits partial revocation of a will by act. Approximately half of the states do not permit partial revocation by act, usually as a matter of interpretation of the applicable statute with a consideration to the difficulty of determining how much of the will is intended to be revoked. If the signature to the will is cancelled, it can be inferred that a total revocation was intended, but partial burnings or other cancellations may not be so clear. When a partial revocation is combined with an attempted, but invalid, addition to the will (e.g., the names of the beneficiaries of two specific bequests are crossed off and transposed without testamentary formalities), the doctrine of dependent relative revocation may be invoked.

F. REVOCATION BY OPERATION OF LAW

Divorce and homicide will revoke a will or parts of a will by operation of law. With a divorce, the provisions granting gifts to a former spouse are declared null and void. The presumption is that if a testator divorced an individual, the testator would not want that individual to still take a previously designated will gift. Similarly, if a beneficiary murders the testator, the presumption arises that the testator would not want that person to inherit his or her property. Exceptions may arise.

A Mississippi slayer statute required an assessment of whether a killing was willful before the killer could be prohibited from inheriting from a spouse. In *Henry v. Toney*, 211 Miss. 93, 50 So.2d 921 (1951), a husband plead guilty to the crime of manslaughter for killing his wife. The question arose as to whether the killing was willful, which would have disabled him from inheriting. The Mississippi Court noted that "a plea of guilty to manslaughter does not necessarily admit a willful killing," and thus cannot be considered conclusive evidence of guilt. The court determined that evidence should have been admitted to shed light on whether the husband's killing of his wife was willful. If it was not, then he would be entitled to inherit from her.

In these jurisdictions, they may impose a constructive trust on the beneficiary to keep the person from profiting from murdering the testator. While the will itself would not be "revoked," the beneficiary would be prevented from enjoying the will gift. Similarly, changes in a will by a codicil or the inability of a beneficiary to take or enjoy the share which the will purportedly gives him or her are not, technically, "revocations" although they have the same effect as far as the beneficiary is concerned.

The provisions for the post-will spouse and for pretermission of children unintentionally omitted from the will are on the definition borderline as to whether they are revocations by operation of law. Uniform Probate Code § 2–508 provides that no change of circumstances other than homicide or divorce, as noted in § 2–803 and § 2–804, revokes a will or part of it. Nevertheless, the Uniform Probate Code has provisions for the omitted post-will spouse (§ 2–301), pretermitted children (§ 2–302) and detailed provisions for a forced share to the spouse which have the effect of overruling portions of the will.

Uniform Probate Code § 2–804 provides that nonprobate provisions and dispositive and appointive provisions of a will in favor of a spouse or a relative of the ex-spouse are revoked by divorce or annulment (and revived if the couple remarries). Sometimes spouses file for divorce and then reunite before it is finalized. Legendary actress and comedian Lucille Ball sought to divorce Desi Arnaz. They reunited before the final degree was granted. Under this scenario, any gifts to the spouse continue. Many jurisdictions do not have statutes comparable to the Uniform Probate Code provision and therefore have the unbalanced position that marriage revokes a will (or part of it) while divorce does not.

G. LOST WILLS

It is possible to have a valid will which has not been revoked, but which cannot be proved because of the absence of the required degree of proof. Consider for example the wills that were burned during the fires that engulfed the twin towers on September 11, 2001. Some states have statutory provisions for the proof of "lost" wills, but the vast majority of states leave the proof of the terms of the document, in the absence of the document itself, to the general law of evidence, requiring, however, "clear" proof of the terms of the will.

The statutes concerning the proof of lost wills generally impose greater standards for proof of the lost will and restrict the number of reasons for the loss which are accepted. Thus, the only wills which may be admitted as lost wills under a typical statute might be those which are shown to be "in existence" at the death of the testator, fraudulently destroyed before his death without his knowledge, or destroyed by public calamity such as the 9/11 tragedy. Each of the grounds requires interpretation and raises new questions. For example, is a will "in existence" if it is in physical existence (the paper document exists) or legal existence (the will, as a concept, has not been revoked)? Is the "fraudulent" destruction capable of being expanded by a "constructive" fraud, e.g., where the attorney entrusted with the original will accidentally destroys it? How public must a public calamity be?

Statutes may require two witnesses to prove the terms of the will. The "missing" or "lost" will is the meeting point of a number of wills doctrines: The will may never have been created. If created, it may have been intentionally revoked by the testator and proof of either the intention and destruction or the secure possession (which raises the presumption of destruction with intention to revoke) may be available. In those cases, there is no valid will. It is possible that some person fraudulently destroyed the will document, leaving the will as a concept to be proved if there is evidence of the will's terms. If there is proof of a will, but no proof of destruction which falls into either of the two categories presented (by testator or fraudulently by another), the will is not revoked, but can be proved only by clear evidence of its contents (or two witnesses if such are required by a statute).

For example, what if Testator leaves his valid will in his automobile which is compacted? There was no intention to revoke the will at that time, but Testator decides, eventually, that he does not want to recreate the document and that he prefers to die intestate. Is the will revoked? Testator has not done an act of revocation with the intention to revoke. The usual course is to say that the will is not revoked. If the terms of the will could not be proved, T has a valid, unrevoked but not proved will. If the terms of the will could be proved, it would be admitted to probate unless a "lost will" statute imposes a greater set of conditions (e.g., that the destruction be without his knowledge or fraudulent or that the will be proved by two witnesses).

H. REVIVAL

Under certain circumstances, a testator can revive a revoked will. The testator can re-execute the revoked document, by creating a new will with the same terms or incorporate by reference the original document and attach a copy to the new document.

Jurisdictions vary as to whether a will can be always or never revived. Within any particular jurisdiction, a particular approach has been adopted and the only issue is whether the testator has clearly indicated a desire contrary to the statutory approach.

For example The Uniform Probate Code will revive a will's provisions concerning a former spouse, otherwise revoked by divorce or annulment, when the parties remarry.

Uniform Probate Code § 2–509 addresses revival or revoked wills. Different presumptions arise when the original revocation was partial or complete. In the case of a complete revocation there is no revival unless "it is evident from the circumstances of the revocation of the subsequent will or from the testator's contemporary or subsequent declarations that the testator intended the previous will to take effect as executed." This approach is probably the most common because it states that a prior will is not revived by revocation of the revoking instrument unless the testator's intention to the contrary is established. Note that revival usually involves the elimination of written revocations and usually does not involve revocations by act. UPC § 2–509(a) would permit revival based upon circumstances of the revocation or the testator's declarations.

Revival can be distinguished from dependent relative revocation in a manner similar to distinguishing a divorce from an annulment. In revival, there was a revocation for a period of time. In divorce, there was a marriage for a period of time. In dependent relative revocation situations, the application of the doctrine results in a finding that there never was a revocation, just as an annulment finds that there never was a marriage.

I. DEPENDENT RELATIVE REVOCATION

1. THEORIES AND APPROACHES

Dependent relative revocation eliminates a revocation of a testamentary document or part of it, and revives it as the testator's will. The must be a valid will, an otherwise valid revocation of part or all of the will, and some reason why that revocation will not carry out the intention of the testator. The revocation of the valid will is said to be dependent upon the validity of some other disposition (usually a subsequent, but imperfectly executed, purported will).

For example, suppose Testator previously created valid Will #1, attempts to revoke it with Will #2. Believing the second document to be a valid will, Testator destroys Will #1. Did Testator die testate if it turns out Will #2 is invalid? The second document is not a will; the first one has been revoked. Testator died intestate unless the court determines that dependent relative revocation should apply to revive Will #1.

Another approach to dependent relative revocation is more mechanical. It looks to the connection between (rather than a comparison of) the revocation and the ineffective disposition. For example, suppose Testator crosses off the signature on his valid will, intending to write a new will, but dies before writing the new will. Is the old will revoked? In most cases, the mere intention to make a new will should not be enough, but if the revocation and new will were found to be part of "one scheme," dependent relative revocation might apply. Courts examine the circumstances to determine the intention of the testator and carry it out as closely as possible.

Terminology of "mistake" is often used in this field. It is possible to say in the examples given above that the revocation of the first instrument was a mistake. In the first example, there was no intention to revoke by an act of revocation because T was under the mistaken impression that the revocation clause in the second instrument had been effective to revoke the will. Perhaps "mistake" is too broad a term for this usage because there are situations on both sides of the dependent relative revocation situation which could use the same terminology. On one side is a mistaken destruction of the will without intention to revoke, e.g., an accidental burning. Here, there is no intention to revoke. On the other side is the claim by the disgruntled former beneficiary that the testator did "not understand" him and made a "mistake" in revoking the bequest to him.

Some jurisdictions decline to apply dependent relative revocation to eliminate a written revocation, although accepting it to declare an act of revocation is ineffective. The justification for the distinction is that the act is inherently ambiguous. The court is seen as having the power to construe the ambiguous act to determine what the testator did, but not to disregard an express statement to carry out the court's conception of what the testator should have done. The inherently ambiguous nature of the acts of revocation is also cited as the reason for the admission of extrinsic evidence to prove the circumstances of the revocation.

Dependent relative revocation goes against many of the trends in the law of wills: The strict interpretation of and demand for rigid adherence to the specific language of the statutes concerning the making and revocation of wills and the philosophy of the parol evidence rule are given little weight in the case by case determinations of whether dependent relative revocation should apply. The court in making the decision should consider the testamentary pattern of the decedent (the terms of the prior wills and the direction they were taking in regard to intestacy), the respective shares and identities of the beneficiaries under the old and purportedly new will, the nature of the defect which prevents the purported new will from taking effect, the trustworthiness of the evidence of the reasons for the testator's desire to make the changes and the proximity of the desired objective to the prior testamentary plans and as contrasted to intestacy. The court cannot make a new will, but it can scrape away revocations to breathe new life into an old will that achieves the same objective.

2. INTERACTION WITH OTHER WILLS DOCTRINES

Dependent relative revocation presents difficulties in addition to doctrinal differences and the uncertainties inherent in an equitable doctrine which is applied on a case by case basis. Often dependent relative revocation is an alternate theory applied after some preliminary theory (revival, mortmain, beneficially interested witness, partial revocation by act, interlineation) has been applied. Additionally, dependent relative revocation could apply internally or externally to a will, i.e., to part or all of it.

The type of revocation may be very material in this area. Some courts apply revival only to written revocations, probably on the basis that acts of revocation are instantly effective. Some courts resist applying dependent relative revocation to written revocations because they are less ambiguous than acts.

In *In re Kaufman's Estate*, 155 P.2d 831 (Cal. 1945), the California Supreme Court applied dependent relative revocation to make Will #2 a codicil to Will #1. It did this despite express language to the contrary in the document and testimony that the testator, after having the effect of the mortmain statute and the difference between wills and codicils explained to him stated, "No, I want a new Will. I don't want a Codicil." The Mississippi Supreme Court reached the opposite result, stressing the written nature of the revocation, in *Crosby v. Alton Ochsner Medical Foundation*, 276 So.2d 661 (Miss. 1973).

To summarize, doctrine of dependent relative revocation and revival can be used by courts to cure a mistake by the testator to enable the testator to die testate, instead of intestate.

CHAPTER 5
WILL COMPONENTS

A. CODICILS

A codicil is a separate document that supplements or changes a previous will without wholly revoking the prior will. It must conform to the requirements to make a will. In determining that a particular document is a codicil, a court arrives at three conclusions:

1. The subsequent document satisfies the requirements of the applicable statute of wills;
2. There is in existence a prior document which also satisfies the requirements for testamentary formality; and
3. The later document does not expressly or by necessary inference revoke the entire prior document.

A testamentary document could be written at different times. If two or more of the parts are capable of standing alone as far as the requirements for testamentary formalities, then the earliest is the "will" and all supplements (at least until the point at which the original will is entirely superseded) are codicils. If the testamentary formalities are satisfied by only one of the documents, it is the will. Changes to a formal will after it is executed generally require a complete re-performance of all the testamentary formalities in order to be valid.

For example, a testator could execute what he thinks is a valid will, but it is later determined to be invalid for reasons unknown to him. For example, one of the two required witnesses did not sign the will. The testator subsequently validly executes a document called a "codicil" which makes a slight change in the purported original will. A valid codicil incorporates the invalid will and makes it provisions valid.

This approach treats the two documents as one document, i.e., a will executed at the time of the codicil. Any internal discrepancies could be resolved by constructional rules about later portions (even in the same document) prevailing over the former. The intent of the testator is used as a guiding principle.

B. INTEGRATION

Integration of a will is the act of deciding what parts constitute the will. Integration problems are more frequently encountered in jurisdictions which permit holographic wills. The term integration is used in both an external and internal sense

1. EXTERNAL INTEGRATION

External integration is the process of determining what *pages* constitute the will. The pages which constitute the will are exactly those pages which the testator intended to be his or her will—but how is the intention determined? Where the several writings are connected by sequence of thought, folded together or physically forming one document, they are integrated if it may reasonably be inferred that the testator meant all the papers together to constitute his will.

Formal (witnessed) wills may pose another problem. If the applicable statute of wills requires that the will be subscribed "at the end," the addition of a page to the document below the signature page may appear to cause the entire will to fail. Usually, the court will focus upon what pages were present at the time that the testator signed or acknowledged the document to the witnesses as "my will." If there is no evidence, the court may indulge in the presumption that pages below the signature were added after execution, thereby admitting to probate the pages before the signature while giving no effect to the subsequently added pages.

2. INTERNAL INTEGRATION

When there are different writings by the testator, often on the same page, internal integration is the process of determining what *writings* (as opposed to what pages) constitute the will or will and codicil(s). Again the touchstone for formal (witnessed) wills is to admit the writings which were present when the document was executed. In the case of holographic wills, however, courts have tended to admit all writings which are in the handwriting of the testator. A construction preference may exist which would exclude items not in the testator's handwriting and not obviously intended by him or her to be incorporated into the will, e.g., a printed letterhead when the jurisdiction required that the will be "entirely" in the handwriting of the testator.

For example, what if the testator wrote entirely in her own handwriting 21 pages of dispositive provisions? The materials used (type of paper and ink) and provisions (references to persons born and dying between the relevant dates) indicate that the will was written in three stages. Each of the pages has the testator's name written on it, and there are three different dates on the document. What, if anything should be admitted to probate? Is it a will or a will and codicils? Probably the most common, but not the only position, would be to treat the document as one 21-page will and admit it to probate. Another approach would be to proclaim it a will with two codicils. An unfortunate possibility would be to hold that the document could not be admitted to probate because it has no certain date (since it has three possible "certain" dates). Utilizing such an approach, it is possible that Louisiana might invalidate the document as an olographic will.

C. REPUBLICATION

A codicil republishes a will. Re-execution of the will in accordance with the testamentary formalities also republishes a will. The republication gives a new point in time to the testamentary scheme.

There are situations in which the time of the will makes a significant difference. Subsequently acquired property may be disposed of through the residuary clause.

If a beneficiary was dead at the time a will was made, the bequest was void, as opposed to being "lapsed." Anti-lapse statutes sometimes keep gifts in the estate by providing a substitute taker. Some anti-lapse statutes have been construed to apply only to bequests made to persons who died after the will was executed and not to void gifts to persons who were dead at the time the will was written If the beneficiary died after execution of the will, then the republication of the will made the gift void, as opposed to a lapsed gift and the anti-lapse statute might not apply.

In a prior era, Mortmain statutes limited the amount which a testator may give to a charity in a will executed within a statutory period (often 30 days, 90 days or 6 months) of death. Thus, a testator who writes a will leaving his estate to charity (to the deprivation of relatives within the "protected class" of the particular statute) could live for a year or more and avoid the "time" limitation of such a statute.

If, however, the testator wrote a codicil which "republished" the will (even though not enlarging the bequest to charity) and then died within the statutory period, the codicil might trigger the mortmain restrictions. Many jurisdictions construed the republication provision not to apply in this situation because the purpose of the statute (to restrain improvident death-bed bequests which were to the detriment of certain relatives) was not served by the republication theory.

The following are several situations where republication by codicil remains relevant. First, in many situations, a revocation, exercise or bequest is required to be made by a will which was executed "after" some other event. For example, a gift *causa mortis* may be revoked by a will executed after the gift was made, but is generally not revoked by a will made prior to the gift. A power of appointment may be created by an instrument which provides that the power will be exercised only by a will executed "after" the power was created. A statute or a marital settlement agreement between the divorcing spouses may provide that all bequests, powers and nominations made by wills executed "prior to" the divorce or settlement agreement are revoked or renounced.

Should a codicil to the prior will republish it to revoke the gift *causa mortis*, exercise the power of appointment or renew the bequest, conferring a power or nomination as personal representative or guardian of a former spouse? It should probably be viewed as a matter of the intention of the testator (combined with the intention of the person creating the power in the power of appointment situation).

Should an otherwise unrelated codicil serve to revoke the gift *causa mortis* if there is no clear intent? Here the issue is more difficult. Courts could be expected to arrive at different conclusions on that issue as well as the issue whether the residuary clause of a pre-power will is republished to be considered as "executed" after the creation of the power. In this case, the protection imposed by the creator of the power might tilt the scale in favor of non-exercise, especially when the change made in the codicil is unrelated or minor.

On the other hand, a pre-divorce will with a post-divorce codicil probably should be considered to be "re-executed" so that the bequests and nominations to the former spouse are preserved. Here, other factors (such as whether the alternate taker by intestacy is a new spouse or more remote relatives) might be considered by the court in a particular case, if it did not feel bound by prior cases.

Second, where there are multiple documents or contradictory provisions, the later provision is usually held to control. The concept of republication artificially gives a new date to an older bequest or other provision. If all the provisions concerned are in the testamentary documents, to say that each codicil republished both the will and the prior codicils would be to ignore the actual timing of the documents.

Third, when pretermission applies only to children (or issue) born after the making of the will and in the post-will spouse situations, the pre-birth or premarital will can be republished by a post-birth or post-marital codicil. If the provisions of the codicil show that the testator contemplated the birth or marriage in making the codicil, republication is obviously appropriate. What effect should a codicil which makes some unrelated change have? For example, if T left his entire estate to his brother, married and had a child and then wrote a codicil which changed his corporate executor, who should receive T's estate?

Fourth, incorporation by reference often includes as one of its requirements that the document being incorporated "be in existence" at the time that the incorporating document is written. If T executes a will on 1 January and purports to include provisions in a letter to be written and dated on 2 February, can a 3 March codicil republish the will to make the incorporation complete? It probably should.

Fifth, when there are changes in the beneficiaries, such as class gifts in which members could be added by birth or deleted by death between the date of the will and the date of the codicil, which date should the will's "now" refer to? The original date seems likely, but this may not carry out the intention of the testator, either because of a desire to include subsequent members or the operation of other policies of the law. For example, T provides "I make no provision for my children now living." in a will, has another child born and writes a codicil making an unrelated change in the will.

Sixth, where there are changes in the items bequeathed, e.g., changes which trigger the concepts of ademption by satisfaction or extinction, accretions, abatement or exoneration, does the bequest as of the time of the will or as of the time of the codicil pass by a will which is republished by the codicil?

These situations exemplify problems that can arise with republication by codicil.

D. INCORPORATION BY REFERENCE

It is common drafting practice to "incorporate by reference" an existing writing into a pleading, contract or other legal document. Rather than copying the exact words of the existing document, it is described and a photocopy is often attached to the incorporation document. This standard practice, however, encounters difficulty with statutory requirements for a will. If the will is holographic, the attachment may not be "in the handwriting" of the decedent. If the will is formal, an attachment may violate the requirement that the testator or the witnesses "subscribe" "at the end" of the will. If the applicable statute does not require subscription at the end, it is possible that the incorporated document may not be present at the time the will is signed in which case the question arises whether the testator has "declared" it to be a part of his or her will.

The document which is incorporated is usually *not* treated as a part of the will itself, but as an external source from which the meaning of the will can be completed. This maintains the distinction between "integration" of pages which constitute the will and "incorporation by reference" which is a figurative, rather than literal, integration. It is treated *as if* it were integrated.

Fear of fraudulent substitutions is probably the basis for the legal insistence upon compliance with certain conditions in order to incorporate a document into a will by reference. The testator is not allowed to "waive" the protections of the statute of wills as to a document which does not have testamentary formalities. The requirements for incorporation by reference into a will are sometimes stated to be the following:

1. The document to be incorporated is in existence at the time the will is executed. This requirement is rigidly applied in order to obtain certainty, even though the will is not effective

until death. The desire to dispose of property by a list "to be made later" is carried out only by the relatively unique provisions of Uniform Probate Code § 2–513, dealing with tangible articles of personalty disposed of by a written statement or list.

2. The incorporating document must manifest the intention to incorporate the provisions of the incorporated document. This essential requirement stresses the fact that it is the intention of the testator, within the bounds permitted by law, which governs.

3. The incorporated document must be sufficiently described to permit its identification. This is simply a variation on the theme that the intention must be discernible in order to be carried out. The descriptions could vary from lawyerlike precision (accompanied by inclusion of a photocopy) to the hopelessly vague. Some courts stress the reverse side of this requirement—that the incorporated document comply with the description—as a separate requirement.

4. Some, but not all, statements of the requirements for incorporation by reference include the requirement that the incorporating document refer to the incorporated document as being in existence (in addition to the requirement that it actually be in existence). This less understandable requirement is deleted from many decisional and statutory statements

of the rule, such as Uniform Probate Code § 2–510.

Most states now permit incorporation by reference into wills, if the foregoing conditions are complied with. In the states which permit holographic wills, most of them permit the incorporation *by reference* of non-holographic material, even though *actual* incorporation (i.e., integration) would make the will invalid because not "entirely" in the handwriting of the decedent.

A specialized statute, designed to resolve problems encountered in the theories of integration, incorporation by reference and reference to facts of independent significance is the Uniform Testamentary Additions to Trusts Act, also found as Uniform Probate Code § 2–511. This provision authorizes "pour-overs" by will to trusts, without regard to the chronology of creation, funding and amendment.

E. INDEPENDENT LEGAL SIGNIFICANCE

Under Uniform Probate Code § 2–512, a "will may dispose of property by reference to acts and events that have significance apart from their effect upon the dispositions made by the will, whether they occur before or after the execution of the will or before or after the testator's death." The rigid insistence of the law that all of the provisions of the will be within the will's four corners and known at the time of execution has caused the defeat of many attempted bequests. This code provision can eliminate some harsh outcomes.

Courts regularly accept a bequest of "the residue" of my estate (the extent and character of which is known only at or after death) to "my heirs" (who are determined at the time of death). In such a bequest, the identity of both the property given and the recipient is determined by reference to a fact having significance independent of the testamentary plan. Similarly, a bequest of "all automobiles which I own at my death" to "such of my children as survive me" will be resolved by reliance upon facts outside of the will. A gift of "the contents of my safe deposit box" to "the person with whom I dine on Christmas in the year before my death" is more difficult and may be ineffective unless it can be proven with absolute certainty. Few courts will give effect to a bequest of "the sum of money which I mentioned to my attorney" to "a certain person to be designated by me to my attorney." This amounts to an attempt to create a secret trust. The attorney may be "independent" and "legal," but the dispositions have no significance apart from the testamentary scheme.

CHAPTER 6

BENEFICIARIES

A. INTRODUCTION

Beneficiaries are recipients of estate gifts. Beneficiaries must be human. Gifts to animals have been revoked or reformed to give resources to a human caregiver of the animal. During the antebellum period of United States history when humans could be enslaved and considered property, a slaveholder had to first free the enslaved person(s) before leaving him or her or them estate gifts.

To take under a valid, unrevoked will which is not lost and which contains a clear disposition of a decedent's estate, the purported beneficiary must meet the following criteria. Individuals must be alive at the time of the testator's death, and not have renounced their gift or murdered the decedent. Even if the individual did not murder the decedent, but an ancestor (such as a parent) did, the beneficiary may lose the right to take a will gift. A purported beneficiary will also lose the ability to take if he or she is not a human (such as a gift to a pet).

A testator may contract to make a will which binds the testator in equity to make a certain disposition, thus causing a purported beneficiary to forfeit a gift. The enforcement of such a contract usually involves imposing a constructive trust upon the will beneficiary for the benefit of the contract beneficiary.

The joint action of the testator and the beneficiary is involved in the following situations:

- The testator inserts a survivorship clause in the will and the beneficiary dies within that period.
- The testator inserts a no-contest, or "in terrorem" clause, in the will that beneficiaries trigger by initiating a challenge to the will.
- A property settlement agreement between the testator and the beneficiary includes a provision by which the beneficiary contractually waives his or her interest in the testator's estate.
- The testator gives, and the beneficiary accepts, a gift during life which is intended as an "advancement" against the share which the beneficiary would otherwise receive at the death of the testator.
- The beneficiary owes money to the testator which is unpaid at death, triggering a "set-off" or "retainer" right to be exercised by the personal representative of the testator.

B. BENEFICIARY'S NATURE OR ACTION

1. ALIENS, ANIMALS, CHARITIES, CORPORATIONS AND FELONS

Uniform Probate Code § 2–111 provides that "No individual is disqualified to take as an heir because the individual or an individual through whom he [or she] claims is or has been an alien." In this context, the word alien refers to a non-citizen as opposed to someone from another planet as illustrated in numerous science fiction movies.

Although restrictions on the ownership of land by **aliens** can be traced to feudal traditions, some states have enacted restrictions on alien inheritance only in the 20th Century. These restrictions have been severely limited, but not dealt a complete death blow, by *Zschernig v. Miller*, 389 U.S. 429 (1968), which upheld an Oregon "reciprocity" statute requiring the beneficiary to demonstrate that a citizen of Oregon could inherit in the foreign country the same as a citizen of that country before the beneficiary could inherit in Oregon the same as a resident citizen. As applied, the Court found the statute to be an unconstitutional interference with the federal government's conduct of international relations.

Subject to this and the further limitation that a treaty would prevail over such statutes, some states have retained statutory restrictions upon the rights of aliens to inherit. The statutory limitations are of the reciprocal ("You show me yours . . .") or the impounding type, requiring the alien to "appear and claim" ("Come and get it."). In these statutes, drafting and construction to avoid problems raised by the equal protection clause of the Fourteenth Amendment usually draw a line between the resident and the non-resident alien, with the former being more constitutionally favored.

A direct gift to an **animal** fails, although many jurisdictions construe it as a direct bequest to a human person who is named with or otherwise linked with the animal purported beneficiary. These courts often give the bequest practical effect through the concept of the "honorary trust." Uniform Probate Code § 2–907 expressly permits "a trust for the care of a designated domestic or pet animal."

For the most part, mortmain statutes, which restricted gifts to **charities,** have been eliminated. Those that remain are diverse in approach and complicated by judicial interpretation. The statutes restrict the amount (a set percentage or all) which a decedent can leave by will to charities. Often the statutes apply only to bequests in wills executed within a certain period of death (30 days, 3 months, 6 months) and only to the wills of decedents who are survived by certain classes of relatives.

Corporations and **government entities**, such as municipalities, states and the United States government, have been held at various times to be ineligible to receive bequests because they are not "persons." Generally, this type of limitation has been removed by defining "person" as in Uniform Probate Code § 1–201(34) to include organizations.

At common law, a **felon** lost all civil rights, including the right to receive property by inheritance or will. Most states today permit a felon to inherit and deal with property (including the making of wills), but there may be residual restrictions and exceptions.

2. DEATH OF THE BENEFICIARY

A beneficiary may die before the testator, at the same time as the beneficiary (simultaneous death), or after the beneficiary. Except for the Uniform Probate Code § 2–104 requirement that an heir survive the intestate by 120 hours, there is generally no requirement that an *heir* (i.e., intestate taker) survive the decedent by more than an instant. The testator, of course, can attach any survivorship condition that he desires to any bequest. John F. Kennedy Jr.'s will, for example required that his beneficiaries "be living on the thirtieth day after" his death. Unfortunately, John F. Kennedy Jr. and his wife Carolyn Bessette-Kennedy perished in a plane crash together, and thus gifts to her were void.

This problem of close-in-time deaths also arises in mass casualty events, such as earthquakes, hurricanes, and shootings. After Robb Elementary School teacher Irma Garcia who died in the shooting at the Uvalde, Texas, grade school, her husband, Joe died two days later from a heart attack. Because of the closeness in time between their deaths, their demise potentially triggered statues, such as the Uniform Simultaneous Death Act. That act seeks to avoid the cost and delay of multiple probates. It provides that, under circumstances where two individuals died close in time (such as within four days) or where there is no sufficient evidence that two or more persons died other than simultaneously, the property of each "shall be disposed of as if he had survived" separately. Thus, the possible heir or will beneficiary is deemed to have predeceased the person whose estate is being distributed.

This problem occurred in *Estate of Parisi*, 328 Ill. App.3d 75 (2002), where the bodies of the father and daughter were discovered on the same day, and there was insufficient evidence to establish order of death. The court ordered that heirship had to be determined separately for the father's and daughter's estates.

In intestacy, one must survive the predecessor in interest in order to become the "heir." What happens when a will beneficiary predeceases the testator? At common law a distinction was made between the will beneficiary who was dead at the time that the will was written (in which case the bequest was "void") and the will beneficiary who died between the time that the will was written and the death of the testator. In the latter case, the bequest was said to "lapse" or fail.

Almost all jurisdictions have enacted some form of "anti-lapse" statute which provides an alternate taker for a predeceased beneficiary. The following statutes show the range of anti-lapse statutes.

Uniform Probate Code § 2–603 applies to "a grandparent, a descendant of a grandparent, or a stepchild of . . . the testator" and provides that a substitute gift is created in the devisee's surviving descendants. They take by representation the property to which the devisee would have been entitled had the devisee survived the testator.

Anti-lapse statutes vary widely as to the required relationship of the predeceased beneficiary to the testator. There are six basic categories as indicated on the anti-lapse table.

- Category #1, followed by four states, requires the beneficiary to be a child or other descendant of the testator.
- Category #2, followed by five states, permits the beneficiary to be either a descendant of the testator or a descendant of a parent of the testator. This would qualify siblings and their offspring.
- Category #3, followed in 13 states and the Uniform Probate Code, applies anti-lapse provisions to the testator's grandparents or lineal descendants of the grandparents. This permits aunts, uncles, cousins and their offspring to take.
- Category #4, followed in ten states, applies to testator's grandparents, descendants of grandparents, or a stepchild of the testator.
- Category #5, followed in ten states, applies to any relative of the testator. California Probate Code § 21110, which is in category #5, provides that:

  (a) . . . if a transferee is dead . . . , the issue of the deceased transferee take in the transferee's place . . . [and]

  (c) As used in this section, "transferee" means a person who is kindred of the transferor or kindred of a surviving, deceased, or former spouse of the transferor.

- Category #6 is the broadest of all as it applies to any devisee or legatee and the person does not have to be related to the testator. It applies in eight states.

TABLE 5-1
ANTI-LAPSE TABLE

CATEGORY 1	CATEGORY 2	CATEGORY 3	CATEGORY 4	CATEGORY 5	CATEGORY 6
CHILD OR OTHER DESCENDANT OF THE TESTATOR	DESCENDANT OF THE TESTATOR OR A DESCENDANT OF A PARENT OF THE TESTATOR	GRANDPARENT OR LINEAL DESCENDANT OF A GRANDPARENT OF THE TESTATOR	GRANDPARENT, DESCENDANT OF A GRANDPARENT, OR A STEPCHILD OF THE TESTATOR	A RELATIVE OF THE TESTATOR	A DEVISEE OR LEGATEE
(4 STATES)	(5 STATES)	(13 STATES)	(10 STATES)	(10 STATES)	(9 STATES)
Arkansas, Indiana, Illinois, Mississippi	Connecticut, Louisiana, New York, Pennsylvania, Texas	Alabama, Colorado, Delaware, Florida, Idaho, Maine, Minnesota, North Carolina, North Dakota, South Carolina, Virginia, Washington, Wyoming	Alaska, Arizona, Hawaii, Michigan, Montana, New jersey, New Mexico, South Dakota, Utah, Wisconsin	California, Kansas, Massachusetts, Missouri, Nebraska, Nevada, Ohio, Oklahoma, Oregon, Vermont	Georgia, Iowa, Kentucky, Maryland, New Hampshire, Rhode Island, Tennessee, West Virginia

All statutes acknowledge the universal rule that the application of the anti-lapse statute is a matter of the testator's intention. A clear statement of intention to the contrary excludes the application of the anti-lapse statute. Some state statutes, but not all, expressly apply to class gifts and save the gift for descendants of the deceased beneficiary as opposed to redistributing the deceased member's share to other class members.

The anti-lapse statutes are also available for use by analogy to two related fields: Failure of bequests for reasons other than death (e.g., a renunciation statute which phrases the alternate takers as "those persons who would take if the renouncing beneficiary were dead") and will substitutes.

The Uniform Probate Code § 2–706 extends the anti-lapse coverage to will substitutes, such as life insurance, retirement plans, payable on death accounts, and transfer on death registrations. The Uniform Probate Code § 2–707 extends anti-lapse provisions to trusts.

3. RENUNCIATION (DISCLAIMER)

At common law it was possible to renounce or disclaim an estate gift, but not possible to renounce an *intestate* succession. Many jurisdictions have changed this rule to permit disclaimer of an intestate share also. Generally, the disclaimer was done to avoid creditors, minimize taxes, or achieve some imperfectly executed, but known, intention of the testator. Some courts have invalidated disclaimers used to avoid creditors as being fraudulent or a preferential transfer.

The Uniform Disclaimer of Property Interests Act (1999), inserted as Uniform Probate Code §§ 2–1101 through 2–1117, clarifies and broadens the power to disclaim interests.

Who receives the disclaimed property? First, the governing instrument is examined to see if there is an effective alternate disposition in the event of disclaimer. If there is not, the disclaimed property passes "as if the disclaimant had died." This may trigger the applicable anti-lapse statute.

For transfer tax purposes, Internal Revenue Code § 2518 imposes the additional requirement that the disclaimer be given in writing within nine-month period after the later of: "(A) the day on which the transfer creating the interest in such person is made, or (B) the day on which such person attains age 21." Therefore, a disclaimer can be effective for state property law purposes under the Uniform Probate Code, but ineffective for transfer tax purposes under Internal Revenue Code § 2518.

4. SLAYERS AS BENEFICIARIES

According to the Associated Press, on March 23, 2007, a Brazilian housewife was convicted and sentenced to 19 years in prison for killing her husband, chopping his body into small pieces and frying it. Had this event taken place in the United States, the housewife would be prohibited from receiving testamentary and will substitute gifts. When it comes to murdering a spouse, three zones of variation exist: the legal theory, the type of slaying, and the type of property involved.

a. Legal Theories

If the source of the law is a statute prohibiting the slayer from taking, the problem usually centers on whether the type of slaying and the type of property interest are within the statutory language and, if not, whether the statute should be extended by analogy. Statutes proceed in only one direction—prohibiting the slayer from taking, so the issue is whether this statute has extended this far.

If there is no statute which applies or can be extended by analogy, then the court will determine whether a slayer will be allowed to receive the property of his or her predecessor in interest. Three possible judicial approaches exist. The first approach is to allow the slayer to take. This is justified on the theory of legislative inaction. ("If the legislature had desired to prohibit such an inheritance, it could have so provided.") Although there is no constitutional "right" to inherit, some of the impetus for allowing the slayer to take has constitutional overtones of various provisions, including due process, equal protection, ex post facto, cruel and unusual punishment, and the dislike of forfeitures as in the bill of attainder provision.

The most direct approach for a court in the opposite direction is a prohibition of inheritance similar to, but without the authority of, a statute. Modernly, some courts have adopted this approach.

At the beginning of the twentieth century, legal writers and courts were reluctant both to let the slayer receive the property of the victim and to admit that courts made, rather than "found," the law. Thus, the device of the "constructive trust" was utilized. The courts stated that the slaying heir or will beneficiary was entitled to receive by intestacy or, but then imposed a "constructive" trust upon the slaying heir or will beneficiary for the benefit of the persons who would "otherwise" have received the property. This verbal fiction of a trust imposed by operation of law was used to achieve the same effect as if the inheritance or bequest was denied to the heir or will beneficiary.

If the slayer is denied or is held to be a constructive trustee, who takes or is entitled to the beneficial enjoyment? It is unlikely that one would draft a will with a provision revoking any bequest to a person responsible for the death of the testator. Provisions for the death of a beneficiary could be extended to cover the barred slayer—but should the anti-lapse statute be applied if the beneficiaries and alternate takers are within its terms? To extend the anti-lapse clause to theoretical deaths would allow one to take "through" a person who could not take, but to deny the application of the anti-lapse clause would be to visit the sins of the parent upon the child and revive a portion of the antiquated concept of "corruption of the blood."

Should other persons be allowed to benefit as a result of the slayer's action? If the slayer is married to the heir or if there are other persons who "benefit" from the "wrong" of the slaying, should they also be prohibited from taking? Some jurisdictions bar the slayer and his or her issue from inheriting.

b. Type of Slaying

The course in Criminal Law teaches that killing of a human being ranges in degree of culpability from justified and accidental through negligent to various degrees of manslaughter and murder. Obviously, the more culpable the killing (and the fewer sympathetic circumstances as in the so-called "mercy killing"), the more likely the court or statute is to deny the killer's right to take. When a statute demands a certain degree of murder or manslaughter or a certain burden of proof, it is difficult for the court to extend the purpose of the statute to a lesser amount. Some statutes, for example, require a criminal burden of proof (to be consistent in the findings of fault) and thereby are inconsistent in making the determinations of the criminal court conclusive on the civil court.

c. Type of Property

Although most statutes and court decisions are consistent between realty and personalty and between testate and intestate estates, many do not extend their application beyond the probate estate to will substitutes. The life insurance situation introduces another possibility: Relief of the insurance company from the obligation to pay to anyone when the beneficiary has murdered the insured. This would bring to the life insurance area the rule applied in the casualty insurance area: If an arsonist cannot collect fire insurance on his or her building, why should a murderer collect life insurance on his or her victim? Normally, however, the company is required to pay the proceeds and the only questions involved are whether the beneficiary should be allowed to take the proceeds and, if not, who is the alternate taker?

It is easy to apply the equitable doctrine of denying the slayer any rights under a trust, but generally it is more difficult to determine, under the typically complicated scheme of distribution of a trust, the identity of the alternate takers. Who should take when the trust instrument provides for distribution among persons "living at the time of the death" of a murdered life tenant? Similarly, if the slayer is one of the takers in default of exercise of a power of appointment, who takes his share if he is deprived because of his murder of the person possessing the power?

The most difficult of the will substitutes and the most likely to be encountered in practice is the joint tenancy situation in which one joint tenant slays the other. Once it is decided that the slayer will not be allowed to enlarge his or her share, one encounters the problem that a killer cannot be deprived of his or her "own" property because of the murder. The two doctrines clash because of the common law concept that each of the owners of joint tenancy property owns the entire property, subject to the right of survivorship of the other joint tenants. If a joint tenant slays another joint tenant and it is decided that the slayer cannot take the "share" of the victim, the possible alternatives include all of the following:

- Create a tenancy in common as if the slayer terminated the joint tenancy.
- Deprive the slayer of all interest in the property and thereby raise great problems of forfeiture.
- Retain the joint tenancy between the slayer and some alternate taker of the victim, e.g., the victim's heir.

- Deprive the slayer of all except a life estate (or a life estate in one half), thereby having a constructive resurrection.
- Deprive the slayer of all except the cash value of a life estate, adding a constructive sale to the constructive resurrection.
- Deprive the slayer of all of the joint tenancy which he or she did not originally contribute. This approach, taken from the death tax field, is usually applied when the victim contributed more than one half.

There are other variations in the fictions which can be applied in trying to resolve the knotty problems of the slaying joint tenant. Many of these involve the use of the constructive trust fiction.

Uniform Probate Code § 2–803 attempts a comprehensive approach to the succession rights of one who "feloniously and intentionally" kills a predecessor in interest, insured, joint tenant, etc. but acknowledges that qualified employee plans may not be subject to state law because of preemption by the provisions of the federal Employee Retirement Income Security Act of 1974 (ERISA).

C. TESTATOR'S ACTION: CONTRACTS TO MAKE A WILL

A contract to make a will is an agreement by one party to devise or bequeath property to another, such promise being made in consideration of a promise or action by the purported beneficiary. The contract to make a will is enforced by a court of equity in appropriate cases. Normally, this enforcement is through the means of a constructive trust. Two typical situations in which a contract to make a will may exist.

In Example #1, on the one hand, Testator induces Friend to move into Testator's house and tend to Testator's needs for the balance of Testator's life in exchange for Testator's promise to devise the house and one-half of the residue of Testator's estate to Friend.

In Example #2, on the other hand, Husband and Wife, both having children by prior (terminated) marriages, marry each other. They agree that the survivor should be entitled to use all of the property for his or her life and that the balance remaining after the death of the second of them should be divided one-half each to the descendants of each of them.

If the contract is fully carried out by both parties, the only difficulties are the tax treatment of the amounts received in Example #1 and the relative priorities of the beneficiaries as opposed to creditors of the estate. Normally, the creditors would be satisfied prior to the gratuitous will beneficiary, but in Example #1, Friend is also a creditor. If Friend is unable to enforce the contract, Friend may still be able to claim the value of Friend's services which were performed within the period of the statute of limitations.

A special provision of the Statute of Frauds may apply to a contract to devise realty. Often an exception, such as full performance by the other party to the contract, is available. Additionally, a document which is ineffective as a will (e.g., because of lack of formalities or revocation) may be effective as written evidence of the contract or its terms.

Uniform Probate Code § 2–514 provides that contracts to make a will may be established under three conditions. First, provisions of a will may state material provisions of the contract. Second, the will may expressly reference the contract and extrinsic evidence may be used to prove the terms of the contract. Third, there may be a writing signed by the decedent evidencing the contract. Further, the Uniform Probate Code § 2–514 makes clear that the "execution of a joint will or mutual wills does not create a presumption of a contract not to revoke the will or wills."

Performance by the party who is to make the will may be incomplete. If Testator in Example #1 were to write a will with the provisions for Friend which were promised, but Testator then revoked the will, the court of equity might be called upon to enforce an "implied covenant of good faith and fair dealing" to enforce the contract by constructive trust upon the heirs of Testator. Note that the heirs are not being punished for any wrongdoing. The court is instead preventing their unjust enrichment. Similarly, in Example #2, if Husband died having left all his property to Wife, Wife might be prevented by the court from giving away the property, although she might be entitled to use it for her necessary living expenses. Wife would therefore be like the owner of a legal life estate (who is not permitted to use principal), but Wife might have some of the rights of a beneficiary of a "discretionary trust" (in which so much of the principal as is necessary to maintain her standard of living can be consumed).

In Example #2, the "Joint Will" form, in which both parties sign the same document, may be used. This form suggests that a contract was intended. If a contract is found to exist, certainty of disposition is obtained at the expense of flexibility. Another form which could be used in satisfaction of a contract (or which might not indicate a contract at all) is the "Reciprocal Wills" in which mirror image provisions are made. Thus, in Example #2, Husband's will would give the property to Wife for life (with, perhaps, some power of invasion or appointment) and the remainder one-half to Husband's issue and one-half to Wife's issue. Wife's will, in turn, would make similar provisions for Husband and the identical disposition among the issue of Husband and Wife. The presence of a pair of reciprocal wills does not by itself prove a contract, but is consistent with the existence of a contract. The contract may also exist independent of the wills which were written. Thus, the wills of Husband and Wife might give a fee simple to the survivor, with or without a remainder over in the event of the prior death of the beneficiary. In the case of a will which purports to give a fee simple to the survivor (or any disposition which does not comport with the contract), the contract will be enforced, by constructive trust, if properly proved.

D. JOINT ACTION OF TESTATOR AND BENEFICIARY

1. NO-CONTEST ("IN TERROREM") CLAUSES

A no-contest clause attempts to punish any will beneficiary who participates in a will contest by forfeiture of the share which the beneficiary would otherwise have taken. A very simple no-contest clause might state: "If any beneficiary contests this will, he shall take nothing under this will."

No-contest clauses are a type of conditional bequest. The condition—that the beneficiary refrain from instituting a contest of the testator's will—is generally regarded as "lawful" although strictly construed. No-contest clauses are distinct from "disinheritance" clauses, which are attempts to avoid pretermission and post-will spouse provisions by providing "I intentionally make no provision for my heirs." Nevertheless, both clauses are commonly found together.

No-contest clauses usually are ineffective for a number of reasons. First, many assets are not in the probate estate. The clause only terminates the rights to the probate estate, not will substitutes, such as joint tenancy, life insurance etc.

Second, not all challenges to a will are "contests" of a will. For example, pretermission and post-will spouse claims and the forced share of a spouse are not asserted in a "contest" of the will, even though they limit its effectiveness. Similarly, petitions to construe or interpret the will or to deprive a beneficiary of his or her share for any of the reasons described in this chapter are not "contests" of the validity of a will *as a will*. The contest of a will is a formal proceeding challenging the will as a vehicle, i.e., the *external* validity of a will. There are also all the problems of *internal* validity by which a provision in an otherwise valid will is ineffective for some stated reason. The particular challenge to the will or its effectiveness must be proscribed.

Third, no-contest clauses tend to be strictly construed because they are in the nature of a forfeiture. The particular act of the beneficiary must fall within the terminology of the testator. This tendency toward strict interpretation has led to longer and more complicated no-contest clauses.

Fourth, the clauses only work to deprive a beneficiary of some portion of the estate which he or she would otherwise have received. Thus, a disinherited child will not be deterred by a no-contest clause unless the will makes a substantial provision for him if he does not contest.

Fifth, an effective bequest to an alternate taker is usually necessary in order to divert the bequest, especially when there is an attempt to disinherit an heir. A will which makes no dispositive provision except "I give nothing to my heirs" gives the entire estate to the heirs. Uniform Probate Code § 2–101(b) is unique in permitting a negative will.

Sixth, a successful will challenge defeats the will *and* the no-contest clause contained in it. Therefore, only an unsuccessful will contest is punished.

Finally, even an unsuccessful will contest which clearly falls within the language of an unambiguous no-contest clause may not be enforced in some jurisdictions, if the contest was entered into in good faith. The reluctance of the court to close its doors to legitimate inquiry and the court's dislike of forfeiture combine to justify a good faith questioning of the validity of the will.

2. CONDITIONAL BEQUESTS, EQUITABLE CHARGES AND ELECTIONS

a. Conditional Bequests

Any lawful condition can be imposed upon the will as a whole or upon any bequest within the will. Consider the following examples.

> EXAMPLE #1: T's will provides: "I give $1,000 to my friend, X, provided he survives me." Valid and usual.
>
> EXAMPLE #2: T's will provides: "I give $1,000 to my friend, X, provided he kills my wife." Invalid.
>
> EXAMPLE #3: T's will provides: "I give my automobile to my older son, provided he gives his automobile to my younger son." Valid and reasonable. Note that the testator sets up an election here and attempts to dispose of property which he does not own. It is more difficult when the election involves property which the testator may have believed he had the right to dispose of, e.g., joint tenancy property.

EXAMPLE #4: T's will provides: "I give $1,000 to my son provided he never marries." Traditionally, this type of restraint upon future action (Contrast "provided he is unmarried at the time of my death") has been declared invalid, even if the son is a priest.

EXAMPLE #5: T's will provides: "If my daughter is divorced or widowed, I give her an annuity of $120,000 a year." The validity of this bequest may turn on the motivation: Was it an (invalid) effort to induce divorce or murder or was it a (valid) desire to provide for the daughter if the wage-earning husband should not be available?

Many of the conditional bequests are similar to situations in which the question is whether there is any beneficiary, e.g., bequests to an animal, for a monument or to burn the money or raze a house. It is possible to phrase the same potential bequests as conditional bequests: "I give to X, provided he . . ." cares for an animal, builds a monument, burns the other money or razes a building. Courts differ in their acceptance of these bequests in either form, but the conditional form is more acceptable in most cases.

b. Equitable Charges

An equitable charge arises when a testator devises property to a person subject to the payment of a certain sum of money to a third person. For example, Testator gives his farm, Blackacre, to his son, "provided he pays his sister $500 a month for her life." The annuity which Testator attempts to create for his daughter is not a trust. A court of equity will enforce the annuity by an "equitable charge" upon the farm. Note that the equitable charge may be a cloud on the title of the farm preventing the son from selling or refinancing it.

A court of equity determines that it is appropriate to enforce the testator plan for a piece of property. Analysis of whether to impose such a charge must take account of a great many factors including the terms and duration of the charge, the reasons for it and alternatives to it and other difficulties (such as the cloud on title) which it may cause.

c. Elections

The forced share of a spouse is an election set up by operation of law. An election may also be involved in conditional bequests (whether expressly made conditional or not) which attempt to dispose of property of someone other than the testator, as in Example #3, above, including the attempt to dispose of property held in joint tenancy to someone other than the joint tenant. Must the joint tenant give the property which had been held in joint tenancy in accordance with the will in order to take the bequests under the will? In election situations, there is a right which the beneficiary can refuse, but the refusal also involves a loss of all other rights under the will in most cases.

3. PROPERTY SETTLEMENT AGREEMENT

Uniform Probate Code § 2–804 and some jurisdictions state that divorce revokes a will by operation of law. The rule is not universal. In other jurisdictions, a property settlement agreement may waive the rights to take under (or against) a will or by intestacy, including the rights to exempt property, family allowance, and the right to serve as personal representative. This is simply an offshoot of the disclaimer doctrine, but it has the added contractual flavor.

Generally, property settlement agreements are strictly construed so that a waiver of each individual right must be included. The property settlement may not become effective because of the non-entry of a final decree of divorce before death. If it is final and effective, the agreement's terms are as enforceable as any disclaimer.

4. ADVANCEMENTS AND ADEMPTION BY SATISFACTION

If an intestate "advances" the heir's share by giving it to the heir apparent during the intestate's lifetime, the doctrine of "advancement" calls for an adjustment of the fractional share of the estate which the heir takes. (Naturally, the doctrine is inapplicable in sole heir situations; it is a doctrine for equalizing shares among co-heirs.) The adjustment calls for a figurative adding back of the value of the lifetime gift to the intestate estate to compute the figuratively enlarged estate for distribution and charging the heir who received the advancement with the value of the gift up to the total amount of his or her intestate share. It is not required that an heir return any excess since that would defeat the testator's intention to make the gift during lifetime.

The concept of the advancement is to carry out the intention of the decedent that the lifetime gift be applied against the ultimate share of the heir or will beneficiary. Many jurisdictions require a greater amount of evidence of such intention, such as a writing, because of the possibility of misunderstanding. See Uniform Probate Code §§ 2–109 and 2–609.

Some jurisdictions go to the opposite extreme and assume that a large gift to a child is intended as an advancement. In the middle are those jurisdictions that neither set up a presumption that there is an advancement in large gifts to issue, nor require a writing to verify the intention of the testator that it was an advancement.

Ademption by satisfaction, sometimes simply called "satisfaction" to avoid confusion with ademption by extinction, is similar in theme to advancements. For example, after writing a will, the testator makes a lifetime gift of the same property (or amount of money) to the intended will beneficiary. The will gift may be considered satisfied by the lifetime gift.

Courts have made many distinctions concerning ademption by satisfaction, reaching diverse results on such issues as whether the doctrine applies to realty, residuary bequests or *pro tanto* satisfactions and whether a presumption arises when the amount given is to descendants of the testator. Generally, most courts apply the doctrine to one of the residuary takers. It is immaterial if the living gift is to the sole residuary taker. It is possible to have an ademption by satisfaction of a portion of a bequest, but both a *pro tanto* satisfaction and a satisfaction not in the same kind raise questions as to whether they were intended as satisfactions.

> EXAMPLE: T's valid will devises Blackacre, now worth $100,000, to T's son, S, and the residue to a friend, F. T gives $50,000 cash to his son, S. Is there an ademption by satisfaction?

Without further evidence of intention, the differing amounts and types of property indicate that an advancement was not intended. Most courts state that the doctrine of ademption by satisfaction does not apply to realty. Of course, if the exact property was given to the beneficiary, there would be an ademption by extinction and the bequest would fail. On the other hand, some courts presume an advancement or ademption by satisfaction when there is a substantial gift from parent to child.

Two problems of timing are associated with advancements. Normally the gifts are valued at the time of the gift, and the estate is valued at the time of death. The advancement may increase or decrease in value. Thus, in the Example, Blackacre could decrease in value to $50,000 and the $50,000 cash given the son could increase or decrease. The other problem of timing is that the will must precede the gift in order for the issue of ademption by satisfaction to arise. Thus, in the Example, if T wrote a codicil to his will after the gift was made to S, the codicil might "republish" the will to make the doctrine of ademption by extinction inapplicable.

In situations in which the person who has received the putative advancement or ademption by satisfaction dies before the donor, it is obvious that there cannot be any "advancement" to the heir because the heir apparent did not achieve that status. It would be extremely unusual to charge an heir with an advancement made to another person who was the heir apparent, even when the heir and the heir apparent are closely related. Related difficult areas include heirs who, having received an advancement, renounce the bequest or murder the predecessor.

Often in a family situation it is difficult to tell whether the donor intended a normal gift, an advancement or a loan. This preliminary determination points toward the applicable doctrines.

5. SET-OFF (RETAINER)

If a will beneficiary owes money to the testator, most jurisdictions permit the personal representative to "set-off" the amount of the debt against the bequest. The doctrine is more likely to be applied when the debt is liquidated and the bequest is fungible. It is unlikely that the personal representative would be allowed to offset a personal injury claim against a bequest of copyright royalties and Blackacre, at least not until a court determined the value of each.

The difficult areas of this doctrine include instances in which the will beneficiary is not the one to take the bequest (e.g., because of death, renunciation or murder) and instances in which the debt is barred (e.g., by the statute of limitations or bankruptcy of the beneficiary). Jurisdictions vary in their treatment of both issues.

Part 8 of the Uniform Probate Code addresses creditors' claims. Section 3–811 permits the personal representative to deduct any counterclaim that the estate has against a claimant. Specification § 3–811 provides:

> In determining a claim against an estate a court shall reduce the amount allowed by the amount of any counterclaims and, if the counterclaims exceed the claim, render a judgment against the claimant in the amount of the excess. A counterclaim, liquidated or unliquidated, may arise from a transaction other than that upon which the claim is based. A counterclaim may give rise to relief exceeding in amount or different in kind from that sought in the claim.

This section implies that the ability of the personal representative to reduce the amount of a claim against the estate by a counterclaim against a creditor is similar to the right to set-off a claim by a beneficiary and thereby reduce the amount which the estate pays to the beneficiary.

CHAPTER 7
ESTATE PROPERTY

A. TYPES OF BEQUESTS AND DEVISES

All of the problems in this chapter address the division of a testator's estate among multiple takers. The guiding rule is that the testator's intention governs. The approach is first to seek the particular testator's intention. Only if that cannot be determined, then ascertain what rule governs the division of the estate.

A common approach utilizes the characterization of each bequest and devise into one of a number of categories—specific, demonstrative, general, annuity and residual. This classifies the bequest by its wording. The consequences of the various doctrines flow from the classification.

An alternative approach focuses upon the function involved (abatement, accretion etc.) and decides whether the bequest is specific, general etc. for the purpose of this function. It is often difficult to tell whether a court is using the characterization or functional approach.

The various classes of bequests and devises are defined as follows:

1. SPECIFIC BEQUESTS OR DEVISES

A bequest or devise of a particular and uniquely identifiable item is "specific." Realty has a tradition of being considered "specific" because each parcel is unique. A devise of "all the realty I own at the time of my death" is probably better classified as general or residual, rather than specific, even if the testator owned only one parcel of realty at all times.

There may be some confusion and sloppiness in use of the term "specific." For example, one may "specify" a sum of money, e.g. $5,000, but that sum, although "specified," is technically not a "specific" bequest because the funds are fungible and do not necessarily come from a unique source. On the other hand, a bequest or devise of the oil painting of Grandfather is specific. The uniqueness of the asset suggests that its value is not a sufficient replacement for it if it does not exist in the testator's estate at his death. Stated another way, the law infers that the testator wanted to give the particular item and not merely the value of the thing.

2. DEMONSTRATIVE BEQUESTS

The demonstrative bequest (a demonstrative devise is quite rare) is characterized by a two-part bequest. The testator bequeaths a sum of money, but also indicates the source of the funds. If the source is existent and is sufficient, no problem arises. If, however, the source is nonexistent or insufficient, the question arises whether the bequest can be distinguished from a specific bequest.

A specific bequest of an item which is not existent causes the gift to fail, but generally the demonstrative bequest does not fail when the fund or property from which the amount or quantity is to be paid no longer exists. Thus a bequest of "$10,000 from my savings account at First National Bank" will generally pass $10,000 from a solvent estate even if the savings account is not in existence at the time of death. However, a bequest of "my savings account at First National Bank" would fail if no such account existed.

A third possibility is that the bequest might require interpretation. For example, the testator had certificates of deposit, but no savings account. Did the testator mean "certificate of deposit" when he said "savings account"? The court can make a determination of testator's intent.

3. GENERAL BEQUESTS AND DEVISES

General bequests and devises are the catch-all classification of bequests. If a bequest is not specific, nor demonstrative, nor residual, it is "general." Some jurisdictions also segregate other types of bequests and devises, e.g., annuities, but there does not seem to be any functional difference.

At times the distinction between general and residual may be immaterial; e.g., a bequest of "my entire estate" is general, but will have the same effect as a residual bequest ("the balance of my estate").

A general bequest or devise is derived from the general (as opposed to specific) assets of the estate and is not dependent upon the existence of the particular thing bequeathed or devised.

> EXAMPLE: Testator's will bequeaths "100 shares of Apple stock" to A and devises "160 acres of farmland in Washington County,

Minnesota," to B. Although testator's estate is solvent, it does not include any such stock or land.

If the bequest and devise in the example are interpreted as being "specific," the doctrine of ademption will apply and both gifts fail since they do not exists in the testator's estate. If, however, the bequests are construed as "general," they will be construed as instructions to the executor to purchase such assets, utilizing funds of the estate. Most bequests of money are correctly characterized as "general pecuniary legacies" if they are not demonstrative. It is common to treat bequests of a certain number of shares of stock to be general rather than specific, which avoids extinguishing the gift.

4. RESIDUAL BEQUESTS AND DEVISES

The residual bequest or devise gives whatever assets are left in the estate after the satisfaction of all debts, expenses of administration, taxes, and all other bequests. Although last in line, it may be the major part of the estate.

The residual taker is like the owner of common stock of a corporation. As the size and net worth of the estate (or corporation) increases, the benefit is bestowed upon the residual taker (or common stockholder). Conversely, as the size and net worth of the estate (or corporation) shrinks, the share of the residual taker (or common stockholder) decreases.

Bequests which fail for any reason pass as the testator directs alternative takers. In the absence of such provision, they pass as provided by statute, e.g., an anti-lapse statute. Unless a statutory or will provision requires otherwise, failed bequests fall into the residue.

When residuary gift fails, the majority of jurisdictions state that the failed part of the residue passes by intestacy (rather than to the other residual takers) unless the testator provides to the contrary. A large minority of states by decision or by statutory provision similar to Uniform Probate Code § 2–604 permit the residue of a residue so that the remaining residual takers share the failed portion of the residual bequest (except in anti-lapse situations). As the Characterization and Functional Analysis of Bequests chart illustrates, the dividing line of the functions is generally between "specific" and not specific or between "residual" and not residual.

TABLE 7-1
Characterization and Functional Analysis of Bequests

FUNCTION/BEQUEST:	SPECIFIC	GENERAL, ANNUITY, & DEMONSTRATIVE	RESIDUE
Abatement, to Pay:			
—Debts, Admin. Exp.	Last	Used After Residue	First
—Other Bequests:	Exempt	Not Used for Others	Used
(Federal Estate Tax is Often Prorated by Statute.)			
ACCRETION	Takes	Does Not Take	Takes

ADEMPTION	Applies	Does Not Apply
EXONERATION	Applies	Not Exonerated, But May Be Applied to Exonerate

B. ABATEMENT

Abatement permits gifts to be lessened or eliminated if the estate is insufficient to provide the gifts mentioned. Issues arise when the estate is not as generous as the testator's dispositive scheme and because the spouse, pretermitted issue, taxing authorities or creditors take their shares before the will beneficiaries. In all cases involved in this chapter, the estate must be solvent after the payment of expenses of administration, taxes and debts.

If the estate is insolvent, there is nothing over which the multiple beneficiaries can fight. If there is only a single beneficiary, his or her fight is with the spouse, pretermitted issue, taxing authority or creditor, rather than other beneficiaries.

Unless otherwise provided by the testator or by statute, the residue of the estate (or any portion which would pass by intestacy) is used first to satisfy the various claimants against the estate, then the other bequests abate in proportion to their value, except that some (but not necessarily all) specific bequests may be spared the imposition of the burden if to do so would destroy their value.

EXAMPLE: T's will bequeaths an oil painting of Grandmother, worth $1,000, to A, cash of $4,000 to B and the residue to C. The total gross estate is $10,000, including the value of the painting;

there are expenses, taxes and debts of $6,000. Who receives how much?

In the example, the residual bequest to C is used first to pay the expenses of administration and debts. If there is federal estate tax, a statute may require that it be "equitably prorated" in accordance with the value of each bequest. Assuming no such proration, how is the remaining $1,000 of expenses and debts to be charged between A and B?

On the one hand, many courts would spare the specific bequest because of its indivisibility. The $1,000 value is coincidental; it is the item itself which the testator intended to pass and to charge a portion of the expenses of administration and debts to it might force a sale of the very item which the testator desired to give in kind. In this example, B would receive $3,000, C would receive nothing and A would receive the painting undiminished in value.

On the other hand, some courts would apply abatement proportionately to the value (or such apportionment would be appropriate if A were also the beneficiary of a cash bequest, e.g., $2,000). Thus, in abatement, a specific bequest is the most favored and the residual bequest is least favored. The themes of abatement are avoidance of the destruction of the specific item, use of the residue (or portion of the probate estate not disposed of by will) and apportionment in accordance with value among the remaining bequests if further abatement is necessary.

C. ACCRETION

Accretion is the growth of an item bequeathed between the time the will was written and the testator's death. It is used here to include the possibility of shrinkage, as well as growth. There can also be a growth between the date of death and the date that the estate is distributed. In this latter case, the growth (or shrinkage) of a specific bequest clearly passes with it and the residual bequests receive the additional growth unless the testator or a statute provides otherwise.

The growth can be of various sorts. No account is ordinarily taken of shrinkage due to inflation. Thus, a 1990 bequest of $100,000 by a decedent dying in 2022 will pass $100,000 in 2022 (or whenever distribution is made) purchasing power, not the purchasing power of 1990. Similarly, growth due to income separated and paid is not considered.

> EXAMPLE: T bequeaths 100 shares of each of A, B and C Corporations to beneficiary in a 1990 will. Between the date of the will and T's death, each of the corporations has the same earnings, but they react differently. A Corporation pays $1,000 in dividends; B Corporation declares a 10% stock dividend in multiple years; and C Corporation simply increases in value.

Specific bequests tend to carry their growth with them so that the 10% stock dividend might pass with a specific bequest of the B Stock. It is not certain that the bequest would be treated as specific, even if the number of shares owned coincided with the number bequeathed. Here, however, we are applying a doctrine which benefits, rather than destroys, the bequest (cf. ademption) and construction of the bequest as "specific" is more likely.

Although general bequests do not ordinarily carry separated and reinvested income as in the case of B Corporation, the bequest of C Corporation does carry the increase in value. Increases and decreases in value tend to be disregarded. If there were a two-for-one stock split, the specific bequest is more likely to pass 200 shares than the general bequest; it is also more likely that the bequest would be construed as "specific" in such a case. Mutual funds with the options of reinvesting the "capital gains portion" of dividends pose particular problems in this area.

Can a testator vary his testamentary plan by choosing to reinvest the capital gains distributions (and obtain additional certificates of beneficial interest)? Generally, yes. The theme of accretion is to keep intact the item specifically bequeathed (but not necessarily its value, income or purchasing power) with any portions not given to (or taken from) the specific bequests being given to (or taken from) the residue. As far as growth is concerned, the specific bequest and the residual bequests are favored at the expense of other bequests.

D. ADEMPTION BY EXTINCTION

Ademption arises when the subject matter of a specific bequest is changed or not a part of the testator's estate at his death. Possibly some states still follow the principle of "in specie" ademption enunciated by the English courts in the late 18th Century. If the item is not present in specie (i.e., exactly in the kind specified), the bequest fails, regardless of the testator's intention. Probably the better view and that held by a large minority is that the intention of the testator controls. This leads to a series of issues when ademption is possible.

First, is the bequest specific? Construing the bequest or devise as demonstrative or general may avoid the ademption issue, but be too broad a stroke because of the effect upon other functions, such as abatement and accretions upon the bequest so construed.

Second, is it changed materially? A "mere" change in form or value may be deemed "immaterial" in order to avoid ademption.

Third, is the item bequeathed traceable and identifiable even though changed? Tracing is similar to, but lacks the equitable flavor of tracing the trust res.

Fourth, does the testator's intention govern? Here, the doctrinal split explained above must be dealt with. If the testator's intent does govern, the further issues arise:

Fifth, what was this particular testator's intention?

Finally, as of when is the intention relevant? Often there are at least two points in time—the time that the will was written and the time of the change—and other possible times such as the time of codicils, further changes or death. Do we discern the intention only from the will or from the surrounding circumstances? This leads to issues as to what evidence is, or should be, admitted.

In approaching ademption issues, it is often helpful to consider the type of asset bequeathed (realty, promissory notes, securities, automobiles, etc.) and the type of change involved. For example, realty which is condemned represents the least volitional change in the asset bequeathed. Conversions or pay-offs of bonds, mortgages and other securities may occur without much participation by the testator. Realty could be sold with a mortgage taken back as security for a promissory note upon which the maker defaults. Upon foreclosure, what is the effect upon a devise of the property by the purchaser or by the seller?

The many possible changes in corporate securities create the issues mentioned under accretions, plus others: Stock redemptions, options and rights (which require the addition of cash), splits and stock and cash dividends all must be dealt with.

> EXAMPLE: T's valid will makes the following bequests and the changes indicated occur after the will was written:
>
> > A. "To A, my pink Lenox chinaware, 34 pieces." (Only 30 pieces have been found; there is no information concerning any other pieces.)
> >
> > B. "To B, the oil painting titled 'Solitude.' " (T gave the painting to B two years ago.)

C. "To C, my John Hancock life insurance policy." (The company paid the proceeds to K, the beneficiary designated in the policy.)

D. "To D, my Tesla." (Two years after the will was written, T traded the Tesla and paid an additional $14,000 for a Mercedes sedan.)

E. "To E, my Corvette sports car." (T was killed in an accident which destroyed the Corvette; the automobile insurance company paid $27,000 to T's executor for the total loss.)

F. "To F, my Google stock." (The 100 shares owned when the will was written split 2 for 1 and then had stock "warrants" which T exercised by paying $500 to obtain 10 more shares. T died owning 210 shares of Google.)

G. "To G, 100 shares of Microsoft stock." (T owned 100 shares when the will was written, but sold them two years ago and purchased 200 shares of Apple.)

H. "To H, the Smith $100,000 promissory note." (The note, secured by a mortgage, had an unpaid balance of $95,000 when the will was written. Monthly payments of $2000 have reduced principal $20,000 and paid $30,000 interest, leaving an unpaid balance at death of $75,000.)

I. "To I, Greenacre." (At the time the will was written, Greenacre was owned free and clear. T mortgaged the property and used the funds, plus $750,000 of additional funds, to build a small apartment house on Greenacre.)

J. "To J, the residue of my estate." (J gets what's left.)

What does each beneficiary receive?

Is ademption an issue for each of the bequests? Perhaps the 100 shares of Microsoft stock (G) is a general bequest which would be treated as a direction to the executor to purchase from the otherwise residual assets 100 shares of Microsoft stock.

In the case of the oil painting (B) that was given during T's lifetime to the beneficiary, we have an ademption by satisfaction, rather than extinction. The will bequest will be, and should be, ineffective to pass the value of the painting to the person who already has the painting.

The life insurance policy is not part of the probate estate and therefore the attempted gift is extinguished. The will is ineffective to change beneficiaries, and there are no proceeds to which it could be traced. Thus, C's bequest fails in all jurisdictions.

In all the bequests except the residual there was a change so that the item in the estate was not the same item that T owned at the time that the will was written. The strictest application of the "in specie" test would cause all of the bequests to be adeemed, even those in which the value increased such as the Google stock (F) and Greenacre (J), because they have been disposed of, destroyed, lost or substantially changed.

Ademption is less likely to be applied when there is a lesser degree of change, as with the chinaware (A), Google stock (F) and promissory note (H). In the last case, change is typical of the asset. There is an ambiguity concerning the change in form of the Corvette (E). If the death occurred before the wreck, ademption is not an issue. Rather, it is an issue of the executor's duty to insure and retroactive application of that duty from the time the executor qualifies. It is more likely that the damage occurred before the death. There is little law on simultaneous death and destruction of the item bequeathed.

In the case of the Lenox chinaware (A), the four pieces are adeemed, but it is unlikely that the remaining 30 will also be adeemed because the set is not exactly as described. The change was material as to four pieces, but not as to the remaining 30. A should receive the 30 pieces.

If the Microsoft stock (G) is construed as a specific bequest, can the conversion into Apple stock be treated as a mere "change in form?" The facts are unclear as to whether there were additional funds invested as in the cases of the Tesla (D) and Greenacre (I). It is easier to resist ademption when the funds can be traced, undiluted, into another asset. Commingling of funds tends to defeat tracing. The involuntary conversion of the Corvette (E) is the best example of a substantial change which should not cause an ademption of the item bequeathed.

A more formal approach to Greenacre (I), especially in a state with the "title theory" for mortgages, treats the mortgaging of realty specifically devised as an ademption. This seems unreasonable especially when the proceeds are reinvested in the property.

The promissory note (H) typifies many ademption problems: The note itself has dropped in purchasing power and unpaid balance, but these changes are immaterial. The monthly payments, even if traced, are probably adeemed, even as to the principal portion. The interest paid before death would almost never be given to the will beneficiary, although accumulated and unpaid interest probably would pass with the note and mortgage. If additional amounts were advanced and a new note given for the new and old debts, then the accretion problems found in the Tesla (D), Google stock (F) and Greenacre (I) situations would also be involved.

The Google stock (F) bequest will pass the 210 shares owned at death. A more difficult situation arises when the bequest is worded "my *100 shares of* Google stock." In that case, the application of tracing forces the words of the will to take on new meaning: "100" means "210" just as "100 Microsoft" in G might become "200 Apple" and "Tesla" in D becomes "Mercedes sedan." The hardest case for determining the intent of T to mean something other than the words which were used in the Tesla (D) voluntarily converted with the additional investment.

It is suggested that you review the foregoing problem until you feel comfortable with the answers and are able to make the distinctions between the bequests outlined above. Review item I in the example and note that two different ademption issues arise because the testator subsequently mortgaged realty which was specifically devised. First, is the net value of the property devised adeemed because of the mortgage? Second, is the value of the debt not a partial ademption, i.e., is the devisee entitled to have the property "exonerated" of its debt?

E. EXONERATION

In criminal law, exoneration refers to a person cleared of a crime after additional evidence (such as DNA testing) has surfaced. In wills law, exoneration refers to whether the person has the right to have an asset cleared of a debt, such as a mortgage. Uniform Probate Code § 2–607 provides that, "A specific devise passes subject to any mortgage interest existing at the date of death, without right of exoneration, regardless of a general directive in the will to pay debts." This means the recipient has no right to receive the property without the mortgage.

However, the personal representative may find it advantageous to the estate to pay off some or all of the debt secured by the property devised; e.g., it may be wise to continue the monthly payments on a promissory note secured by the property devised or bequeathed. If there is no exoneration, the beneficiary is placed in a position where he or she must contribute the funds necessary to reimburse the other beneficiaries. If there is exoneration, the source of the funds within the estate is the property not disposed of by will, if any, and if not, the residuary estate, if any.

If there is no residuary estate, there is a split of authority as to whether general bequests can be used to exonerate. Specific bequests and devises are exonerated themselves and are not subject to abatement for the exoneration of other specific bequests or devises.

CHAPTER 8

INTERPRETATION

Interpretation of the terms of a will does not lend itself to facile explanation. For each trend or technique, there seems to be an opposing trend or technique. In some cases rigid rules of future interests dictate what the testator is deemed to have intended by a certain word. In other cases, typically when an "ambiguity" is found, words take on entirely new meanings.

Recall that the application of wills doctrines may give an unexpected meaning to words: Anti-lapse and ademption doctrines may cause a bequest of "My 100 shares of Microsoft stock to my brothers" to be interpreted as "200 shares of Apple to my nieces." This happens because the Testator sold the Microsoft stock and purchased Apple and because the brothers died leaving their daughters (Testator's nieces) as their descendants.

The interpretation process relies, foremost, on the "intention of the testator." In search of that intention, various techniques have been used. Most words have varying degrees of clarity. Some words, especially "technical" words such as "heir" have precise meanings which will be attributed to the testator unless it is obvious that he did not intend them. (For example, a will which starts "This is my will if I die intestate. . . .")

The more usual legal approach to a word is Justice Holmes' much quoted assertion, "A word is not a crystal, transparent and unchanged, it is the skin of a living thought and may vary greatly in color and content according to the circumstances and time in which it is used." Beyond this approach is the circular and less helpful semantic approach by which the word is deemed to mean whatever the user intended it to mean.

A sampler of interpretation principles includes the following:

- All the testamentary writings should be construed together to be consistent, if possible. If they are inconsistent, the later will prevail.
- The will should be construed to avoid partial or complete intestacy, but the courts will not write the will for the testator.
- Words are to be taken in their ordinary sense and technical words are given their technical meaning, except that any contrary intention by the testator can be shown and given effect.

As an examination technique in this area, the presence of quotation marks or other indicia of direct quotation offers the material about which interpretation may be sought. Three typical areas for interpretation are as follows.

First, what passes under a bequest of "belongings," "bonds," "business," "cash," "contents," "dwelling," "funds," "household," "money," "personal" property, estate, effects or things, "possessions," or "securities"? Pay close attention to the document and the list of items in the estate.

Second, who takes under certain descriptions such as "child," "first cousin," "devisee," "family," "spouse," "off-springs" or "relations"? This is why it's important to graft a family tree.

Third, what is the effect of certain provisions? For example, a gift to a class which includes a person specifically excluded in another provision of the will may mean the person is excluded from the class gift. When the percentages do not total 100, the gift amount may appreciate proportionally to reach 100 percent. If there is a dispute as to whether a fee simple or a life estate is given to a beneficiary, the question becomes whether there was a second beneficiary to follow the life estate. If not, the gift is most often construed as one in fee simple. Sometimes the gifts may be as vague as bequests for "college education" or "maintenance." The personal representative may interpret this language start paying college bills or rent.

In the event of disputes, courts will try to discern the intent of the testator to interpret the will.

CHAPTER 9
CREATION OF TRUSTS

A. TRUSTS CONTRASTED TO WILLS

The subject matter of Trusts, unlike Wills, is evenly divided between creation and administration. To create a trust requires a res (trust property), trustee(s), settlor/trustor, beneficiary, and trust purposes.

The Restatement Third, Trusts and the Uniform Trust Code have helped bring more certainty to trust principles. While wills was predominately based upon statutes, trusts are based more upon case law. Trusts are the child of the Courts of Equity. Both wills and trusts focus upon what part of the estate is distributed to whom. Trusts, additionally, focus upon the duties of the person making the distribution and how distribution is achieved.

B. DEFINING A "TRUST"

A trust is a device whereby a trustee manages property for one or more beneficiaries. The settlor or trustor is the person establishing the trust. The trustee is person responsible for managing the trust assets and holds the legal title. The beneficiary is the person who benefits from the trust assets, and holds the equitable title. The trust res is the trust property. While a private trust can be created without a trustee other than the creator, it will fail if the settlor fails to name a beneficiary beyond himself or herself or fails to name the trust property. Finally, there must be a trust purpose that defines the trustee's active duties toward managing the trust property. Otherwise, the trust is considered a dry trust and non-existent.

The trust relationship imposes "fiduciary" duties upon the trustee for the benefit of the beneficiary. These fiduciary duties are the life-blood of the relationship.

A trust arises when the owner of property separates the benefits from the burdens of ownership by giving them to different people beyond just the owner. Normally the benefits and burdens of property ownership are in the same person. For example, an owner of an apartment house would be entitled to collect rents (a benefit) and would be required to make repairs and pay taxes (burdens).

The owner would then receive the net benefit (or have the net loss). If the owner wanted to separate the benefits and burdens, he could create a trust by delivering legal title to one person (the trustee) and the equitable (or beneficial) title to another (the beneficiary). The trustee would then have duties imposed upon her by the terms of the trust instrument and by general trust law. The beneficiary would have only the benefits (perhaps reduced slightly by the trustee's fees). The trustee would have the power (unless denied by the trust instrument) and perhaps even the duty (perhaps even if prohibited by the trust instrument) to sell the apartment house and reinvest the proceeds for the benefit of the beneficiary.

A trust separates legal title and equitable title (i.e., the "ownership" protected by the respective courts of law and of equity). A trust is a relationship which requires the existence of some property interest, the "res."

The elements of a trust can be visualized as an electrical plug. The two prongs are the negative aspects of ownership (the duties) that are assumed by the trustee, and the positive aspects (the benefits of ownership) that are received by the beneficiary. The relationship is in regard to the property, the res, and is created by the intention of the settlor or trustor, the creator of the trust. Given these elements, the court of equity made them significant by imposing duties that are the electrical current or life of the trust. We examine those duties in the last portion of this nutshell.

THE PARTIES TO THE TRUST RELATIONSHIP

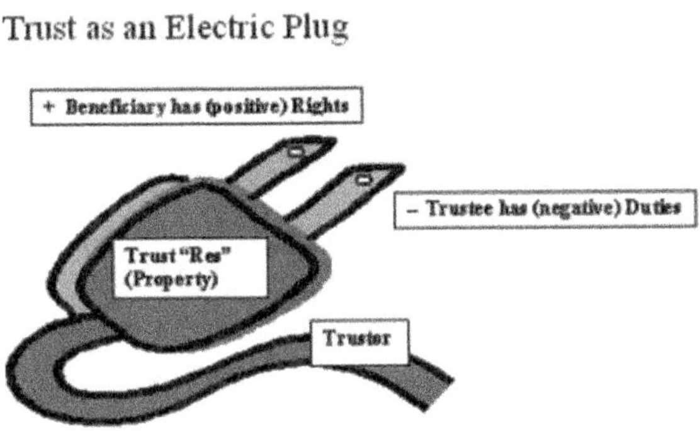

C. CONTRASTING A TRUST AGAINST OTHER RELATIONSHIPS

The edges of the trust definition can be explored by comparing and contrasting the trust with other relationships, such as agency, custodianship, personal representatives, bailments, power of appointments, security arrangements, contracts, and the imperfect gift. All are explored in this section.

1. AGENCY VS. TRUST

Both the trust and the agency are fiduciary relationships in which one person acts for another. Both may involve property, although an agency need not concern property while a trust always does. An agency is terminated upon the death or incapacity of either agent or principal because it is a continuing consensual relationship. A "durable" power of attorney, permitted by many state statutes, is an exception for incapacity of the principal.

A trust, once created, exists as long as permitted by the trust terms so long as it doesn't run afoul of the Rule against Perpetuities. The principal is liable for the acts of the agent done within the scope of employment, but neither the trustor nor the beneficiary is liable for the acts of the trustee. This is so even when the trustee's acts cause a diminution of the trust estate.

Both trusts and agencies come in a variety of forms. An agency is more like a puppeteer (the principal) governing the acts and limiting the discretion of the marionette (the agent). The principal has greater control of the acts of the agent and is therefore liable for the agent's acts. On the other hand, a trustee is normally free of control by the settlor and the beneficiary, although a certain amount of control can be retained through the creation or retention of a power to terminate or revoke or to replace the trustee. The beneficiary need not consent to the acts of the trustee and does not have a day-to-day control.

The agent seldom has title, while the trustee always does. The range of acts permitted to the agent is smaller than the range of acts permitted to a trustee. Examination of the understanding of the parties as to the amount of control which the agent or trustee is to have is probably the best means for distinguishing the two relationships. Examples of agencies are the employer-employee relation, powers of attorney, escrows and most custodial arrangements.

2. CUSTODIANSHIPS VS. TRUSTS

A custodianship, similar to a trust, involves property given by one person to a second to be held and managed under fiduciary principles for a third person. The legal title, under the Uniform Transfers (or Gifts) to Minors Act, is in the minor, but the custodian has full powers of management, sale and reinvestment.

Like a trustee, the custodian can make broad decisions including the decision to sell the property involved and is totally free of any control by the donor who created the arrangement. Delivery to the custodian is a sufficient delivery to complete the irrevocable gift for property and tax reasons, whereas one cannot normally make a completed delivery to one's own agent (since the agent would be under a duty to return it, if directed by the principal). The distinction is less material in the case of the custodianship because most of the troublesome differences have been eliminated by the statutory provisions.

3. PERSONAL REPRESENTATIVES VS. TRUSTS

A person who is unable to act in his or her own behalf may have a "representative" appointed to care for his or her person or estate. The personal representative may be an executor, administrator, guardian, conservator, committee, curator, or other appropriate individual(s). The personal representative of the estate (whether or not the protected person is deceased) is a fiduciary dealing with the property of another, but none of the arrangements falls within the classic definitions of a "trust."

Generally, the relationships are established in accordance with a statute. A deceased person may be represented by an executor (if chosen by the decedent's will) or administrator (if not so chosen) or the generic "personal representative" title used by the Uniform Probate Code. A living person may be unable to manage his or her property because of some permanent or temporary legal disability such as minority. Each state provides for the appointment of a representative of one or more names to manage the property of such person.

Normally the personal representative is appointed by the court, although nomination by will or the involved person is often permitted. Supervision of the representative is by the court, with limited discretion. Title is usually in the beneficiary rather than the representative. The historic derivation of the relationship is the court of law, rather than the court of equity.

4. BAILMENTS VS. TRUSTS

A bailment is the delivery of personal property by the owner to another for the performance of some act (shipment, storage, cleaning, repair). For example, a person creates a bailment when he asks his friend to keep his piano until he can find another suitable home. The friend must return the piano to the owner upon request in essentially the same condition as provided. If the item is not returned upon it requests, it becomes subject to a possessory lien for the reasonable charges for the item. This can be spelled out in a bailment agreement.

Like a trust, a bailment is involved with property. Unlike a trust, a bailment is not possible for real property. Temporary loans of real property require loan or rental agreements. All bailments and rentals are limited in scope. The bailee and renter take possession (rather than title) to the property. This is not a fiduciary relationship, and has its origin in property law rather than equity. Trusts tend to be longer-lasting and more formal than bailments.

If the subject of the bailment is lost, destroyed or decreased in value without fault on the part of the bailee, the loss is borne by the bailor. By contrast, a trustee has a higher duty to preserve the trust property and may be liable for a loss which occurs without fault on his or her part.

5. POWER OF APPOINTMENTS VS. TRUSTS

A power of appointment is the power in one person to designate who shall be the owner or recipient of property. Powers of appointment deal with the ownership attribute of property. The *donee* of the power exercises it to appoint to one or more permissible *appointees*.

Generally, there are no management powers associated with a power of appointment unlike with a trust. A power is not a duty to appoint, and thus it need not be exercised. If it is not exercised, the property subject to the power goes to (or remains in) the "takers in default of appointment." The power to give away is an attribute of ownership which can be separated out of the bundle of interests and given to another. If one decides to allow another to designate who shall receive or enjoy property, the person so chosen is said to be the donee of a power of appointment.

The power is an ownership right. It is not held subject to any fiduciary duties, although it can be limited and efforts to evade the limitation would be "in fraud" of the power. Like a trust, a power of appointment relates to property. Unlike a trust, it can be exercised only once as to any particular property.

Since a power of appointment is a right which exists in one person to divert the ownership, it is necessary that another person have the title until the power is exercised or eliminated. Often the holder in the interim is a trustee. Thus, a power of appointment is usually found contained in a trust although such an arrangement is not necessary.

A power could be *general* permitting one to appoint to oneself or *special* permitting one to appoint only to or among a certain group of persons, which usually does not include the donee of the power.

> EXAMPLE #1: Testator's will bequeaths "my entire estate to my son, John, to be used for my daughter, Ann." This sounds in management for another and is probably a trust.

> EXAMPLE #2: Testator's will bequeaths "my furniture to my children, my son John to pick who gets which item." John has a general power of appointment and can appoint to himself, but there may be a question whether he can take all items or whether he is limited to equalizing the shares.

6. SECURITY ARRANGEMENTS VS. TRUSTS

Security arrangements such as mortgages, pledges, liens and equitable charges are designed to provide protection to a lender. The title to the property which comprises the security may apparently or actually be given to a lender by a borrower, subject to a condition of repayment. The trust form is used as a security arrangement in the "trust deed" in which the borrower gives title to property to a third person as security for a debt.

The law of mortgages contains both the "title theory" in which the lender obtains title to the property and the more prevalent "lien theory" in which the interest of the lender is seen as "merely" a lien or a security interest with the borrower remaining the owner of the title to the property. Equity interacted with the law of mortgages to create the "right of redemption" by which a mortgagor who had defaulted on the express terms of the mortgage was nevertheless entitled to title upon curing the default. This was, in effect, an equitable demotion of the borrower's breach from material to immaterial status.

Some security arrangements have their origins in equity and are therefore similar to trusts. The equitable lien (a lien recognized in equity even though not complying with legal formalities) and the equitable charge (a charge upon the property imposed by a court of equity) both give an interest related to the property, but not the property itself. For example, Testator dies, survived by his two children, and a will that provides: "I give Orange-acre to my son, S, provided he pays his sister, D, $5,000 a year for her life." The legal and equitable title to Orange-acre has been devised to S, but D has an equitable charge upon Orange-acre, a security interest, for the payment of the $5,000 annuity.

The distinction between a security interest and a trust is similar to the difference in a corporate organization between a bondholder and a shareholder. The bondholder has a debt, fixed in amount, which normally takes priority in payment. The shareholder owns the "equity" interest and benefits from or is burdened with any increase or decrease in value. After the debt is paid, the security holder no longer has a value in the property and the shareholder has the entire ownership.

The key to distinguishing a trust from a debt (or a contract or other relationship) is the intention manifested by the settlor. It is objectively determined by what the parties said and did.

7. CONTRACTS VS. TRUSTS

The distinction between a trust and various types of contracts is important for procedural reasons. The statute of limitations may limit oral contracts to a year, whereas trusts may last for decades or longer. Tracing of proceeds when the promisor-trustee is insolvent is important for both contracts and trusts. Higher fiduciary standards govern a trustee than parties to most contracts. The equitable jurisdiction over trusts possibly does not exist in certain law courts, especially small claims and conciliation-type courts.

8. THE IMPERFECT GIFT VS. TRUST

A gift is a voluntary, gratuitous transfer of interest in property from one to another. To be a valid gift, the donor must intend the transfer to be a gift, must deliver the gift, and the gift must be accepted by the donee. The delivery may be actual (direct transfer of item); symbolic (deed to land), or constructive (keys to the car). If the donee is already in possession of personal property (such as a bailee) when the donor intends to make a gift, then no further delivery is necessary. Once accepted, a gift is normally irrevocable, although one species of gift, the gift *causa mortis*, is revocable.

A gift *causa mortis* is one made in anticipation of death. For this gift to be effective the donor must be stricken with some disorder that makes death imminent; death must ensue as a result of a disorder; the gift must be conditioned on death from this disorder; and the donor must actually deliver the gift. If the donor does not die, the gift is revoked.

Trusts and gifts interrelate in that a trust traditionally is created by a gift. Trusts are capable of being revocable, whereas only the gift *causa mortis* is. A gift is a one-time transaction, while the trust creates an ongoing relationship.

Trusts relate to the desires of persons to hold on to property until death, but also to indicate who should have the property upon death. Please note, "Equity will not transform an imperfect [usually because of a failure of delivery] gift into a trust, but if the gift is incomplete by reason of some technicality [e.g., delivery] and if the essential elements of a trust are established, the manifest intention of the donor may be sustained through a trust." The first part stresses the legal requirement of delivery; the second part permits a loophole in cases where the intention of the donor (usually dead at the time the controversy is to be resolved) is "clear."

D. QUIZ ON TRUSTS VS. OTHER RELATIONSHIPS

QUESTIONS

1. A delivers his automobile to B and directs B to keep the automobile for one month and then to deliver it to C. What arrangement might this be? Why? What facts would change your decision?

2. A transfers by signed deed and registration certificates to B a commercial garage and lot, together with three automobiles with directions to B to sell the garage, lot and automobiles and to invest the proceeds and pay the income to C for life and, upon C's death, to deliver the principal to D. What arrangement is this most likely to be labeled?

3. A devises Redacre to B "on the condition that B pay $1,000" to C. Would B commit a breach of trust by conveying to D without having made payment to C?

ANSWERS

1. This is probably a bailment, rather than a trust. It is a delivery of personal property to be stored and then delivered. B does not seem to have any discretion to use, or duty to make productive, the automobile. Compare the situation if it were a taxicab and all parties involved were taxi drivers. Had A given B the title documents, power to sell and directions to use the property and deliver the proceeds to C, a trust would have been created.

2. Here the delivery of title, power to deal, longer existence of the relationship and broader powers of B

indicate that he is a trustee. Additionally, the division of the equitable estate into life estate to C and remainder to D is a typical trust disposition. This case contrasts with question number 1 to show the effect of additional details in deciding what arrangement has been made.

3. The fixed sum (as opposed to an ownership of Redacre) payable to C sounds in debt and the means of creating the arrangement (a will) suggests that an equitable charge, rather than a trust, has been created. Property subject to an equitable charge can be transferred; a bona fide purchaser for value without notice cuts off outstanding equities; if the conveyance was not to such a purchaser, then the charge remains on the property. There is no breach of trust unless there is a trust (or other fiduciary relationship). An equitable charge, although enforced in equity, does not impose equitable duties.

CHAPTER 10

ELEMENTS OF A TRUST

Section 402 of the Uniform Trust Code establishes five requirements for creation of a trust. It provides that a trust is created only if:

(1) the settlor has capacity to create a trust;

(2) the settlor indicates an intention to create the trust;

(3) the trust has a definite beneficiary or is:

(A) a charitable trust;

(B) a trust for the care of an animal, as provided in Section 408; or

(C) a trust for a noncharitable purpose, as provided in Section 409;

(4) the trustee has duties to perform; and

(5) the same person is not the sole trustee and sole beneficiary.

The required elements of a trust are thus (1) transfer of (2) trust property, the res, by (3) the settlor to (4) a trustee for (5) the beneficiary.

A. THE TRANSFER OF PROPERTY

In order to make a transfer during life or by will, a settlor must have the legal capacity required for the form of transfer. Thus a minor, incompetent, or other person suffering under legal disability cannot form the intention to make a gift during lifetime.

Both the Restatement of Trusts and the Uniform Trust Code set forth methods of creating trusts. The Restatement, Third, Trusts § 10 provides that a trust may be created by:

> (a) a transfer by the will of a property owner to another person as trustee for one or more persons; or
>
> (b) a transfer inter vivos by a property owner to another person as trustee for one or more persons; or
>
> (c) a declaration by an owner of property that he or she holds that property as trustee for one or more persons; or
>
> (d) an exercise of a power of appointment by appointing property to a person as trustee for one or more persons who are objects of the power; or
>
> (e) a promise or beneficiary designation that creates enforceable rights in a person who immediately or later holds those rights as trustee, or who pursuant to those rights later receives property as trustee, for one or more persons.

Under the Uniform Trust Code § 401, a trust may be created by:

> (1) transfer of property to another person as trustee during the settlor's lifetime or by will or other disposition taking effect upon the settlor's death;

(2) declaration by the owner of property that the owner holds identifiable property as trustee; or

(3) exercise of a power of appointment in favor of a trustee.

In summary, a trust could be created gratuitously or contractually during life or at death by the owner of (or possessor of a power of appointment over) the property. Each method of creating the trust must comply with the formalities required. Often trusts are classified by their method of creation and called "testamentary" (if created by will and therefore effective at death) or inter vivos (created while living).

Is a writing required to create a trust? The answer is yes for real property, otherwise there will be problems with particular jurisdictions' statute of frauds. Writings are seldom required for a trust of personal property. Section 407 of the Uniform Trust Code permits oral trusts. It provides that unless required by a statute other than the Uniform Trust Code, "a trust need not be evidenced by a trust instrument, but the creation of an oral trust and its terms may be established only by clear and convincing evidence."

Lawyers who are preparing trusts for their clients generally prepare a formal trust instrument, deeds for realty, and instruments of transfer for personal property. The trustee formally accepts the trust and the beneficiary is notified of the existence of the trust and furnished a copy of the trust instrument. This is the formal method of creating a trust.

The settlor must manifest the intention to create a trust in a way which can be objectively determined. Secret intention is insufficient if there is no outward indication of intent.

The use of precatory language, such as expressing a wish that something be done, may negate the intent to create a trust. For example, Pam leaves $100,000 to Alfred with "the hope that Alfred will care for Erin," or she leaves her farm to Justin with "my wish and desire that Amber should live on the land during his life." Neither of these statements typically create a trust, but rather a moral obligation unenforceable by law.

With a moral obligation, the settlor expresses a wish, but does not legally require a specific outcome, such as that Alfred must care for Erin. Thus, Alfred may spend the $100,000 as he desires. With a legal obligation, Alfred would be required to use the $100,000 for the benefit of Erin because he would hold it in trust for her. In creating a trust, the testator settles binding duties upon the trustee. In accord with Uniform Trust Code § 404, a trust may be created "only to the extent its purposes are lawful, not contrary to public policy, and possible to achieve." The Restatement (Third) of Trusts § 29, invalidates an intended trust if: "(a) its purpose is unlawful or its performance calls for the commission of a criminal or tortious act; (b) it violates rules relating to perpetuities; or (c) it is contrary to public policy."

In the following situations, the testator (T) devises the residue of his estate to the beneficiary (B) with the following additional language. Is a trust created?

EXAMPLE #1: " . . . hoping she will keep Condoland in the family." This is now generally held not to show an intention to create a trust; the uncertainty of the identity of the beneficiaries (other than B) is probably the key factor.

EXAMPLE #2: " . . . desiring that she give it at her death to my son." Older cases held this to create a trust with life estate in B and equitable remainder to the son so that B could not make a contrary disposition of the property in her will. More modernly, this probably would not create a trust, but each case would be decided on its own merits.

EXAMPLE #3: " . . . provided that she leaves all of her estate at her death to my son." Here, the language is stronger and would create a trust if T had the power to create a trust. However, the property which T attempts to dispose of ("*her* estate") includes property over which T does not have the power directly to create a trust. It may be treated as a bequest on condition or as a species of contract to make a will, imposing an equitable (if not legal) duty upon B to bequeath her property as requested if she desires to take the benefits of T's estate.

EXAMPLE #4: " . . . so that he can go to college." Or: " . . . hoping that he will buy a new home." Or: " . . . suggesting that he devote himself to the service of mankind." Or: " . . . recommending that he conduct himself like a gentleman." All of these bequests would probably be treated as outright bequests with surplus language to which no effect will be given. Note that what might be construed as a condition is ignored when it is in the nature of suggestions for self-improvement, unless the language is very clear, e.g., " . . . provided, however, that he refrains from drinking any alcoholic beverage for two years. If he does not so refrain, this bequest shall fail and pass instead to. . . ."

EXAMPLE #5: T purchases life insurance on T's life, naming B as beneficiary. T tells B of the policy and "suggests" that the money be used in a certain way. The facts of each individual case will tip the scale one way or the other and different courts might well find different results on what appears to be the same fact situation.

EXAMPLE #6: In clause #1 of the Will, T gives his estate outright to B with no language of condition or trust. In clause #2, T purports to dispose of the same property "after B dies." Whether a life estate only or a fee simple was created in B is a matter upon which disagreement is likely. The intention of the testator is controlling, but two clear intentions make either result possible. The scale may be tipped by factors such as the relationship of the parties and tax consequences, but the intention of the testator to impose binding duties upon them is the determining factor.

B. TRUST RES/PROPERTY

The Restatement (Third) of Trusts § 40 permits a trustee to "hold in trust any interest in any type of property." Thus, the trust res may be real, personal, or intellectual property. It may be tangible or intangible, so long as it is in existence, capable of being earmarked and assigned.

The following quiz may be helpful in sorting out items which are not yet property, those which are not assignable and those which lack the specificity required for a trust res.

C. QUIZ ON THE TRUST RES

QUESTIONS

1. S declares in an otherwise effective instrument a trust of any and all profits he should make in the future from dealings on the stock market. Is there a valid trust?

2. Same facts as Problem #1, above, except that S declared himself trustee of $100,000 to be used for trading in the stock market, the principal of $100,000 to be returned to S at the end of the year. The profits, if any, of the trading are to be kept in trust for S's children. Valid trust?

3. A theatrical producer, owning the stage and movie rights to the not-yet-produced "My Fair Lady," purports to transfer five percent of his share of the profits from the stage and movie rights as the sole asset of the trust. Is there a valid trust?

4. T executes a trust instrument, but does not act in relation to the trust res other than to sign an "Authorization" to the trustee to collect the assets of the

trust. T dies before the authorization is acted upon. Valid trust?

5. T executes a trust instrument as described in Problem #4, but adds the following clause to the "Authorization": "I hereby transfer all my right, title and interest in the estate of my father to this trust." The father is still living, but has no spouse, no other children and no will.

6. Same facts as Problem #5, except that the father died, intestate, last week.

7. If the only property transferred to the purported trust was the right to receive the proceeds of a life insurance policy (i.e., the policy itself was not transferred, but the trustee was named as the "beneficiary" of the life insurance contract), is there a valid trust?

8. If the only assets of the purported trust consisted of a leasehold interest and a patent or copyright, which is an intangible property right with a limited duration, would there be a valid trust?

9. If in Problem #8, above, the lease contained a clause prohibiting the tenant from assigning or sub-leasing the premises, would the tenant of the lease be able to make a valid trust of the leasehold interest only? Would the landlord be able to do so?

10. D owes C money. D offers a novation by creating a trust for C's children. Is there a valid trust?

11. D owes C money. C purports to create a trust of D's debt to C. Valid trust?

12. If S, the owner of an undivided one-half of certain realty and personalty (in which X owns the other undivided one-half), purports to establish a trust of his undivided one-half interest, is it a valid trust?

13. If S, being the owner of 500 cattle, purports to create a trust of 50 cattle from the herd, is it a valid trust if they are not separated, ear-marked or otherwise sorted out from the remaining 450?

14. If S, the owner of $5,000 in cash, purports to establish a trust of $1,000, but does not segregate a particular $1,000 of his cash, is it a valid trust?

15. S purports to establish a trust by writing his personal check for $1,000; when, if at all, does it become a trust? Will there be a trust if S dies before the check is "cashed"?

16. S, being uncertain of the amount of wealth that he has, purports to establish a trust of five percent of his wealth. Is it a valid trust? What if the attempt is by his will, to become effective on his death, and therefore includes what will be future income, viewed from the time that the will is executed? Is it a valid trust? When? Will it include "future" income?

ANSWERS

1. *Brainard v. Commissioner*, 91 F.2d 880 (7th Cir. 1937) held that there was no trust because property not yet in existence cannot be the subject of a trust.

2. Although next year's apple crop may not be enough of a property interest to be a trust res, the orchard, even for one year, can be. Thus, a valid trust exists.

3. In *Speelman v. Pascal*, 178 N.E.2d 723 (N.Y. 1961), a close case, such an assignment of future profits was deemed to be a sufficient trust res. Delivery had been made by a writing reciting a consideration. Equity will enforce, in appropriate cases, assignments of a future interest, if supported by an adequate consideration; but a gratuitous assignment of future property would become effective only

after it became a property interest and the settlor reaffirmed the original assignment. Restatement, Third, Trusts § 41 (2003) says that "An expectation or hope of receiving property in the future, or an interest that has not come into existence or has ceased to exist, cannot be held in trust."

4. There is no valid trust until the res is transferred to the trustee. An authorization to the trustee to collect the trust assets was held to be an agency which terminated upon the death of the settlor in *Farmers' Loan & Trust Co. v. Winthrop*, 144 N.E. 686 (N.Y. 1924).

5. There is still no valid trust, even though the document is in form sufficient to effect a present transfer. There is no property interest to pass since "No one is the heir of a living person." The expectancy of an inheritance, bequest or devise is not sufficient property to be a trust res. (Contrast the contractual assignment in Problem #3.)

6. A valid trust would be created, even in jurisdictions which hold that title to realty, or the entire estate, vests in the personal representative (the administrator here) and even though the administrator has not yet been appointed. The right of the heir is now vested and can be a trust res.

7 Possibly the designation of the trustee as the contractual third party beneficiary of a life insurance policy is sufficient property to be a trust res, but the issue has been resolved in many states by statute, expressly permitting such an "unfunded life insurance trust" with the incidents of ownership of the policy (or merely the beneficiary designation, as here) as the sole trust corpus. This is an extremely close case in the absence of a statute because of the similarity of life insurance to an inheritance during the life of the person insured.

8. A valid trust can be created even though the res has a short lifetime. These wasting assets create problems for

the trustees because their cash return is not entirely income but a combination of both principal and income. A portion of the cash return should replace the expiring asset.

9. An asset which cannot be transferred cannot be the trust res. The prohibition upon the tenant assigning would probably prevent a trust from arising. On the other hand, the landlord could create a trust of the underlying property, subject to the lease, or of the rights the landlord has under the lease. In the latter case, the trust res would be a wasting asset; it is doubtful that a court would transform the prohibition against assignment by the tenant into a mutual prohibition. If the lease called for prior landlord approval of the assignee, the trust would arise upon such approval (or actions which make the approval unnecessary, such as actions which give rise to an estoppel). If the lease called for an additional payment rather than imposing a blanket prohibition, the lease could probably be a valid trust res. The payment should probably be the responsibility of the transferor, but it is possible that the trustee would take the leasehold, subject to the obligation to pay the amount called for in the lease.

10. No trust is created because one cannot create a trust out of a debt which he or she owes. A debt is a liability, not an asset. The amount owed has not been segregated out and specified among the assets of D. See *Molera v. Cooper*, 160 P. 231 (Cal. 1916).

11. On the other hand, the creditor in a debt situation has an asset which can be a trust res. It is a chose in action against D.

12. A valid trust can be created of an undivided interest in a particular parcel even though it is not possible to say which part of the whole is subject to the trust. There is seldom any dispute about the presence of an undivided interest in trust; there may be a conflict of interests if the

trustee is the owner of another portion of the property in the trustee's own right. Similarly, separate shares of a corporation, although not representing the entire ownership, could be a trust res.

13. However, the attempt to make a trust of "50 head out of 500 head" instead of an "undivided one-tenth of 500 head" may cause the trust to fail for want of specificity of the identity of the trust res. If a cow dies, is it part of the trust or not? If there are five calves born to the 500 cattle, how many of the calves are in the trust? Note that if a trust is found (which is remotely possible), the trustee will have the immediate duty of separating and earmarking or otherwise identifying the cattle which are in the trust.

14. Classic trust theory says that a failure to segregate an identifiable portion of the trust will make the trust res too indefinite. Thus a trust of "$1,000 out of this $5,000" will not be effective. Cf., a trust of "one-fifth of this $5,000" which would probably be a valid trust res. Should the existence of a trust turn on the felicity of the phrasing?

15. The settlor's personal check is merely a direction to the bank to pay an amount; it is an authorization, as in Problem #4 above. When the check is negotiated, the funds are separated and the trust has a res. Statutes permitting a bank to honor checks after the death of the maker are designed for the protection of the banks and possibly may not be sufficient to permit a post-death negotiation to create a trust.

16. A trust of 5 percent of one's fortune (whether 5 percent of each asset or the value of 5 percent) might well fail for lack of specificity, if made during lifetime. Contrast the 5 percent of certain contract rights in Problem #3 and further contrast an assignment of "an undivided one-twentieth" as more acceptable, despite the same approach. A trust to become effective on death is "testamentary" and

must conform to the statute of wills; if it does, it is a valid will and the 5 percent value can be, and is, determined. An attempt to create a trust to arise in the future fails for want of a present transfer.

In the foregoing problems, future property is involved in Problems 1 through 7; Problem 8 dealt with wasting assets; Problems 4, 5, and 9 focused on problems of assignment. Problems 10, 11 and 15 dealt with a trust of one's own debt while Problems 11 through 16 dealt with the specificity required of the trust res and the acceptability of undivided shares of a specified thing as a trust res.

D. THE SETTLOR

The settlor of a trust transfers the trust res with the intention to create a trust by imposing fiduciary duties upon the trustee in relation to the res for the benefit of the beneficiaries. The same persons may be beneficiary or trustee in addition to being the settlor. The areas of interest of the settlor's role therefore revolve around his or her ability to transfer the property and form the intention to create a trust. The following requirements must be met.

First, the settlor must be the owner of the property or otherwise legally qualified to transfer it. The donee of a power of appointment is legally qualified to transfer it, but not the "owner" of the property.

Second, the settlor must have the capacity necessary to make the transfer and form the intention to create a trust. Section 402 of the Uniform Trust Code provides with regard to settlor issues that a trust is created if: "(1) the settlor has capacity to create a trust; [and] (2) the settlor indicates an intention to create the trust." Further, section 601 requires that the capacity required "to create, amend, revoke, or add property to a revocable trust, or to direct the actions of the trustee of a revocable trust, is the same as that required to make a will."

Third, the settlor must manifest intention to create a trust. While the trust can be created without communication of the settlor's intention to the beneficiaries and the trustee, an outward expression of his intention in writing or to a third person is required. An undisclosed secret intention to form a trust is insufficient.

Fourth, the settlor can retain some or all of the legal title or the beneficial interest, but not all of both, since the trust is created by separating the legal title from the beneficial interest. The retention of the legal title is involved in the self-declaration of trust; in that case, the beneficial interest, or a part of it, must be given to another person. The retention of a beneficial interest can be express or implied. Any portion of the beneficial interest not disposed of expressly is retained. The implied retention is reflected in the concept of "Resulting Trusts."

Fifth, the settlor can retain powers over a trust which would not be permitted in a common law gift and which do not make him a beneficiary, in the strict sense, of the trust. The power of revocation is the most obvious of these powers.

At common law, irrevocability is deemed such an essential element of gifts that an attempt to make a revocable gift is unsuccessful. On the other hand, the equitable trust can be made partly or completely revocable (or terminable by someone other than the settlor). Thus, a donor wishing to retain control cannot do so unless a trust is used. Related powers include the power to amend the trust or to control the trustee in certain areas, such as investment or time or amount of distributions of income and principal.

At common law, trusts were presumed to be irrevocable unless expressly stated to be revocable. Uniform Trust Code § 602(a) reverses this presumption; the trust is revocable unless stated to the contrary. It provides, "Unless the terms of a trust expressly provide that the trust is irrevocable, the settlor may revoke or amend the trust."

E. THE TRUSTEE

The appointment of an original or successor trustee is made by the settlor in the trust instrument. If the settlor does not provide for an original or successor trustee who is able and willing to serve, appointment will be made by the court having jurisdiction over the trust.

The trustee can be any person or entity capable of taking or conveying legal title including individuals, corporations and governmental units. Unincorporated associations, such as lodges or social clubs, are generally incapable of taking or conveying title. Therefore, they may not serve as trustees.

A trust could be created with no trustee being named initially. If the settlor transfers the equitable title to the beneficiary, he has manifested the intention to create a trust. The settlor will retain the legal title for failure to convey it to someone else. If he is dead, the legal title is vested in his heirs or will beneficiaries, but the equitable title remains in the trust beneficiaries.

Equity will not allow a trust to fail for want of a trustee except in the very rare situation in which the settlor manifested the intention that the trust should not come into existence unless this particular person served as trustee and that person is not available. Such a personal trusteeship is seldom found. Section 204 of the Uniform Trust Code provides that if a trust has no trustee, venue for a judicial proceeding for the appointment of a trustee will be either (a) in the county of the state in which a beneficiary resides; (b) in a county in which any trust property is located; or (c) in the county in which the decedent's estate was or is being administered if the trust is created by will.

It is not necessary for the settlor to inform the trustee of the trust in order for the trust to arise, but the failure to notify the trustee tends to indicate that the settlor had not yet finalized his or her intention to create a trust.

A trustee can choose to accept or decline the original appointment. Uniform Trust Code § 701(a) sets out conditions under which a person designated as trustee will be deemed to have accepted the trusteeship. A designated trustee can accept "by substantially complying with a method of acceptance provided in the terms of the trust" or "if the terms of the trust do not provide a method or the method provided in the terms is not expressly made exclusive, by accepting delivery of the trust property, exercising powers or performing duties as trustee or otherwise indicating acceptance of the trusteeship."

Acceptance is necessary in order for the trustee to be liable for his or her acts as trustee, but the acceptance is often said to relate back to the time of the creation of the trust. Normally acceptance or disclaimer of the trustee position is an irreversible decision. Acceptance may be express or may be implied from the circumstances such as participation in the creation of the trust, failure to decline after being made aware of the trust, or dealing with the trust property in a way that is consistent only with the existence of a trust relationship.

Delivery of the legal title to the trust property must comply with the legal requirements for transfer of that type of interest and the type of creation. An imperfect transfer of legal title to the trustee causes the legal title to remain with the settlor or his heirs or will beneficiaries, but does not prevent a trust from arising if the equitable title was transferred to the beneficiaries.

Any designated person who has not yet accepted the trusteeship may reject the trusteeship under Uniform Trust Code § 701(b), which provides, "A person designated as trustee who has not yet accepted the trusteeship may reject the trusteeship. A designated trustee who does not accept the trusteeship within a reasonable time after knowing of the designation is deemed to have rejected the trusteeship."

Once accepted a trusteeship often cannot be resigned except as provided in the trust instrument or by permission of the court having supervision over the trust. Section 705 of the Uniform Trust Code permits the trustee to resign "(1) upon at least thirty days' notice to the qualified beneficiaries, the settlor, if living, and all co-trustees; or (2) with the approval of the court."

The trustee may be the settlor or may be a beneficiary or both. The only impermissible combination occurs if a sole trustee is the sole beneficiary. In such a situation, the legal and equitable titles are said to merge into a fee simple title in the settler. If there is another trustee (or another beneficiary), a trust is created.

Co-trustees (or cotrustees) normally have full responsibility for the entire trust. Section 703(a) of the Uniform Trust Code states that co-trustees "who are unable to reach a unanimous decision may act by majority decision." Further § 703(b) requires that if "a vacancy occurs in a cotrusteeship, the remaining cotrustees may act for the trust." All trustees must participate in trust decisions unless a co-trustee is "unavailable to perform the function because of absence, illness, disqualification under other law, or other temporary incapacity" under Uniform Trust Code § 703(c). A co-trustee may also delegate the performance of a function to another trustee. Unavailability of one trustee permits the remaining ones or a majority of the remaining ones to act for the trust under Uniform Trust Code § 703(d) to achieve the trust purposes or avoid injury to trust property.

A trustee may not delegate to a co-trustee the performance of a function the settlor reasonably expected the trustees to perform jointly under Uniform Trust Code § 703(e). Except as otherwise provided in Uniform Trust Code § 703(g), a trustee who does not join in an action of another trustee is not liable for the action. Uniform Trust Code § 703(g) requires each trustee to exercise reasonable care to: (1) prevent a co-trustee from committing a serious breach of trust; and (2) compel a co-trustee to redress a serious breach of trust. A dissenting trustee, under Uniform Trust Code § 703(h) who joins in an action at the direction of the majority of the trustees and who notified any co-trustee of the dissent at or before the time of the action is not liable for the action unless the action is a serious breach of trust.

It is possible that the settlor divided the tasks between two or more persons, e.g., Trustee #1 to manage apartment houses and Trustee #2 to manage a farm, both in the same trust. It is also possible to have persons who are quasi-trustees in the sense that they are advisors to the trustee in such matters as investment, but are not involved in the day-to-day operations of the trust. These advisors are also fiduciaries and are bound by the same principles as the trustee even though they have a more limited role. Although the settlor has the power to divide up the tasks of the trustee among co-trustees, the co-trustees do not have the same power. It would be an improper delegation of the trustee powers for the trustees to make such a division.

Co-trustees take legal title as joint tenants, even in jurisdictions which would not otherwise find the co-ownership to be a joint tenancy because of statutory requirements that a joint tenancy be expressly declared or because of the lack of the four unities required by common law. Thus, if one co-trustee dies, the other co-trustee automatically succeeds to the legal title. Upon the death of the last of the trustees, the legal title descends to his or her heirs or will beneficiaries, but there is no beneficial enjoyment involved. Therefore, the surviving spouse of a trustee has no dower (or statutory equivalent) rights in trust property.

A trustee can resign as permitted in the trust instrument, by the court having supervision of the trust, with the consent of all the beneficiaries if they are competent, or with thirty days' notice to the qualified beneficiaries and all co-trustees. It is common drafting practice to include a provision permitting the trustee to resign. If the trustee seeks permission of the court, the judge examines the situation from the viewpoint of the beneficiaries, not the trustee. A form of estoppel can be applied to the extent the trust beneficiaries are *sui juris* and consent to the resignation of the trustee; however, those who are not able to consent or who did not do so could impose liability upon the trustee for failure to act.

A trustee can be removed as provided in the trust instrument or by a court having jurisdiction over the trust. The trust instrument may reserve the power to the settlor or give the power to third persons, including beneficiaries, to remove the trustee.

Section 706(a) of the Uniform Trust Code provides that the settlor, a co-trustee, or a beneficiary "may request the court to remove a trustee, or a trustee may be removed by the court on its own initiative." Section 706(b) permits the court to remove a trustee if: (1) the trustee has committed a serious breach of trust; or (2) lack of cooperation among co-trustees substantially impairs the administration of the trust. Further, a court may determine that removal of a trustee best serves the interests of the beneficiaries because of unfitness, unwillingness, or persistent failure of the trustee to administer the trust effectively. Finally, a court may find that removal of the trustee best serves the interests of all the beneficiaries and is not inconsistent with a material purpose of the trust, and a suitable co-trustee or successor trustee is available when a substantial change of circumstances may necessitate removal.

Removal is considered a strict measure and is not lightly done. Breaches of trust duty, including those giving rise to a liability to the beneficiaries, will not necessarily be sufficient cause for removal of the trustee. Disagreements or conflicts with the beneficiaries are similarly not causes for removal. The trustee may have an adverse interest, as beneficiary or otherwise; but such an adverse interest, if known to the settlor at the creation of the trust, will not serve as a basis for removal. The original appointment by the settlor is deemed to be an acceptance of a conflict of interests then existing.

However, acquisition of an adverse interest after the trust is created may lead to removal of the trustee for conflict of interests.

F. THE BENEFICIARY

Any "person who would have capacity to take and hold legal title to the intended trust property has capacity to be a beneficiary of a trust of that property; ordinarily, a person who lacks capacity to hold legal title to property may not be a trust beneficiary," according to Restatement of Trusts, Third § 43 (2012). Two mutually exclusive types of beneficiaries exist: the charitable beneficiary and the private beneficiary. The two types differ in the following ways:

- *Ascertainability and Enforcement.* Generally, beneficiaries of a private trust must be ascertainable, or established, to enforce a trust. Uniform Trust Code § 402(b) states that a beneficiary is definite "if the beneficiary can be ascertained now or in the future, subject to any applicable rule against perpetuities." The beneficiaries of a charitable trust are unascertainable, meaning that the settlor does not know the persons who benefit from his or her largess. Note, however, that Uniform Trust Code § 409 permits the creation of a noncharitable trust without ascertainable beneficiaries (such as unborn grandchildren) for a period of up to 21 years. Charitable trusts are enforced by the attorney general, and the settlor in jurisdictions adopting Uniform Trust Code § 405(c).

- *Rule Against Perpetuities.* A settlor may establish a remainder gift to a charity to follow another charity (Owner leaves Tree-acre to Beta Charity so long as Beta distributes food to the poor, then to Carta Charity) without violating the Rule against Perpetuities, even though it may take longer than 21 years for the second gift to vest (i.e., for Carta Charity to receive its gift). This charitable exemption permits a condition (i.e., distributing food to the poor) to be imposed and enforced indefinitely. A remainder gift to an individual following a gift charity (Owner leaves Tree-acre to Beta Charity so long as Beta distributes food to the poor, then to Cousin Joyce) may violate the Rule against Perpetuities as it may take forever before Tree-acre vests in Cousin Lori. A gift to a charity may be vested for Rule against Perpetuities purposes and may be exempt from limitations upon the duration of a trust under conditions which would make a private trust invalid, such as a direction to pay the income only "forever" without a disposition of the principal of the trust.

- *Tax Advantages.* The charitable trust may enjoy various tax advantages such as full exclusion from taxation. Private trusts must pay applicable federal, state, and local income taxes.

- *Cy Pres*. Charitable trusts have the ability to use the *cy pres* doctrine to carry out the general charitable purpose of a trust when the original purpose becomes impossible.

1. PRIVATE TRUST BENEFICIARIES

As previously noted, a beneficiary may also have other roles (settlor or trustee) in the trust with only one combination producing no trust: The sole trustee cannot be the sole beneficiary because duties would neither exist nor be enforced by the trustee-beneficiary.

Although notice to, and acceptance by, a beneficiary of a private trust is not necessary in order to create a trust, it is necessary that the beneficiary be capable of taking beneficial title and be ascertained or ascertainable.

a. Capacity

Any person with capacity to take and hold legal title can be a beneficiary to a trust. A minor or incompetent can be the owner of a beneficial interest in a trust. Occasionally a state will limit ownership of property (or certain types of property, such as farmland) by aliens (foreigners) or corporations. In such cases, it is a matter of interpretation of the statute whether ownership in trust is prohibited, but generally the prohibition does extend to such indirect ownership also.

b. Unincorporated Association

A typical unincorporated association is the fraternal organization, lodge or "fund" which has not formally incorporated or established itself within any of the traditional forms of organization. The unincorporated association may have a formal constitution and bylaws and elaborate internal rules or it may be simply a group of persons with a common interest, such as a bowling league.

Unincorporated associations occupy the ambiguous area between a formal corporation and a class gift. Comment e to the Restatement, Third, Trusts § 43, indicates that an unincorporated association has a capacity to be the beneficiary of a trust during the perpetuities period. Afterwards, the trust would be severed and distributed according to the terms of the trust to either the ascertainable association members or converted to a resulting trust to benefit the settlor, his or her heirs, or assigns. Many jurisdictions have enacted statutes eliminating the common law rule prohibiting unincorporated associations from taking legal title.

A few jurisdictions refuse to recognize an unincorporated association as a juristic entity; it does not legally exist. Therefore, in those jurisdictions, the beneficial interest belongs to the members of the association. If the settlor intended a gift in trust to the members of the group, the beneficiaries can be determined if the group is "frozen in time" (e.g., the members of the association as of the time of the creation of the trust or some other time).

The fringes of the unincorporated association blend into the category of "class gifts." Both deal with groups of people who are identified by some common characteristic. Fraternities are clear examples of unincorporated associations (unless they have formally incorporated) while "my descendants" is a clear example of a class gift. The spectators at a specified sporting event could be viewed as an unincorporated association while the members of the teams could be considered as borderline between a class and an unincorporated association.

c. Class Gifts—Construction

It is extremely common that the beneficiaries of a trust be designated as a class, such as "my children" or "my nieces and nephews." The class members must be ascertainable and determined. A number of interpretation problems and unique rules of future interests arise whenever a class gift is involved. Anti-lapse statutes may apply to class gifts and save a gift to a class member for a related person.

As of when is the membership of the class determined? A class gift could be viewed as a tube extending through time. The sides of the tube are the description of the class's common characteristics—"my issue" or "my employees." The tube is capable of being open at either end—new members can be added and older members can be dropped from the class. Sometimes an end is sealed by nature or the terms of the class gift: I will have no further "employees" after I cease any business.

A class gift needs to be frozen in time in order to determine the identity of the particular members who are the beneficiaries. The settlor's express language, an inference of intention or a combination, freezes the class.

In his will, legendary singer Elvis Presley created a class of "My daughter, Lisa Marie Presley, and any other lawful issue I might have." Further, he stated, "Upon the death of both my said father and my said grandmother, the Trustee is directed to divide the Residuary Trust into separate and equal trusts, creating one such equal trust for each of my lawful children then surviving and one such equal trust for the living issue collectively, if any, of any deceased child of mine. This trust does defined the class members as "lawful issue." When Deborah Delaine Presley sued Elvis' executors to become a beneficiary of his estate as his illegitimate daughter, the court rejected her claim as the class was limited to Elvis' children from lawful marriages. In the case of *Presley v. Hanks*, 782 S.W.2d 482 (Tenn. App., Jul 20, 1989), the court mentioned that after Elvis had successfully defended against a paternity suit in California he deliberately added the word lawful with reference to any of his children.

In another example, the use of the term "now living" or "then surviving" gives a reference to some particular point in time. The point may be obscured even when such words are used. "Now" in a will could refer to the time of writing or to the time of the testator's death. "Then surviving" after multiple life estates is unclear unless expressly stated to be "the last to die of" them. Does one who dies, leaving issue, "survive" through the issue?

The vesting certainty for the Rule against Perpetuities requires that both ends of the class gift be sealed—no further additions can be made and no condition precedent (such as survival) can exist for any member of the class. This is considered particularly important where DNA tests can add to a class indefinitely with additional individuals discovering connections to the settler. Generally, members of a class take equally (except that "by right of representation" is often used with gifts to "issue" of someone).

d. Class Gifts—Ascertainability of Members

Class gifts use categories, such as "my nephews," rather than names to identify people. These categories can be ambiguous because of particular circumstances (Does "issue" include adopted or illegitimate issue? Is an aunt's husband an "uncle"?) or because of the particular term used ("friend"). In *Clark v. Campbell*, 133 A. 166 (N.H. 1926) a trust for the testator's "friends" was held void for indefiniteness of beneficiaries even though the term could have been construed to refer to persons referred to in other parts of the same will as "friends." The next step up in definiteness is "relatives," a term which is sometimes construed to mean the heirs or next of kin related by blood, but could also be construed as too indefinite if one counts those related by marriage.

e. Class Gift—Partial Ascertainability

The beneficiaries of a private trust must *all* be determined with certainty. If all of the persons who comprise the class cannot be determined, the trust fails as to that class. It is still possible, however, that the attempt to pass property to the members of the class may be valid as either a power of appointment or an outright gift to the trustee. Thus, in the case of a bequest "to my friend, John Doe, to distribute among my friends" a valid general power of appointment may have been created permitting John Doe to distribute the property to himself as well as to others.

Even though a trust's binding obligations upon the trustee do not exist, the donee has the power to appoint to anyone, including himself, if the language is construed to create a general power of appointment. Similarly, a bequest "To my friend John Doe so that he can take care of my relatives, if necessary" may be construed as precatory language connected to an outright gift to John Doe (and therefore valid) rather than a trust (and potentially invalid for indefiniteness of beneficiaries).

> EXAMPLE: T devises the residue of his estate to A "[a] in trust [b] for my relatives [c] as A may select [d] excluding himself." Without the language in quotation marks, or without the "in trust" the residual bequest might be construed as an outright bequest to A. By itself the "in trust" indicates (but is not conclusive) that no beneficial interest was intended to pass to the "trustee." If it is a trust, the beneficiaries shown

in "[b]" may be too indefinite to constitute a class; often "relatives" will be construed to mean "heirs" or "next of kin." If too indefinite to be a trust, such a term, however, when combined with the clause in "[c]" indicates that a power of appointment was intended. The power would probably be general except for the language of "[d]" but that language is sufficient to change the power from general to special while reinforcing the power of appointment interpretation of the entire bequest. Probably the best interpretation of the clause as written is that it created a valid special power of appointment in trust with the legal title in A and the equitable title in default of appointment remaining in the heirs of the testator.

The Restatement tests for the ascertainability of the members of a class vary for direct gifts and powers of appointment. Restatement, Third, Trusts § 45 insists that only "members of a definite class of persons can be the beneficiaries of a trust." Comment a to this rule indicates that a class of persons is definite "if the identity of all the individuals comprising its membership is ascertainable at the time the trust is created or will become ascertainable within the period and terms of the rule against perpetuities. A class is not indefinite for this purpose merely because it consists of a changing or shifting group, the number of whose members may increase or decrease."

Restatement, Third, Trusts § 46 provides that if "the transferee is directed to distribute the property to such members of the indefinite class as the transferee shall select, the transferee holds the property in trust with power but no duty to distribute the property to such class members as the transferee may select; to whatever extent the power (presumptively personal) is not exercised, the transferee will then hold for reversionary beneficiaries implied by law." This indicates that should the transferee elect not to distribute the property to the class members, then the transferee must hold the property for reversionary beneficiaries and cannot keep it for himself or herself.

2. INCIDENTAL BENEFICIARIES

Not everyone who benefits from a trust is a beneficiary of the trust. The test is the settlor's intention to benefit, not the economic benefit. The distinction is important for procedural reasons, since an incidental beneficiary often does not have standing to challenge the trustee's actions or inaction.

> EXAMPLE: T creates a trust for the benefit of A and directs that the trustee shall invest in common stock of Microsoft, Inc. The corporation does not have a beneficial interest in the trust sense and does not have standing to sue to enforce the terms including the express provision for investment of the trust.

Other examples of incidental beneficiaries are schools at which "true" beneficiaries are enrolled with tuition paid out of the trust, creditors of a "true" beneficiary for whom the trust will pay debts and governmental entities which would otherwise expend funds for the care of a "true" beneficiary.

The concept of "incidental" beneficiary is used to deny enforcement of trust terms by those only tangentially concerned with the trust; it could be viewed as the court's decision that the interest of the incidental beneficiary is too obscure or attenuated to be enforced. The concept probably should not be expanded further, but it does serve as an explanation and bridge to the concept that the recipient of largess from a "charitable trust" is not the "true" beneficiary; the public is the beneficiary and the recipient of the largess is "merely" an "incidental" beneficiary.

3. CHARITABLE TRUSTS

A charitable trust must have a charitable purpose, indefinite beneficiaries, and a trustee as indicated by the trust. The *cy pres* doctrine permits reformation of a trust to fulfill a general charitable purpose by getting near to the original purpose.

a. Charitable Purposes

Section 405(a) of the Uniform Trust Code provides that a "charitable trust may be created for the relief of poverty, the advancement of education or religion, the promotion of health, governmental or municipal purposes, or other purposes the achievement of which is beneficial to the community." The idea of what is charitable may change from time to time and from place to place.

i. Poverty

Relief of poverty is and has traditionally been a charitable purpose, even though the definition of poverty has varied considerably. It is obvious that some of the commodities and services considered to be basic today would have been luxuries of the rich four centuries ago, considering the diet, shelter and transportation differences. To the extent that anyone receives economic benefits as an individual beneficiary of a charitable trust, he or she is further removed from poverty.

Relief of poverty is probably one of the oldest of the charitable purposes. More modernly there has been a tendency for governmental units to assume the task of relieving poverty thus blending two charitable purposes.

A trust for "the poor" is charitable, but a trust does not have to be exclusively for the poor in order to be charitable. A gift or bequest in trust for "the poor" (like a similar disposition "for charitable purposes") can be applied for purposes which fit within the designation. If the trustee is unwilling to go forward, the court will assist in "framing a scheme" for the charitable disposition. For example, Uniform Trust Code § 405(b) provides that if the terms of a charitable trust do not indicate a particular charitable purpose or beneficiary, "the court may select one or more charitable purposes or beneficiaries. The selection must be consistent with the settlor's intention to the extent it can be ascertained." A trust which benefits the wealthy as well as the poor is still capable of being charitable even though it does not fall within the "poverty" classification.

Private individuals can be "incidental" beneficiaries and they need not be totally destitute in order for the trust which benefits them to be charitable, but both the recipients' identities and their degree of poverty affect the probability that the purpose will be found to be relief of poverty. If the persons who are to benefit are not a sufficiently large and indefinite class, in the words of Austin Wakeman Scott, "that the community is interested in the enforcement of the trust" it is not a charitable trust.

A trust for named individuals who are poor is not considered a charitable trust, but geographic, age and gender limitations ("poor, old women of Roseville") are permitted. On the border line is a trust for "my poor relatives" which might be upheld as a private trust if the beneficiaries can be ascertained. Perhaps the non-charitable nature can be explained in terms of the settlor's charitable intent being less than the intent to keep the economic benefits within his or her blood line.

ii. Education

Aid to any of the elements of the traditional learning process—institution, teachers or students—is an educational purpose, as are the creation of programs (research, dissemination of information, etc.) and the creation of allied institutions (museums and libraries).

Some testators overestimate the value of their personal writings, works or collections. An otherwise valid charitable trust to publish unpublishable writings or preserve the home of an undistinguished person as a museum will generally fail as a charitable trust because it is not of sufficient value to the community as a whole.

iii. Religion

Generally trusts for the advancement of religion of all types are upheld in the United States today. The advancement may be in the form of direct payment to a church or rabbi, minister or priest or it may be associated with religious work (missions, pamphlets etc.) or accessories (choir, organs, etc.).

A close area is a religious purpose which is connected to the personality of the testator, such as maintenance of a grave. This trust may be upheld as an "honorary trust." It fails as a private express trust because the beneficiary cannot be ascertained.

Established churches have had less difficulty in gaining acceptance as being for charitable purposes than newer religions. Some denominations such as the Church of Christ, Scientist (Christian Scientists) and the Church of the Latter Day Saints of Jesus Christ (Mormons) have evolved entirely within the United States from initial small groups.

It is not a simple task to separate those churches in their initial years from other sects which were less successful (such as that of Joanna Southcote who declared that she was pregnant by the Holy Ghost and would give birth to a second Messiah). Generally, trusts for the benefit of such religious groups are upheld as charitable unless the court decides that the religion is so absurd as to be irrational. Such a course of conduct pits the pre-convictions of the judge against the religious convictions of the settlor of the trust.

iv. Governmental

Governmental purposes which are considered to be charitable include direct gifts to a governmental unit and gifts for creation or maintenance of public works (streets, libraries, bridges, firehouses, etc.) as well as for more intangible purposes such as fostering peace or preparing for war.

Trusts seeking to change the law (or the identity of the persons who administer it) walk the borderline between the permissible governmental function of peaceful and orderly change of the law and the impermissible "political" function which is not deemed to be charitable. Federal income tax law denies a charitable deduction for contributions to an organization which seeks to influence legislation. Rarely will an individual's political campaign be deemed charitable, although the individual may be the leading spokesperson for some particular governmental policy.

Increasingly, governmental functions are tending to include most of the other charitable functions, such as relief of poverty, and advancement of education and public health. Whether such a public approach will exclude or expand private charity has not been fully determined.

v. Generally Beneficial to the Community

Potentially charitable trusts require analysis to fit them within any category of charitable trusts. Although many cases are clear, there are an equal number of instances in which the purposes have difficulty fitting the previous categories (Poverty, Education, Public Health, Religion or Government). If analysis does not permit such labeling, there is still the possibility that the trust purpose is one which will benefit the community generally. Into this category fit, or attempt to fit, trusts for the protection of animals generally, and the promotion of sports and health, among other purposes. Not all of these purposes will be deemed to be charitable. The following guidelines may assist both in this general category and in the more specific categories already described:

- Generality of purpose is not fatal. The court will enforce, at the instance of the attorney general, a trust for "charity" as well as a trust for "education" or "relief of poverty."

- Private profit is generally fatal to a charitable purpose. Thus, a non-profit hospital is a charity while a proprietary hospital is not a charity (even if it does not, in fact, have a profit).

- Taint of personal interest, as opposed to personal attitude, tends to result in non-charitable classification. A trust for the relief of poverty of the grantor or his or her relatives will tend to be deemed non-charitable unless the group encompassed by the term "relatives" is extremely large. Often, it is permissible to give a preference to one's own relatives, e.g., by establishing a scholarship for education with such a preference.

- Smallness of the number of potential recipients of largess, while fatal only if the group is absolutely limited, tends to indicate that a private benefit was sought. An award could be established which honored only one person at a time, but which potentially would honor a great number over a period of time. Such an award would be for a charitable purpose.

- Social utility is measured to some degree. Thus amateur sports (e.g., fox-hunting or yacht racing) are less likely to be held to be charitable purposes than the preservation of animals or the study of boat design. Professional sports, of course, involve proprietary institutions and therefore seldom, if ever, will be found to be charitable. Contrast the governmental role of providing a stadium for the same sports.

- The language used may build a stronger case, but is not determinative by itself. For example, a contribution to "improve the breed" of race-horses which in fact is designed to support professional horse racing will probably be deemed to be non-charitable. A skilled draftsman can aid interpretation but cannot transform every idiosyncrasy into a charity. A trust for the "education and relief of poverty of Antarctic penguins" (if not interpreted to make better sense) should fail no matter how diligently the draftsperson evokes the terms of charity.

- Uniqueness or unpopularity of the cause generally must be rather extreme in order for the trust to fail. Individual courts differ on what is a wholly invalid purpose.

b. *Cy Pres*

The *cy pres* ("as near" as possible) doctrine permits preservation of charitable trusts by seeking the nearest practical alternative to a charitable trust which would otherwise fail or be ineffective. Section 413(a) of the Uniform Trust Code provides, "if a particular charitable purpose revert to the settlor or the settlor's successors in interest; and (3) the court may apply *cy pres* to modify or terminate the trust by directing that the trust property be applied or distributed, in whole or in part, in a manner consistent with the settlor's charitable purposes."

The classic example of a court using the *cy pres* doctrine arose *Jackson v. Phillips*, 96 Mass. 539 (1867) in which a testator who died in 1861 attempted to create a trust for the purpose of putting an end to slavery. After the Civil War, the trust corpus was used for the education of former slaves to render them more capable of self-government.

Consider the elements of *cy pres*:

i. A Trust

The *cy pres* doctrine arose in trusts and remains in that field predominantly, but there has been an occasional expansion beyond the pure trust situation, especially when non-trust charitable dispositions are involved. A similar but unrelated doctrine of flexibility which also exists in trust law is "deviation" which permits a change in the administrative provisions of a trust (as opposed to a change of the dispositive provisions which is involved in *cy pres*).

ii. Evidencing General Charitable Intent

If the charitableness of the settlor is narrowly construed to be limited to the impossible purpose only, the trust will fail. The principle of construction here is to carry out the settlor's charitable intention unless it does not contain a general charitable intent. The court is, in effect, asking itself: Given the circumstances and the language used in the instrument at the time the trust was created, would the settlor have desired that the property be diverted to another charitable use of a similar nature if the exact use specified could not be complied with?

iii. Which Was Initially Valid

There has been some weakening of this requirement so that *cy pres* has been applied in a few cases when the trust's charitable purpose was illegal, impossible or impractical at all times.

iv. *Becomes Impossible, Illegal or Impractical, or Wasteful*

Such events trigger the *cy pres* doctrine. The difficulty may be insufficient funds for the purpose directed, a total change in the laws, elimination of the disease or problem involved, or a waste of resources. Examples include large centers for the treatment of tuberculosis, poliomyelitis or smallpox, or trust created to obtain the vote for women after a Constitutional Amendment had already been passed.

Impracticality is the difficult area here. If it is merely difficult but still possible to fulfill the settlor's object, the court is reluctant to change the original purpose. A detailed examination is required of a purpose which is possible but difficult.

Currently the *cy pres* doctrine is invoked in situations in which the testator-settlor imposed a racial, religious or other "suspect category" restriction upon the incidental beneficiaries who receive trust benefits. In *Evans v. Abney*, 396 U.S. 435 (1970), the Georgia Trial and Supreme Court decided that since the sole charitable intention of the settlor was to maintain a public park for white persons only, the purpose had become impossible under the law. The park reverted to the settlor's heirs when the Georgia courts and the United States Supreme Court refused to apply *cy pres*.

c. Enforcement of Charities (Standing)

The settlor has standing to enforce a charitable trust if such rights are expressly reserved or if the trust was established in a jurisdiction adopting the Uniform Trust Code or under other legal rules granting standing to challenge the administration of the charitable trust. Section 405(c) of the Uniform Trust Code provides, "The settlor of a charitable trust, among others, may maintain a proceeding to enforce the trust." Commentary to the Restatement (Third) of Trusts § 94 makes clear that "A suit for the enforcement of a charitable trust may be maintained only by the Attorney General or other appropriate public officer or by a co-trustee or successor trustee, by a settlor, or by another person who has a special interest in the enforcement of the trust."

Traditionally the state's attorney general is charged with the enforcement of both charitable trusts (sometimes under the Uniform Supervision of Trustees for Charitable Purposes Act) and corporations. The significance is more in the exclusion from standing of persons or organizations which might otherwise be willing to supervise the trust, e.g., an existing charity with similar purposes.

The trustees and an occasional very direct incidental beneficiary (e.g., the professor for whom an endowed chair has been created by charitable trust) may also have standing to enforce the trust.

4. MIXED CHARITABLE AND NON-CHARITABLE PURPOSES

Commentary to Uniform Trust Code § 103 makes clear that when a trust has both charitable and noncharitable beneficiaries, only the charitable portion qualifies as a "charitable trust." Distinctions between the two types of trusts are found in the requirements relating to trust creation and modification. Pursuant to Uniform Trust Code § 405 and § 413, a charitable trust must have a charitable purpose and charitable trusts may be modified or terminated under the doctrine of *cy pres*.

Further, Uniform Trust Code § 411 allows a noncharitable trust to, in certain instances, be terminated or modified with consent of the settlor and all beneficiaries, "even if the modification or termination is inconsistent with a material purpose of the trust," while charitable trusts do not have beneficiaries in the usual sense. Given these distinctions, keep in mind that a split-interest trust is subject to two sets of provisions, one applicable to the charitable interests, the other to the noncharitable interests.

The easy cases of separation are those expressly stated as separate items—e.g., "One half for the poor of my city and one half for my relatives." Despite the settlor's intent that there be one trust, two will be created in certain jurisdictions to preserve validity. Another easy trust to divide is the life estate to an individual (non-charitable) and remainder to charity. One trust for these two purposes should be sufficient.

When both charitable and non-charitable purposes exist and are inseparable, the trust must conform to all the requirements for each type of trust. To be valid as a private trust, the beneficiaries must be ascertained or capable of being ascertained within the period of the Rule against Perpetuities but a trust in which all the beneficiaries are ascertained is not likely to be a charitable trust.

In the usual case of inseparably mixed charitable and non-charitable trusts in which some rule is violated by a part of the trust, the entire trust fails. It may be possible to construe the trust so that only a portion fails. Obviously, if the trusts are separable and the charitable trust violates rules applicable to it or the non-charitable trust violates rules applicable to it, that portion of the trust fails.

Any failed portion of a trust passes to alternative takers if effectively so directed by the settlor. If there is no direction, it returns to him by resulting trust. If he is dead, it passes to his will beneficiaries (the residual takers if not specifically provided for in the will) or heirs.

To keep an inseparably mixed trust from failing, one alternative, rarely used, is to strike the lesser portion, usually the non-charitable part because the charitable trust is generally treated more advantageously. Thus, a trust to build a public library (charitable) and to publish the settlor's undistinguished treatise on "Law and Apes" might be allowed to disregard the second, otherwise inseparable, purpose.

5. HONORARY TRUSTS

The most common areas of the honorary trusts deal with honoring or remembering a dead person or caring for specific animals or things. Uniform Trust Code §§ 408 and 409 specifically permit such trusts.

At common law, such trusts would have been invalid both as a private trust because there are no ascertained human beneficiaries and as a charitable trust because the number of incidental human beneficiaries is too small or non-existent. Now, this type of trust may be created by giving the transferee the power to apply the property for the designated purpose (within the bounds of the Rule against Perpetuities, i.e. not to exceed 21 years), so long as the purpose is not capricious.

a. Dead Persons

Decedents are traditionally honored by burial or cremation, with monuments and graves or tombs and with a ceremony (including flowers) within a reasonable time after death. If a testator wished to provide for perpetual care of his grave, he could do so in most states because permitted by statute. According to Uniform Trust Code § 409, such a noncharitable purpose trust without a definite or definitely ascertainable beneficiary "may not be enforced for more than [21] years." In the absence of statute, a trust for care of a grave would violate the Rule against Perpetuities.

If the trust were for the preservation of a public cemetery or the grave or tomb of a notable person, a valid charitable trust probably exists. A wide latitude is often allowed in monuments and other markers for graves, but the monument must be proportional to the wealth of the decedent and conform both to his preferences and to some sense of appropriateness. In honoring a deceased person, the saying of masses is often considered to be a charitable purpose. In jurisdictions where a trust for the saying of masses is not considered to be a charitable trust, the purpose could be allowed as an honorary trust.

b. Animals

Pets are often the intended recipients of the benefits of a trust. Indeed, in *Estate of Russell*, 444 P.2d 353 (Cal. 1968), the testator left her residuary estate to "H. Quinn & Roxy Russell." Extrinsic evidence was admitted to prove that Roxy Russell was the testator's Airedale dog who died after the will was written but before the testator's demise. Despite Quinn's argument that the testator intended to leave the entire estate to him and he was supposed to care for the dog, the court held that the gift to Roxy Russell failed and passed to the testator's only heir-at-law.

Leona Helmsley left $12 million for the care of her Maltese named Trouble, and thereby created the world's richest dog in 2007. After her relatives sued, the Court lowered Trouble's portion of Helmsley's estate to $2 million. Trouble's caretaker, Carl Lekic, reportedly spent $100,000 annually on her care—including $8,000 for grooming and $1,200 for dog food. Additionally, Trouble, who had faced 20 to 30 death and kidnapping threats, also retained a full-time security guard, according to the ABC News website. Trouble died in December 2010 and was buried near her former owner at the 12,000-square-foot Helmsley family mausoleum in Sleepy Hollow Cemetery in Westchester County, N.Y. Gifts to animals either outright or in trust create the dual problems of no human beneficiary and no human measuring lives for the Rule against Perpetuities period. A trust for the care of animals (or some species of animal), as opposed to a specific animal, can be upheld as charitable. When the testator narrows the benefited animals down to one cat or dog or even "my horses and hounds," the group is too small for a charitable trust and too inhuman for a private trust.

The Uniform Trust Code § 408, fortunately, permits the establishment of trusts for the care of an animal. The animal(s) must be alive during the settlor's lifetime. The trust terminates upon the death of the animal or upon the death of the last surviving animal.

Since animals cannot speak, the trust may be enforced by a person appointed in the terms of the trust or, if no person is so appointed, by a person appointed by the court. Subsection (b) of Uniform Trust Code § 408 permits a "person having an interest in the welfare of the animal may request the court to appoint a person to enforce the trust or to remove a person appointed." Subsection (c) indicates that the trust property "may be applied only to its intended use, except to the extent the court determines that the value of the trust property exceeds the amount required for the intended use." Otherwise, it "must be distributed to the settlor, if then living, otherwise to the settlor's successors in interest."

c. Capricious Purposes

A trust may be deemed capricious if it violates public policy, such as encouraging criminal or tortious conduct, interfering with freedom to marry, encouraging divorce, or limiting religious freedom. Further, the trust purpose must not be frivolous.

What is "capricious" varies from case to case. A trust to brick up or raze a building is probably capricious, but some courts have permitted the demolition of a building. A trust to keep a clock in repair has been deemed capricious, but a similar trust for a clock in a museum might be permitted. One lady successfully insisted that she be buried in her aged sports car, coupling the request with a condition upon a bequest of a substantial amount of money. The beneficiary chose to honor the request rather than contest it.

Some requests for monuments on graves can be capricious, e.g., the court struck down a bequest to pay for a band to play music at the testator's tomb on the anniversaries of his death. Thus, while trusts for capricious purposes generally will not be enforced, even by honorary trust, sometimes they might slide through the system as acceptable.

G. EXPLANATION OF TRUST CLASSIFICATIONS

Trusts can be classified by the manner in which they are created, revocability, voluntariness, special purpose, legality and type of beneficiary. Often the classification is only one attribute, so that the same item may fit a number of classifications. A testamentary charitable trust, for example, combines method of creation and type of beneficiary. The following classifications provide some—but not all possible—types of trusts:

1. PASSIVE AND ACTIVE TRUSTS

A "passive" trust is one in which the trustee has no duty except to transfer the property to the beneficiary. This type of trust was the historical starting point and most common type of trust until the enactment of the Statute of Uses which "executed" (i.e., carried out, not killed) the passive trust by stating that the beneficiary was given the legal title which then merged into the equitable title, destroying the trust.

The only significance today is that a trust in which the only duty of the trustee is to convey title to the beneficiary becomes "passive" and may be deemed to have been carried out by the appropriate Statute of Uses. Almost all trusts which we will encounter are "active" trusts in which the trustee has some additional duty.

This accords with commentary to Uniform Trust Code § 402, which states that trustee "duties are usually active, but a validating duty may also be passive, implying only that the trustee has an obligation not to interfere with the beneficiary's enjoyment of the trust property. Such passive trusts, while valid under this Code, may be terminable under the enacting jurisdiction's Statute of Uses."

2. RESULTING (IMPLIED), CONSTRUCTIVE AND EXPRESS TRUSTS

In the classification of trusts by the degree of voluntariness of their creation, the only three categories are the "resulting" (implied) trust, the "constructive" trust and the "express trust." The resulting or implied trust arises when there has not been a complete and effective disposition of the beneficial interest. For example, S transfers property to T in fee in trust to pay the income to L for life. The remaining undisposed-of portion of the equitable interest (an equitable reversion) remains in S by virtue of an "implied" or "resulting trust."

Similarly if there is a transfer to a trustee without a designation of the intended beneficial interest, it is presumed that a resulting trust was intended. In a few jurisdictions, this rule has been changed by statute for realty so that a conveyance to "T as trustee" without further indication of the trust may be construed as an outright transfer to T.

Constructive trusts are remedial devices to correct fraud upon an express trust or prevent unjust enrichment. In *In re Mahoney's Estate*, 220 A.2d 475 (Vt. 1966), the Vermont Supreme Court indicated that a constructive trust could be imposed upon Charlotte Mahoney to keep her from profiting from shooting and killing her husband Howard. As a constructive trustee, Charlotte would be compelled to convey the property to the heirs or next of kin of Howard.

The "express trust" is the type most commonly dealt with in the Trusts course. All the following classifications are types of express trusts.

3. LEGAL AND ILLEGAL TRUSTS

Thus far, all the classifications of trusts in this book dealt with "legal" trusts. Section 404 of the Uniform Trust Code provides that a trust "may be created only to the extent is purposes are lawful, not contrary to public policy and possible to achieve." Unlawful trusts are invalid. Such a trust may be void at its inception or become voidable later if the purpose changes.

The commentary to Uniform Trust Code § 404 indicates a trust has a purpose which is illegal if "(1) its performance involves the commission of a criminal or tortious act by the trustee; (2) the settlor's purpose in creating the trust was to defraud creditors or others; or (3) the consideration for the creation of the trust was illegal." It further defines purposes violative of public policy as those that "tend to encourage criminal or tortious conduct, that interfere with freedom to marry or encourage divorce, that limit religious freedom, or which are frivolous or capricious."

Breaches of the law could be as flagrant as a direction to a trustee to furnish weapons to prison inmates. Attempts to defraud others could consist of transferring the property in order to avoid creditors, qualify for welfare or clothe another with indicia of wealth. Capricious purposes include such items as destruction of the property.

Attempts to defraud others (typically the spouse or other creditors) may lead to the invalidity of the trust. In the case of the attempt to defraud the spouse's claim, a line is sometimes drawn between present claims for alimony and future claims for the spouse's share of a decedent's estate, with the latter being less protected.

In cases in which some illegality is found, a series of issues arise: How much of the trust fails? Will the condition alone fail or does the gift to which it is attached fail or does the entire trust fail? As to the failed portion of the trust, to whom should it be distributed? In some cases (e.g. attempts to defraud creditors), return to the settlor is not permitted generally. Allowing the property to remain with the beneficiary may tend to encourage the very act which the illegal trust declaration sought to avoid.

4. TESTAMENTARY AND INTER VIVOS (LIVING) TRUSTS

Trusts are further divided by the manner of their creation. Those created by will and effective at the time of the testator's death are called "testamentary" trusts while those created during lifetime are called "inter vivos" or "living" trusts. The significance of the distinction is mainly found in the formalities for creation (a valid will if testamentary, a valid gift or contract or exercise of a power of appointment if inter vivos) and the recipient of property if a resulting trust arises for any reason. Further, a testamentary trust becomes a matter of public record when the will is filed, whereas an inter vivos trust remains private and free of public scrutiny.

Failed portions of a testamentary trust will pass as directed by the decedent's will, whether by specific alternate gift or the residual clause. If the failed trust itself was the (and possibly even if only part of the) residual clause, the failed residuary material passes by intestacy. A failed portion of a living trust goes by resulting trust to the settlor if still living. If he has died between the time of creation and the time that the trust is declared to be partially or completely invalid, the failed property passes by resulting trust to the settlor, through her to any subsequent unrevoked disposition (e.g., a quit-claim of any interest in the property) and, if none, to her estate for distribution in accordance with her will, if any, and if none, to his heirs.

5. REVOCABLE AND IRREVOCABLE TRUSTS

A trust may be partly or completely revocable or irrevocable. Since the power of "revocation" is one which is reserved only by the settlor of a trust, the distinction between revocable and irrevocable exists only for living trusts. (Until the settlor's death, the testamentary trust has not yet been created, although the will creating it is revocable. After her death and the creation of the trust, there is no living person who can "revoke" the trust.)

A similar power to terminate the trust given to one other than the settlor is either a power of termination (if all that is done is to terminate the trust status with the trust property being distributed as provided in the trust instrument or by resulting trust) or a power of appointment (if the person can both terminate the trust *and* direct who shall receive the trust property).

The settlor can declare a trust to be revocable or irrevocable. In the absence of such a declaration, most jurisdictions will deem the trust irrevocable unless expressly made revocable. The opposite rule exists in a few states by statute and in Uniform Trust Code § 602(a). The power to revoke is usually considered to contain the lesser power to amend. If the settlor expressly provides for amendment, but does not provide for revocation, it is a question of interpretation of the power to amend as to whether it can be extended to encompass a complete revocation. An unlimited power to amend probably should be so interpreted.

6. SPENDTHRIFT, SUPPORT, AND DISCRETIONARY TRUSTS

Active express legal private trusts (which typically are also testamentary and irrevocable) may contain one or more of three optional methods of limiting access to the trust assets by the beneficiary and his creditors.

a. Spendthrift Trusts

This type, typically of an equitable life estate, contains express restrictions upon the voluntary or involuntary alienation of the beneficiary's share. Most jurisdictions, but not all, permit such restraints upon alienation, but there has been a tendency to limit the scope of the exemption by statute.

The most difficult creditors to ignore are the (usually former) spouse and minor children who are seeking to enforce court orders for support. Section 503 of the Uniform Trust Code provides that a spendthrift provision is unenforceable against: (1) a beneficiary's child, spouse, or former spouse who has a judgment or court order against the beneficiary for support or maintenance; (2) a judgment creditor who has provided services for the protection of a beneficiary's interest in the trust; and (3) a claim by the appropriate state or the U.S. government.

In *Shelley v. Shelley*, 354 P.2d 282 (Or. 1960), the Supreme Court of Oregon held that the two former spouses and four minor children of Grant Shelley could reach the income of Grant's spendthrift trust to pay claims for alimony and child support. Grant had disappeared and his whereabouts were unknown. The spendthrift trust had been set up by his father to prevent him from alienating his interests, but the court held that his former wives and children had a right to the income that was "reasonable under the circumstances" to support their respective needs. The children had a right to seek distribution from the trust corpus because they were specified in the trust instrument as intended beneficiaries.

A few states permit a settlor to establish a spendthrift trust for his own protection from creditors. Generally, the attempt to do so would probably create a valid trust with an invalid spendthrift clause, since such clauses are not a vital part of the trust. The creditor of the beneficiary usually attempts to reach the beneficiary's interest by a number of equitable analogs to the legal process of attachment; these equitable means include (in various jurisdictions) creditor's bills, garnishment, attachment, sequestration or trustee process.

b. Support Trusts

These trusts tend to have the same effect as a spendthrift trust (and are valid in jurisdictions which do not allow beneficiaries to hide behind a spendthrift clause). Both support and discretionary trusts protect the beneficiary by giving no vested interest to him or her. In the support trust, the trustee is directed to pay so much of the income or principal or both as, in the trustee's discretion, is necessary for the support of the beneficiary.

Naturally, disagreements can arise as to what is encompassed in the term "support" and the intention of the settlor is sought in the trust instrument and surrounding circumstances.

c. Discretionary Trusts

Discretionary trusts give the trustees discretion to decide exactly how much, if any, income or principal or both should be used for the benefit of the beneficiaries. Thus, the beneficiary is only entitled to receive the income and principal according to the standards set forth in the trust. Discretionary trusts may need a trusted family member, or at least someone who cares about the beneficiary, to supervise the distributions.

For example, in *Marsman v. Nasca*, 573 N.E.2d 1025 (Mass.App.Ct. 1991), the trust gave the trustees the "sole and uncontrolled discretion" to pay over amounts of the principal they deem advisable for the comfortable support and maintenance of the trust beneficiary. The court found that this language set an ascertainable standard, namely that the trust was established "to maintain the life beneficiary 'in accordance with the standard which was normal for him before he became a beneficiary of a trust'." The trustee (a lawyer) had a duty to inquire into the needs of the beneficiary. When the trustee did not, he committed a breach of trust.

Like spendthrift trusts, discretionary trusts are subject to claims from former spouses and minor children. The Uniform Trust Code § 504(c) indicates that a trustee who fails to comply with a standard of distribution or abuses a discretion may be ordered by the court to satisfy a judgment or court order against the beneficiary for support or maintenance of the beneficiary's child, spouse, or former spouse. Further, a court can "direct the trustee to pay to the child, spouse, or former spouse such amount as is equitable under the circumstances but not more than the amount the trustee would have been required to distribute to or for the benefit of the beneficiary had the trustee complied with the standard or not abused the discretion."

7. FUNDED AND UNFUNDED LIFE INSURANCE TRUSTS

Trusts can be classified by the assets which they contain. Insurance Trusts are trusts which contain insurance policies upon the life of the settlor or another person (such as the settlor's spouse or parent). The insurance policy may be the only property, and thus it is considered an unfunded trust because it does not yield funds until the death of the insured. If there are additional assets besides the life insurance policy, then it is considered a funded trust.

The trusts are primarily designed for tax features and the funded v. unfunded and revocable v. irrevocable features are therefore the most important. Elaborate provisions of the Internal Revenue Code, and comparable state income tax laws, govern the taxability of the transfers into and from the trust, the payment of premiums and the income and deductions of the life insurance trusts.

8. MASSACHUSETTS BUSINESS TRUSTS AND ILLINOIS LAND TRUSTS

The law of a particular state may permit commercial trusts that are usually created pursuant to a state's business trust act. According to commentary to Uniform Trust Code § 102, these business trusts are often created to "administer specified funds, such as to pay a pension or to manage pooled investments." Massachusetts business trust and the Illinois land trust present two examples.

The Massachusetts business trust is simply an extension of the trust concept into the field of business organizations. Instead of organizing as a partnership or corporation, the trust form is used. Many so-called "mutual funds" are organized as Massachusetts business trusts. An investor, instead of being issued a "share" of stock received a "certificate of beneficial interest" which is approximately the same thing.

The Illinois land trust is used to convert realty into personalty on paper only. Equitable conversion of realty to personalty occurs when one who contracts to sell the realty is regarded as having sold the realty, even though the sales transaction is still in the form of an unexecuted valid contract. Thus, if the seller dies before completing the paperwork which he is legally required to do (i.e., sign and deliver a deed and accept money in exchange) the court of equity will regard the decedent as the owner of personal, rather than real, property.

Most states treat an immediate duty upon the trustee to sell realty as being similar to a contract to sell the realty; the duty to convey is regarded by equity as having been performed. Illinois, however, carries this principle to a logical extreme and regards many long-range duties to sell as if they were immediate duties to sell. Thus, in Illinois, it is possible to convert realty, on paper, into personalty by placing the realty into trust and imposing an ultimate duty upon the trustee to sell the land.

The distinction between personalty and realty is important because it determines the proper jurisdiction to administer the decedent's estate. It, however, does not do so in the case of a trust unless the trust is terminated by its own terms upon the death of the settlor. Because the property is managed and distributed in accordance with its terms, the property is not subject to probate administration. This distinction can be important for state death tax purposes.

Both the Massachusetts business trust and the Illinois land trust are rather obscure, but they illustrate both the tendency to label trusts with many categories and the tendency for local law variations to permit a great variety of trusts.

9. TOTTEN AND *FARKAS V. WILLIAMS* TRUSTS

Some trusts of particular nature derive their name from the cases in which they were found to be valid. Totten trusts, derived from *In re Totten*, 71 N.E. 748 (N.Y. 1904) (more often called savings account or bank-account trusts), are purported trusts in which a depositor in a savings account executes a writing filed with the bank which declares that he or she is the trustee of that account for another person, but retains the passbook and, typically, does no other acts indicating trust intent.

This definition is in accord with the Restatement (Third) of Trusts § 26 (2003), which states that Totten Trusts are created "where a person makes a deposit in an account with a bank or similar financial institution in the depositor's own name 'as trustee' or 'in trust' for another, the presumption is that the depositor intends to establish a 'tentative trust.' The depositor may modify or revoke a tentative trust and may, from time to time, withdraw any or all of the funds on deposit. On the death of the depositor, the trust is enforceable by the beneficiary as to any funds then remaining on deposit, unless the depositor has revoked the trust."

In re Totten considered the trust to be valid, but held that it had special rules as to revocability. It was deemed to be revocable unless acts or statements to the contrary were done or made. This was the opposite of the then general rule that trusts are irrevocable unless stated to the contrary.

The importance of the Totten trust is that it permits a means of indicating a successor to the particular asset (the savings account, a very commonly owned asset) without the expense, bother and formality of a will (i.e., it is a "will substitute") and without the disadvantages of joint tenancy (requiring a present gift of an undivided interest, thereby losing control, flexibility and revocability).

The presence of a Totten trust raises the issue of its validity. Although most jurisdictions permit such a trust (and a number further validate the practice by statute), some decisions have considered such a trust to be too tentative or violative of the purposes of the Statute of Wills. If the Totten trust is valid, additional issues may arise such as whether the revocation can be by will and, if so, whether a residual clause of the will revokes the trust.

Farkas v. Williams, 125 N.E.2d 600 (Ill. 1955) validated what is probably the "thinnest" possible trust. Capitalizing on the fact that no particular trust attribute is essential (revocability, independence of trustee, trustor and beneficiary of each other, independence of the trustee, etc.) a trust was created in which the settlor retained, in one capacity or another, virtually every bit of control over the property. The trust was revocable by the settlor; he was also the life beneficiary with right to direct the trustee to sell the assets of the trust and distribute the proceeds to him and he was also the trustee with a power to sell the assets and terminate the trust. Only if none of these terminating powers was exercised did the remainder pass to another person. The Illinois court upheld the trust and it served as the model for other trusts (predominately for securities) urged upon consumers as a means of "avoiding probate."

The bottom line is that beneficiaries of trusts should be grateful. The settler thought enough of them to establish an instrument and direct that they receive part of their trust property.

CHAPTER 11

TRUSTEE POWERS AND DUTIES

A. IN GENERAL

Trustee powers, duties and liabilities are interrelated. For example, the power to sell and the power to invest are natural outgrowths of the duty to make the trust corpus productive. Liabilities of the trustee arise when a duty is breached.

The primary source of trustee powers and duties is normally the trust instrument, but a writing is only required by the Statute of Frauds for dealings in real property. The settlor's contemporary statements of intention are admissible unless barred by the parol evidence rule. Subsequent may be admissible unless the trust is revocable or amendable. The trust terms may expressly or impliedly give or impose the powers or duties.

Additionally, the law will infer additional powers and duties from the particular trust instrument's provisions or from the general law (decisional or statutory). For example, see the Uniform Probate Code § 7–301 and subsequent sections for a discussion on trust administration.

Courts of equity imposed a series of duties upon individual trustees. When professional trustees appeared on the scene, they sought both broader powers and narrower duties in order to carry out the remaining duties imposed. The courts gave mixed responses to this trend. The professional trustees had greater success with the legislatures. Statutes were enacted permitting a number of practices which would otherwise constitute breaches of strict trust duties—registering securities in the name of a nominee rather than the trustee, combining investments in a common trust fund, etc.

A related fiduciary, the personal representative of a decedent's estate, was more heavily regulated by statute. It has become very common for legislatures to spell out in great detail the powers and duties of the executor or administrator of a decedent's estate. The Uniform Probate Code permits the exercise of powers without direct court supervision when there is no objection by those interested in the estate administration.

The trust instrument may require co-trustees (multiple fiduciaries) to act unanimously or may permit them to act by majority. Section 703(a) of the Uniform Trust Code provides that co-trustees "who are unable to reach a unanimous decision may act by majority decision."

B. POWERS OF THE TRUSTEE

The trustee possesses general powers and specific powers. According to Uniform Trust Code § 815, the trustee has the general powers conferred by the trust. Unless limited by the trust terms, these powers over the trust property "any other powers appropriate to achieve the proper investment, management, and distribution of the trust property;" and "any other powers conferred" by the Uniform Trust Code.

Section 816 of the Uniform Trust Code gives trustee numerous specific powers, including the power to collect trust property, reject additions to the trust, acquire or sell property, deposit money, borrow money and mortgage trust property, acquire stocks and exercise associated ownership rights, acquire and maintain real property, grant options to sell or lease trust property, insure trust property, abandon property of no or insufficient value, pay or contest claims, pay taxes, sign and deliver contracts, and wind down the administration of the trust on termination. These rights and powers are discussed in more detail below.

1. SALES, LEASES AND MORTGAGES

Normally a power of sale of trust assets is found in the trust instrument. If not expressly given, a power may be inferred from the duty to make the property productive, unless there is a specific prohibition against sale. Normally, a prohibition against sale will be given effect, but the court may allow a deviation in the administrative provision prohibiting a sale, if the circumstances warrant such a deviation.

An intention that the property not be sold may also be inferred from the trust instrument. The surrounding circumstances such as the character of the property, like real estate or family corporation stock originally belonging to the settlor, may limit its sale. An authorization to retain certain property is not necessarily a direction to retain the property.

The power of sale is not a completely unfettered discretion. The trustee must still act in a reasonable and prudent manner, obtain a fair price, seek broad exposure to the market, and accept only cash or terms which are reasonably secured. She also must not sell trust property to herself or her close relatives.

Usually the power to lease also exists. For unimproved realty, the power to lease is a reasonable alternative to sale. For other tangible personalty and improved realty, the leasing raises problems of depreciation; with existing leaseholds, patents and copyrights, there is a problem of depletion. In all cases of leases, there is the problem of whether the trustee has power to lease the trust assets for a period longer (or potentially longer) than the trust duration.

The typical trust arrangement involves a life estate and remainder. Can the trustee lease for a period which is different than the life tenant's life? Few lessees could be found for the period of the trust, and the power to lease for a longer period is therefore generally conceded by the court.

Often prospective tenants request that an option to purchase be included with the lease. Generally options to purchase are not permitted to be given by the trustee because of the one-sided nature of such an option. The tenant would ordinarily exercise the option only if the property has increased in value between the times that the option was given and exercised. The trustee has, therefore, abandoned the possibility of getting a higher price by giving an option.

In order for an option to be a proper exercise of the trustee's duty of care, it would have to be shown that the option and lease terms, individually, constitute arrangements which could not otherwise have been made, i.e., the lease would not otherwise have been possible and the sale would not otherwise have been possible at the same terms.

Mortgages or other pledges of trust property in order to secure a loan to the trust are rarely permitted—or wise. Normally, such a power will not be inferred, even if a power of sale is given. Possibly a pledge may be allowed if there is an emergency and court supervision or approval of the mortgage or pledge cannot be obtained in advance.

Generally, loans to the trust are not permitted, even if unsecured. If secured, the probability is that the amount borrowed is less than the probable sale price of the same property. The difference between the mortgage and the sale price is the amount the trustee has "spent" to obtain the loan.

Contrast the situation where the property is received in the trust subject to a mortgage. In that event, the trustee has the option of investing additional trust capital into the asset by paying off the debt secured by the mortgage or of selling the asset which is subject to the mortgage. Although it is common business practice to buy property subject to a mortgage, such investments are often considered improper for a trustee in the absence of specific trust provision authorizing or directing them.

2. INVESTMENTS, IMPROVEMENTS AND EXCHANGES

Investments are not only permitted but are required by the trustee's general duty to make property productive. In making investments, the trustee must exercise due care, be loyal, diversify the investments and earmark the trust assets. These duties are analyzed below. The power to "manage" the trust assets is normally sufficient to imply the power of investment, even if it were not inferred because of the duty to make trust assets productive.

Improvements are often distinguished from repairs on the basis of the greater cost and lifespan of the improvements combined with their tendency to increase the usable lifespan of the asset improved. While the duty to repair is easily inferred, the power to improve is dependent upon express trust language or the need to make the improvement to carry out the purposes of the trust.

The power to improve is not so readily found, but may be granted by the court even if not given by the terms of the trust instrument. An improvement can be viewed as an additional investment in the property being improved; as such, it is necessary that the improvement comply with all the duties of a trustee concerning investments. The duty to diversify is the most likely duty to be breached by the improvement of a trust asset. There may also be a breach of the standard of care.

Exchanges are within the power of a trustee who has the power to do the two things which constitute an exchange—sell asset #1 and purchase asset #2. At times, an exchange may be a better (e.g., for tax reasons) or only (e.g., a corporate reorganization) way of acquiring the new asset. Each of the two parts is examined separately for conformity with the duties required of a trustee; if all are satisfied on both aspects, the exchange is permissible.

3. DISCRETIONARY POWERS

The more common situation in professionally drafted trust instruments is not the absence of a power but the fact that the trustee has been given broad discretion in his, her or its exercise of the power. If discretion is expressly given to the trustee in the exercise of the power, the court will not ordinarily interfere with the exercise or non-exercise of the power unless the action or inaction is beyond the bounds of a reasonable judgment or is the product of dishonesty or improper motive. Improper motives include spite or the furthering of interests of persons (either the trustee or third persons) other than the beneficiary.

The trust instrument which confers the discretion will either impose a standard by which the reasonableness of the exercise can be tested, or it will not. In either case, the court will interfere with the exercise of a valid discretion only when the trustee acts beyond the bounds of reasonable judgment. The imposition of a standard by the trust instrument will aid the court in determining what is beyond the bounds of reasonable judgment. The court will ordinarily allow the trustee full discretion within those bounds even though the court might have acted differently if it were determining the same question.

> EXAMPLE: Settlor bequeaths a fund in trust to Trustee to pay so much of the income and principal as Trustee, in his judgment, should deem necessary for the support, maintenance and education of Monique. The amount necessary to maintain Monique in the style of living to which she is accustomed is reasonably between $4,000 and $6,000 a month. Trustee may expend any amount between $4,000 and $6,000 a month; deviations from that acceptable range are subject to revision by the court. If Trustee expends only $4,000 a month, the remainderman will receive unexpended amounts. Trustee's action may be revised by the court.

The standard imposed upon the trustee may be more specific, as in the Example above, if the standard used was "as is necessary to maintain the standard of living enjoyed by her immediately before my death, having regard to the other assets and the income from them that is available to assist her." The standard could also be so vague as to be no standard whatsoever, such as "whatever she wants," or "keep her happy."

4. DEVIATION

Changes in the administrative, as opposed to dispositive, provisions of a trust are a "deviation" from the trust. Such a deviation is required in cases where the terms are not lawful or are impossible to comply with. The trustee may also ask the court for permission to deviate from other administrative provisions when they do not appear to be in the best interests of the trust or its beneficiaries or were not in the contemplation of the settlor. Note that the deviation is concerned with the administration of the trust and does not (except incidentally) change the shares of any of the beneficiaries. Contrast the charitable trust doctrine of *cy pres* which changes dispositive provisions from one charity to another.

The closest that the doctrine of deviation comes to a change of beneficial interests is an acceleration of the vested interest of the beneficiary, usually a minor, despite a direction to withhold the property until a given age. The pressing present need of the minor for the funds or other property is a sufficient change of circumstances to permit the court to order earlier payment of part or all of the trust property to the needy beneficiary.

One limit to this doctrine is the requirement that the interest of no other beneficiary be impaired by the earlier payment to this beneficiary. Thus, a contingent trust interest which requires, for example, survival in order to take the principal, would not be a proper subject for this deviation from the instruction to withhold the funds until the beneficiary attains a certain age.

C. DUTIES OF THE TRUSTEE

1. LOYALTY (DUTY NOT TO SELF-DEAL)

The greatest duty of a fiduciary is the duty of loyalty. The duty is inherent in the fiduciary relationship and will attach because of the fiduciary relationship and is not derived from particular wording in the trust instrument. This concept of loyalty extends to all fiduciaries, not merely trustees, but is examined here primarily in relation to trustees. The duty is both positive—the duty to administer the trust solely for the benefit of the beneficiary—and negative—the duty not to deal with the beneficiary on the trustee's behalf without full disclosure and fair dealing.

The duty of loyalty is very strong in the trust setting. For example, in *Magruder v. Drury*, 235 U.S. 106 (1914) a breach of trust was found when one of two trustees was also one of two partners in a real estate brokerage which regularly charged ordinary commissions on purchases and sales of notes secured by mortgages. The decedent-settlor had engaged in similar business with the co-trustee during his lifetime. The trustees invested trust funds through the partnership. The commissions charged by the partnership in the ordinary course of business were no larger than it charged others and the trust could not have purchased the investments at a lower price elsewhere.

The *Magruder* court stated that although no wrong was intended and none was in fact done to the trust, the co-trustee could not profit from the trust. He was, accordingly, required to return one-half of the profits made by his two-man partnership from the business with the trust of which he was co-trustee. Note the absence of both causation and actual loss to the trust in this situation. The trustee was required to disgorge profits not because he had done wrong, but because his acts had the appearance of doing wrong. The salutary concept of loyalty requires an extreme disinterest. Perhaps this is a carryover of the concept of having the harem guarded by eunuchs.

In *Matter of Rothko*, 43 NY2d 305 (N.Y. 1977), New York's highest court upheld conclusions of lower courts that Mark Rothko's executors/trustees had engaged in self-dealing when they entered into contracts with galleries to sell works belonging to his estate at deep discounts. Further, the court observed, "If the trustee is guilty of a breach of trust in selling trust property for an inadequate price, he is liable for the difference between the amount he should have received and the amount which he did receive." When a trustee breaches the trust, whether through self-dealing or incompetence, the trustee becomes accountable for the resulting lost funds to the beneficiaries.

This concept of requiring the trustee to account for any potential profit by the trustee is logically extended to all cases in which the trustee sells or buys anything or renders any service (except as trustee) to the trust. Trustees who are casualty insurance salespeople or commission securities salespeople and who sell to the trust face a dilemma because they are required by trust law to return the commission and often forbidden by insurance or securities law from giving discounts.

Attorneys who perform legal services such as defending a lawsuit or giving tax advice may not make a profit from such services. A trustee who serves as his or her own lawyer does not have a choice of which capacity he or she will be compensated in. The only position for which compensation can be claimed is the trustee position. To permit payment to himself or herself as attorney would be to allow him or her to profit from the trusteeship. The only profit permitted is the fee for serving as trustee, even though it is lower than the rates ordinarily charged by the same person when serving as a lawyer.

The trustee who purchases trust assets is similarly placed in the worst possible position by the options which are available to the beneficiaries. They can insist upon a return of the item sold (if it has not been sold to a bona fide purchaser) or claim any profits made by the trustee (whether or not resold) or can confirm the sale.

The trustee is entitled to the return of the purchase price, often with interest, and the amount (or perhaps only the value) of any improvements made to the property if the trustee is required to return the property. Any changes in value of the property between the time of the sale and the time that the beneficiaries are allowed to take action is at the expense of the trustee: If the property goes up in value, the beneficiaries can seek return of the item itself or an accounting of the profits; if the item drops in value, the beneficiaries can ratify the sale.

Good faith of the trustee does not prevent the imposition of liability for the breach of trust, although it is relevant in determining whether further action (such as removal as trustee or denial of commissions) should be taken. The trustee breaches the duty of loyalty simply by buying, directly or indirectly, trust assets. The price paid by the trustee may be as high as, or even higher than, the price which could be obtained from others, but a breach has nevertheless occurred.

One rationale for the strictness of this approach is that the trustee has such control over the manner and advertising of the sale that even a subconscious desire that no other buyer be found must be defended against. It is not a defense to an action by the beneficiaries that the sale was fairly conducted by third persons or conducted by auction, since the third persons and auctioneers were chosen by the trustee.

The trustee cannot do indirectly that which he or she is forbidden to do directly. Thus, the purchase through an intermediary does not prevent liability of the trustee. However, in certain cases, if the trust connection has been broken, the purchase by the trustee is permitted. Thus, if the trustee is no longer trustee or if he or she purchases from one who purchased from the trust, the sale will not be set aside or otherwise subject to attack unless it can be shown that the trustee used information gained while serving as trustee or had prearranged the purchase prior to the resignation or sale to the third party.

The self-benefiting may be the purchase from the trust, the sale to it or an incidental profit or commission on either sale. Sales to the trust pose problems of determining exactly what constitutes the "profit" of the selling trustee.

For example, assume that the trustee purchased an asset at $10,000 in year 1 and then, in year 2 when the asset was worth $30,000, sold it to the trust for $40,000. It is obvious that the excess of the purchase price over the value at the time of sale ($40,000 minus $30,000 = $10,000) should be returned to the trust. Should the difference between the price paid by the trustee in year 1 and the value in year 2 also be recovered? Some authorities say that the issue should be decided by whether the trustee purchased the asset with an intention to sell to the trust and that in the absence of such an intention, the trustee is not required to surrender the "profit."

Consider further, in the same situation, if the selling trustee, in year 3, when the asset was worth $40,000 sold it for $50,000 to a third person or the trustee himself or herself. Are there two breaches or none? What is the measure of damages?

The Uniform Trust Code specifically permits corporate trustees to engage in acts that would normally violate the duty of loyalty. For example, Uniform Trust Code § 802(h)(4) permits trustees to deposit "trust money in a regulated financial-service institution operated by the trustee" so long as the transaction is fair to the beneficiaries. The process of evaluation is often done by the loan department (in which case the bank as trustee would be purchasing services from itself) or by the trust department (in which case any loan not made by the trust department, but made by the loan department would be subject to the charge that the bank had taken a trust opportunity for its own profit).

Often a loan would be too large for a particular trust, but could be shared by a number of small trusts. Mortgage "participations" by which one loan is made by a number of trusts raise a number of problems—earmarking, loyalty and propriety of investment being among them. Investment of the trust assets in stock of the trustee bank may be a breach of the duty of loyalty because other shareholders (and particularly the large shareholders who often control the bank) would not want the market value of the stock to drop. Thus, there would be pressure to continue to hold the trust stock even when there is knowledge in the corporate hierarchy of factors which would cause the value of the shares to drop. The problem is aggravated when the principal trust asset is the controlling stock interest of the trustee bank, for example a testamentary trust of the bank's founder.

As indicated above, the rigors of the duty of loyalty can be eased by statutory provisions (as is often the case for corporate trustees), exculpatory clauses in the trust instrument, court order or beneficiary consent. Such provisions are seldom inferred. For example, in *Magruder v. Drury*, 235 U.S. 106 (1914), described above, the trustee was merely continuing a course of conduct done during the lifetime of the settlor.

Post-death sales of real estate mortgages were breaches of trust even though the trustee had made similar pre-death sales to the settlor; the pre-existing business arrangements were not considered to be an inferred exculpation from breaches of the duty of loyalty. Further, an inference of an exculpatory provision is found in distinctions made between initial and subsequent trust investments. If the settlor placed assets, e.g., stock of the corporate trustee, in the trust, the trustee is not necessarily under a duty to sell the assets even though they might be an improper investment if purchased by the trustee.

One who is a trustee for a number of trusts may purchase from one trust for the benefit of a second trust, but the purchase and sale must be fair to both trusts. The thin line of such absolute fairness and the subjectiveness of what is "fair" combined with the devastating effect of hindsight suggest that it is an unwise experiment.

The concept of loyalty in fiduciary situations has been extended to require fairness in dealings with business opportunities by partners and corporate fiduciaries, e.g., directors. The concept of "corporate opportunity" is directly derived from the theory that a trustee should not profit from his trust.

Uniform Trust Code § 802(c) presumes a conflict of interest when there is a financial transaction between a trustee with his or her spouse; his or her descendants, siblings, parents or their spouses; the trustee's agent or attorney; or with a corporation that the trustee owns a significant interest. All of these transactions would violate the duty of loyalty.

The duty of loyalty also extends to the purchase of adverse interests. For example, if the trust property is subject to a lien or other encumbrance and the trustee acquires the claim in the trustee's individual capacity, it is a breach of trust. On the other hand, a debt owed to the trustee at the time the trustee assumes the office is not necessarily a breach of the duty of loyalty. Naming someone as trustee is not properly used as a means of compromising just debts. Another example of a trust opportunity is a renewal of a lease in which the trust is tenant; the trustee cannot renew in his or her individual capacity.

Trust ownership of a controlling interest in a corporation poses (in addition to problems of proper investment) problems of loyalty in the voting of shares for director and corporate officer positions. If the trustee uses the trust voting power, alone, to elect himself or herself to a compensated position in which he or she had not previously served, there is a breach of the duty of loyalty even though the compensation is earned. It is more difficult when the voting power is merely added to that which was already possessed by the trustee and most difficult to find liability when the individual was in the corporate position prior to becoming trustee.

2. DUTY TO ADMINISTER

Uniform Trust Code § 801 provides that once a person accepts a trusteeship, he or she must "administer the trust in good faith, in accordance with its terms and purposes and the interests of the beneficiaries, and in accordance with this [Code]." The trustee should do what is necessary for the good of the trust and those who are interested in it. The duty to administer applies to both the terms of the trust and to the assets held by the trust. Thus, the trustee is liable for knowledge of and compliance with the terms of the trust (e.g., notifying beneficiaries of their rights and making distributions when required) and is also liable for errors and omissions in the management of the trust property (e.g., failure to maintain properly).

The general duty to administer is the well-spring of many other, more specific duties: The duties of loyalty and impartiality are aspects of proper administration of a trust. The duties to make productive and to account also can be traced to the generic duty to do that which is correct.

The trustee's duty to gather the assets of the trust, preserve and make them productive and distribute them in accordance with the terms of the trust may pose problems which are not specifically dealt with by the trust instrument or other trust duties. The trustee can seek the advice of the appropriate court if the trustee is in doubt. For example, he or she may seek counsel on the wisdom of abandoning a valueless asset or maintaining or defending a claim in litigation.

3. DUTY TO MAKE PRODUCTIVE INVESTMENTS

The duty to make productive investments is express or implied in most trusts, but is not an essential trust duty. The trustee may be appointed for the purpose of preserving real or personal property in its present form and delivering title or possession upon the happening of some event, e.g., attaining age 21 or the payment of a debt. The trustee's duty to deliver realty, chattels or intangibles in kind negates a duty to make productive.

This duty is generally applied in a practical and reasonable manner. If the assets of the trust include an unproductive asset, e.g. undeveloped land, and the duty to make productive exists, e.g., by express provision or implied from trust terms such as a long-term trust with a direction to pay "income" to the beneficiary, the trustee will be allowed a reasonable time to make the property productive.

In the case of undeveloped realty in which there is no duty to deliver the realty title to a beneficiary, it may be possible to rent the property in unimproved condition, e.g., as a farm or city parking lot. If not, the trustee would normally sell the property rather than build upon it. If the unproductive property is money on deposit in a checking account, (as opposed to undeveloped land), the time to invest would be less since the trustee does not have to sell in order to reinvest.

It is not necessary to make every penny of the trust funds productive. A reasonable amount of money can be retained in a checking account in order to pay current trust distributions and expenses. How much is "reasonable" is, of course, a matter of judgment.

There are issues of reasonableness of the amount reserved for anticipated future expenses and distributions, the reasonableness of the amount of time necessary in order to reinvest and possibly only a case of under-productiveness, as opposed to unproductiveness. The liability of the trustee, if any, is usually only for the income which would have been produced. Absent bad faith, there is not reasonable cause to remove a trustee (or deny compensation) for failure to make a trust asset productive.

Nevertheless, a few depression-era cases held trustees liable for failure to make property productive when funds were left too long on deposit, without interest, in banks which failed. Presumably the same rule would be applied today to the extent the amount on deposit exceeded recoveries under federal insurance plans for banks and savings and loan associations. The absence of causation did not bother the courts in imposing liability. A strict penalty was imposed upon the failure to make the property productive. This line of cases does not seem to be consistent with either the general test of "reasonableness" of the duty to make productive or the tendency to seek causation for imposing penalties upon trustees except in cases of failure to earmark.

The pattern for permissible investments consists of an overlay of the trust provisions superimposed upon statutory patterns which are in turn superimposed upon case law. The absence of total certainty in this portion of trust law is the price of case-by-case determination of appropriateness of particular investments. Except when impossible, illegal or impractical due to a change in circumstances, the dictates of the settlor—whether expanding or contracting the permissible investments—must be followed.

Statutory provisions vary from a list of investments which in turn are either permissive (allowing trustees to make other types of investments) or restrictive (considering no other investment to be proper). Statutory provisions of a "prudent man," which became the "prudent investor" rule, was promulgated in Restatement of Trusts 3d § 90 and the Uniform Prudent Investor Act.

The prudent man rule for investments as phrased in *Harvard College v. Amory*, 26 Mass. 446 (1830) stated that a trustee "is to observe how men of prudence, discretion and intelligence manage their own affairs, not in regard to speculation, but in regard to permanent disposition of their funds, considering the probable income, as well as the probable safety of the capital to be invested."

This test stressed two contradictory points—probable income and probable safety. The amount of income which a given amount will produce increases as the degree of risk increases. Thus, a highly speculative investment such as a new business or vacant land purchased as an investment, might produce a great (though uncertain) gain (income) but it also imposes a substantial risk upon the capital.

At the same time, federal governmental bonds tend to be as secure as the monetary system, but produce a very low income because of the small risk. Thus, in the ordinary case neither investment is a proper investment for the entire trust corpus. The bonds might be a proper investment for a portion of the trust, but the new business would generally not be considered proper because it is "speculative."

The prudent **man** rule was changed by The Restatement of Trusts, Third, which introduced the prudent **investor** concept. Section 90, which provides for a general standard of prudent investment, states, "The trustee is under a duty to the beneficiaries to invest and manage the funds of the trust as a prudent investor would, in light of the purposes, terms, distribution requirements, and other circumstances of the trust."

Part (a) requires "the exercise of reasonable care, skill, and caution, and is to be applied to investments not in isolation but in the context of the trust portfolio and as a part of an overall investment strategy, which should incorporate risk and return objectives reasonably suitable to the trust." Part (b) states that "[i]n making and implementing investment decisions, the trustee has a duty to diversify the investments of the trust unless, under the circumstances, it is prudent not to do so."

The Uniform Prudent Investor Act stresses that the standard of prudence in investments is to be applied to the entire portfolio rather than individual investments. The Uniform Trust Code has incorporated the Uniform Prudent Investor Act as its Chapter 17.

In examining investments, no particular investment is always inappropriate or always permissible. This relative validity of investments leads naturally to examination questions in which the student should be able to identify probabilities, reasons for the probabilities and then proceed on the alternate theories that the investment(s) is/are proper or improper.

Certain trends in acceptability can be identified. First, government obligations of the United States, the state in which the trust is administered, other states and cities and governmental bonding districts (within certain limits) are generally the most acceptable traditional trust investments, in the order of preference stated. If the governmental entity has a history of default or declaring bankruptcy, such as when Birmingham declared bankruptcy in 2011 and Detroit declared bankruptcy in 2013, their notes are best avoided by trustees. Government bonds almost always found on statutory lists, favor the remainderman over the income beneficiary by being more safe than income-producing items but they have little protection against inflation. In 2022, the U.S. Treasury Department began issuing Treasury Inflation-Protected Securities, or TIPS, to provide protection against inflation. The principal of a TIPS increases with inflation and decreases with deflation, as measured by the Consumer Price Index. When a

TIPS matures, you are paid the adjusted principal or original principal, whichever is greater. When inflation exceeded 9% in June 2022, these seemed a safer investment for a trust.

Second, debt obligations secured by a first mortgage on real estate which has a value with a good margin over the amount owed is another traditionally first-quality investment. There are dangers that the property may drop in value, that the improvements may be destroyed and the title might be defective. The percentage of value which commercial lenders will lend today (between 70 and 90 percent and up to 97 percent with federal insurance programs) is so high that trusts (unless protected by the federal insurance) cannot compete in the investment market. Second mortgages are considered to be improper investments in most cases, but the amount of the first mortgage might be so small that a second mortgage would not be an improper investment.

Third, corporate bonds, especially for utilities or quasi-governmental organizations are also highly regarded. It is still possible for the bonds to be a poor investment, e.g., in a railroad or airline which has gone through bankruptcy reorganizations in the recent past.

Fourth, equity securities (stock of corporations) are investments which have met increasing approval. Although an investment in a new business is too speculative to be a proper investment in most cases, there are now greater safeguards in the security industry and more established and supervised corporations than at the time that trust investment policies were being formulated. Today, most states permit investments in the common or preferred stock of established companies.

Another investment which has met increasing approval because of federal protection is the unsecured loan to a banking corporation represented by a savings account or certificate of deposit. The latter item usually has a time restriction on withdrawal of funds (backed by forfeiture of income) and is therefore less desirable in a short-term trust. Federal insurance of deposits in banks and savings and loan associations has tended to make proper one part of an otherwise improper investment—unsecured loans.

New businesses and land remain the least appropriate investments. The speculative nature of both makes income uncertain and may risk the principal. A farm or an apartment house requires more skill and attention than the average trustee would possess or be able to devote. Trades and businesses, speculative investments and investments for capital gains are also generally considered improper, although they might be permitted in particular cases.

The Uniform Prudent Investor Act recognizes that mutual funds (trusts or corporations which carry on the business of investing in other businesses) assist diversification. That act permits the delegation of the investment power. There is uncertainty as to the extent to which the trustee's fees (which ordinarily involve compensation for investment decisions, among other actions) should be reduced when management fees are paid to the mutual fund. The allocation of the ordinary income and capital gains distributed by the mutual fund between income and principal beneficiaries may also be a problem.

An otherwise proper investment might be improper because it breaches other duties of the trustee such as the duty to diversify, to be loyal, to be impartial, and to not delegate.

The trustee must use the care and skill of a reasonable person (even if the trustee does not possess such care and skill) and commentators and some courts attempt to impose higher degrees of care and skill upon those professional trustees which advertise expertise in the field of trust management. See Uniform Probate Code § 7–302 and Uniform Trust Code § 806.

The time for determining the appropriateness of an investment is the time that it is made. Of course the litigation process is such that almost all contested cases of investment judgment involve items which time ultimately proved to be poor investments.

4. DUTY TO EARMARK (NOT TO COMMINGLE), NOMINEES

There are two duties involved in "earmarking." First, the trust assets should be separated from all other assets. Second, the assets should be clearly identified as belonging to this trust. Toward this end, § 810 of the Uniform Trust Code requires the trustee to keep adequate records of the administration of the trust, and separate trust property from the trustee's own property. A trustee of two or more separate trusts, however, may jointly invest their assets so long as the trustee keeps records clearly indicating the separate interests.

Trustees must not commingle the assets of the trust with the trustee's personal assets. If done with the intention to misappropriate, the commingling is embezzlement. It is a breach of trust whether or not the intention to appropriate is present.

The court is strictest with this type of commingling because the appearance is the same whether or not the intention to misappropriate is present. The presence of that intention is somewhat subjective and the presence can be determined only after the fact has occurred. Thus, as a matter of preventive law, the courts impose strong penalties upon trustees who commingle trust assets with their own assets.

Assets belonging to third persons, especially other trusts, also need to be kept separate, but the possibility of misappropriation is less severe. The most difficult cases in this area concern multiple (or potentially multiple) trusts created by the same settlor. The strict rule is that the assets of the trusts must be kept separate. Often it is difficult to tell whether a combined trust for many beneficiaries (e.g., children) is intended or whether separate trusts are intended. For income tax purposes, separate trusts are usually desirable. However, if the trusts are separate, the assets need to be separated and unambiguously earmarked for the individual trusts.

A technical breach may occur if the trustee does not realize that separate trusts are involved.

A situation in which potentially separate trusts can exist, but which is usually treated as one trust, occurs when there are additions or "pour-overs" to an existing trust. The settlor may reserve and exercise the right to make additions to his trust while living or by will.

Others may contribute to the trust. For example, a spouse may contribute to the trust created by the other spouse or a grandparent may contribute to a trust established by the parent. The terms of the addition (and sometimes the original trust) dictate whether a separate trust using the same terms is intended; normally the total amount is treated as one trust.

The need to keep trust assets separate is felt most by the person attempting to trace trust assets. Other fiduciary relationships such as attorney-client or the husband-wife situation in community property states involve "tracing" an asset through changes in form to its present status (e.g., realty sold, converted to cash which is used to acquire stock certificates). If the trustee of two or more separate trusts, however, jointly invested their assets and kept records clearly indicating the separate interests, as required by Uniform Trust Code § 810(d), then tracing should be a rather simple matter.

If a fiduciary mixes the "trust" property with his own property, the court may require the fiduciary to separate the interests or to become the guarantor of the value of the fiduciary portion or the court may subject the entire mass to the fiduciary relationship. Equitable principles are involved in such tracing. Many factors are relevant, including the degree of culpability in commingling, the ownership of the portion commingled, the good faith of the fiduciary, and the relative values of the amounts commingled.

The "duty to earmark" involves the obligation of the trustee to mark the asset, as appropriate, with the indicia of ownership by him or her in the fiduciary relationship for the benefit of this particular trust. The method (which takes its name from one method of marking cattle) varies with the type of asset involved. Realty should have record title in the name of the trustee as trustee for the particular trust. Properly recorded trust ownership indicia is notice to prospective purchasers. The registration should be complete, however. Some states permit, by statute, a purchaser to ignore a designation of the record titleholder "as trustee" if there is not a fuller description of the trust.

Earmarking of intangibles which are represented by a document in registered form should be accomplished by the same means as registration of title to land—by describing the trustee "as trustee for the XYZ Trust under the will of John Jones, deceased" or "as trustee under the John Jones Trust created by instrument dated July 1, 2022." Tangible items should be "earmarked" in accordance with their nature. If there is documentation involved with the ownership, such as motor vehicle registration or bills of sale, the trust status should be clearly shown.

The duty to separate and the duty to earmark pose difficult, but not insurmountable, problems for professional fiduciaries. The traditional response of the banking organizations has been not to conform the industry's practice to the law, but to conform the law to the industry's practice.

Statutes excuse many of the practices of combining trust assets and registering assets in the name of the bank without showing trust status or in the name of nominees (often bank officers), thus showing neither the name of the trustee nor the trust status. These "nominee" statutes are almost universal, but they are not uniform. Some statutes permitting registration of trust assets in the names of nominees are restricted to the type of fiduciary (corporate only or some or all trustees, executors etc.) while others are restricted in the type of investment which can be so registered (mortgages, stocks or other named investments or all investments).

When the duty to earmark exists (i.e., it has not been excused or eliminated by the trust instrument or statute) and it has been breached, there is a further question whether causation should be relevant. The older cases did not require causation between the failure to earmark and the loss suffered by the trust. Thus, the trustee who failed to earmark became a guarantor of the principal and often the income of the trust.

A loss occasioned by general economic conditions and which would not have been charged to the trustee in the absence of the technical breach of the duty to earmark was often charged to the trustee.

This strict liability was justified as penalizing the trustee for being careless or ignorant of the proper methods of administration and thereby unnecessarily subjecting the beneficiaries to risks (even though such risks did not come to pass).

5. DUTY TO ACCOUNT

Trustees have a duty to keep beneficiaries informed about the administration of their trusts. A related duty requires trustees to account for trust property, expenditures, and income. The terms "account" and "accounting" are used in two senses. First, the "account" is the table of figures which show the financial condition of the trust, sometimes accompanied by a textual explanation. Second, the action of "account" is an equitable form of action by which fiduciaries (including resulting and constructive trustees) are called before the court to explain their actions as fiduciary. In the barest form, the account is simply financial statements—balance sheets showing the beginning and ending points and a profit and loss statement showing the changes between the two points.

The beginning point of the first account is a statement of the assets received in the trust, which is usually part of the trust instrument for living trusts or the decree of distribution for testamentary trusts. For subsequent accounts, the beginning point is the ending point of the prior account. The account should show all receipts and disbursements, additions and subtractions and gains and losses on sales, exchanges and distributions.

When rights of successive beneficiaries are involved, a breakdown of the items as principal and income is usually included. Finally, the account should end with a "Balance on Hand" which agrees mathematically with the prior balance as adjusted for the intervening action and which can be verified by examination of ownership certificates of the items claimed to be on hand. The trustee should obtain, preserve and have available for inspection by concerned parties documentation (e.g., receipts, canceled checks etc.) for each item. The trustee should also permit examination of the trust assets and the trust books. See also Uniform Probate Code § 7–303(c), which provides that upon "reasonable request, a beneficiary is entitled to a statement of the accounts of the trust annually and on termination of the trust or change of the trustee."

The duty to account has a number of subsidiary duties which can be enlarged or diminished by the trust terms or by statute. Actions of the trustee should be noted by writings which are preserved and available for inspection. The trustee should furnish the beneficiaries information concerning the trust and their shares in it. Any beneficiary can request that the trustee present an accounting. The trustee has a duty to verify facts upon which distributions are made such as death, remarriage, birth, age etc.

The duty to account may become the opening round in resolving intra-trust disputes. As to matters presented in the account, the beneficiary is given notice by an accounting, which may be presented formally through a court or informally and directly to the beneficiary. Failure to object when able to do so constitutes acceptance. Items not in the account (or items falsely presented) do not bar the beneficiary nor the court from examining them at a later time. If the beneficiary seeks to impose liability upon a trustee for something not shown in the account, such as secret profit by the trustee on dealings with the trust property whether or not the duty of loyalty is also breached, the technique is to require the trustee to account for that item.

The beneficiary's response to the trustee's account is to "object" to the inclusion (e.g., trustee expended trust funds for a contested purpose) or exclusion of the particular item. The trustee then has the burden of going forward, but generally makes a prima facie case by presenting receipts or other documentation or testimony in support of the contested items.

Because the duty to account is used as the procedural entry to the court, the duty to account traditionally could not be waived by the settlor of the trust. Some modifications are permissible to the duty, but the attempt to relieve the duty completely is inimical to the trust concept. However, the beneficiaries, if legally competent, may waive an account.

There is great diversity in statutory patterns concerning trust accounts. The variables focus upon whether the settlor can vary the requirement, the manner of creation of the trust (living or testamentary or both) and the desires of professional trustees to limit their liability by securing court approval of their actions.

Statutes are more likely to require accounts from testamentary trustees, often continuing the jurisdiction of the probate court in order to do so. When accounts are required by beneficiary request or statute for living trusts, the court of equity generally is the proper court for the accounting action. The advantage of a court account in which a beneficiary is not required to take the initiative is sometimes offset by the cost, delay and lack of privacy involved in any court action. Some fiduciaries render private accountings to the beneficiaries thus barring later claims by beneficiaries who were *sui juris*.

The court which hears the account and the objections to it may wholly or partly approve or disapprove the account, order corrections, "surcharge" (i.e., state that the trustee is liable for an amount greater than the liability shown in the account), allow or deny trustee's compensation and expenses (including court costs and attorneys' fees) or remove the trustee.

Approval of an account settles all matters truthfully presented in it, and possibly all misrepresentations which the beneficiaries, if competent, could have discovered with reasonable inquiry. The decree, like all decrees, can be reopened if there was fraud, concealment or mistake in the account or the order settling it.

The traditional phrasing of expenditures by the trustee is that the trustee "is entitled to reimbursement" from the trust, but actual practice is to pay the items from the trust and seek approval of the expenditure in the account. Thus, an account which shows disbursements is the occasion to challenge the nature, purpose or amount of the expenditure, but the hypocrisy of the phrasing is normally left untouched.

If the trustee is dealing with the beneficiary for the trustee's own benefit, the most complete and full disclosure is required. The logical extension of this principle is that attempts by the fiduciary, as fiduciary, to reduce or eliminate liability by submitting an account directly to the beneficiary (i.e., not through court proceedings) border on the self-interest field in which a fuller disclosure should be required. Computer printouts submitted directly to beneficiaries by corporate fiduciaries may be inadequate because of complexity or abbreviations.

6. DELEGATION OF DUTIES

Individuals who become agents of a trustee owe "a duty to the trust to exercise reasonable care to comply with the terms of the delegation." A trustee who complies with these terms "is not liable to the beneficiaries or to the trust for an action of the agent to whom the function was delegated."

At common law, trustees had a duty not to delegate the administration of the trust to others. The Uniform Trust Code § 807 specifically indicates that a trustee "may delegate duties and powers that a prudent trustee of comparable skills could properly delegate under the circumstances." In entrusting duties to others, the trustee is required to exercise reasonable care, skill, and caution in selecting an agent, establishing the scope and terms of the delegation, and must periodically review the agent's actions in order to monitor the agent's performance and compliance with the terms of the delegation.

7. DUTY TO DIVERSIFY

The duty of diversification was upgraded by Restatement of Trusts, Third § 90 to be part of the prudent investor rule. In the exercise of the care and skill of a prudent investor, the risk of loss should be spread among various types of investments. Placing the entire trust corpus into one investment (or debts by one obligor) may not be prudent under the circumstances. An easy example of a breach of the duty to diversity (among other duties) would be the deposit of funds in excess of the maximum amount of federal insurance in a bank or savings and loan association account.

Not all courts recognize the duty to diversify as a separate duty. In jurisdictions which decline to recognize the duty to diversify as a separate duty, it is a factor in determining whether an investment is prudent. The theoretical difference is important in determining the appropriate measure of damages.

The failure to diversify may subject the trustee to liability for damages in the amount by which the investment is excessive. If the duty breached is the prudent investor rule, the entire investment (rather than part of it) is improper and the damages are the entire loss.

Circumstances which are relevant in determining both whether the duty to diversify is present and whether, if present, it has been breached, include the following:

- The approach of the particular jurisdiction as to whether there is a separate duty to diversify.
- Language of the trust investment concerning the making and retention of investments. The duty to diversity, if it exists, can be expressly or impliedly waived by the settlor.
- Identity of the person who made the investment. An investment made by a trustee is more likely to be subjected to the duty to diversify than is an original investment by the settlor. Many jurisdictions have statutes which permit the retention of the assets in the form in which received in the trust; those jurisdictions eliminate both the broader duty of care and skill of the prudent investor as well as the subsidiary duty to diversify.
- The extent to which a single investment is, itself, diversified. If the entire trust corpus is invested in one mutual fund or one common trust investment fund, there would be diversification at the level of performing investment, but no diversification at the level of management immediately below the trustee level.

For example, what if a Trustee invests, in his duty as a trustee, the entire trust fund in Spread Mutual Fund, a diversified investment fund, and the fund suffers a large loss because of employee embezzlement. If the jurisdiction recognizes the duty to diversify, the trustee is liable to the beneficiaries to the extent of the loss suffered on the excessive investment.

Thus, if a 30% investment would have been proper, 70% of the loss is charged to the trustee. If the duty to diversify is not a separate duty, the trustee may be liable for failure to exercise the care and skill of a prudent investor. If the embezzlement loss was the same amount to the trust, but occurred in one of the investments by the mutual fund, the duty to diversify is not so obviously violated.

8. DUTY OF IMPARTIALITY

When a trust has two or more beneficiaries, the trustee must act impartially in investing, managing, and distributing the trust property, giving due regard to the beneficiaries' respective interests, according to Uniform Trust Code § 803. Unless permitted or directed by the trust instrument to do otherwise, a trustee must act for the benefit of the trust as a whole and not favor the interests of one beneficiary over another.

The typical trust arrangement consists of a life estate and remainder persons. The life tenant is benefited by the higher return of riskier investments and the remainder persons are benefited by greater safety. Protection against loss due to inflation is more important to remainder persons.

An instance in which the duty of impartiality is tested occurs when a trustee is requested to take certain action by one of several beneficiaries (either consecutive or concurrent). It would appear to be appropriate for the trustee to seek and obtain the approval of all other beneficiaries before doing any act which the trustee would not have done absent the beneficiary request. It may, however, be impossible to seek and obtain approval of unknown or contingent or minor beneficiaries.

The trustee thus acts at the trustee's risk when the trustee follows the suggestions of some, but not all, beneficiaries. The requesting beneficiaries may be estopped from imposing liability upon the trustee for any breach of trust arising out of the requested transaction, but non-consenting beneficiaries are not estopped. The other duties imposed upon a trustee may create a dilemma. For example, the duty to make productive may conflict with the duty to preserve. Indeed, the concept of the prudent investor is one which balances income against preservation.

9. BREACHES OF TRUSTEE DUTIES

The preceding pages described the major trustee duties. Many trust administration problems can be analyzed as if they were an unintentional tort using the prongs of duty, breach, causation, defenses and damages.

a. Duty

The preceding sections described the major trust duties—Loyalty, to Administer, Make Productive, Earmark, Account, Non-Delegation, Diversification, Impartiality and Accounting. Some duties have both positive and negative phrasings; for example, the duty of loyalty includes the duty not to self-deal, and the duty to earmark includes the duty not to commingle. A "breach of trust" is a breach of a trust *duty*.

b. Breach

Because of the higher standards imposed by the fiduciary duties, breaches can more easily be found. The trustee seldom has a *de minimis* defense. It is usually sufficient to explain how the act done is inconsistent with the duty imposed.

c. Causation

Slight, and in some cases nonexistent, causation likens many breach of trust cases more to strict liability than to negligence. For example, a trustee may be liable for the loss in marketable securities which were an appropriate investment, but which declined in value if the trustee failed to earmark the securities. Although earmarking the securities would not have prevented the loss, it would have made it more difficult for the trustee to shift the trustee's own loss securities into the trust portfolio. This aspect of the liability of the trustee for breach of trust is less important than in Torts.

d. Defenses

The exceptions and defenses to charges of breach of trust generally come from one of four sources: exculpatory clauses, statutory authority, court permission, and consent.

i. Exculpatory Clauses

These clauses in the trust instrument may relieve or reduce the trustee's duties, but the trustee cannot be relieved of liability for reckless, intentional or bad faith acts.

Uniform Trust Code § 1008 indicates that a trust term relieving a trustee of liability for breach of trust is unenforceable if it "relieves the trustee of liability for breach of trust committed in bad faith or with reckless indifference to the purposes of the trust or the interests of the beneficiaries; or . . . was inserted as the result of an abuse by the trustee of a fiduciary or confidential relationship to the settlor." Further, if the trustee drafted or caused to be drafted the exculpatory term, then it "is invalid as an abuse of a fiduciary or confidential relationship unless the trustee proves that the exculpatory term is fair under the circumstances and that its existence and contents were adequately communicated to the settlor."

In the *Marsman v. Nasca*, 573 N.E.2d 1025 (Mass.App.Ct. 1991) case, the trustee had drafted the exculpatory clause into the will that contained provisions creating a testamentary trust. James F. Farr, the lawyer-trustee, testified that he discussed the exculpatory clause with Sara, the settlor, and she wanted it included. The court held that "since there was no evidence that the insertion of the clause was an abuse of Farr's fiduciary relationship with Sara at the time of the drawing of her will, the clause is effective."

ii. Statutory Authority for Deviation from Traditionally Required Fiduciary Practices

Statutes may permit corporate trustees to hold securities in the name of a nominee (thus breaching what would otherwise be the duty to earmark) or to use a common trust fund (thus violating the duty to be impartial and loyal to each trust and the duty to keep the trust assets separate). Generally, these statutes are valid. They seldom relieve individual trustees of liability.

iii. Court Permission

Prudence dictates that trustees obtain prior consent before committing an act that might be considered a breach of trust. Nevertheless, some technical breaches may receive retroactive court validation. It then becomes necessary to explain to the court the reason why the general rule should not apply to the situation of this trust.

iv. Express Consent of All Beneficiaries

All beneficiaries must be both fully informed and able to consent to an act that might be considered a breach of trust. The presence of any beneficiary who is not *sui juris* deprives this exception of full force. The requirement of a complete and honest explanation in a non-coercive setting tends to make the consent even rarer. The settlor of a revocable trust can also consent to what would otherwise be a breach of trust.

However, this consent is invalid if it was "induced by improper conduct of the trustee" or the beneficiaries did not know of their rights or of the material facts relating to the breach of trust at the time they gave consent, according to Uniform Trust Code § 1009.

e. Damages

The Uniform Trust Code § 1002 provides that trustees must pay damages for breach of trust. The trustee is liable to the beneficiaries affected by the breach for the greater of: "(1) the amount required to restore the value of the trust property and trust distributions to what they would have been had the breach not occurred; or (2) the profit the trustee made by reason of the breach." When there are multiple trustees, they may be required to contribute to damages depending on whether they individually contributed to the breach or received a benefit from the breach of trust.

In addition to money damages for breach of trust, other equitable forms of relief may be imposed, such as rescission of a transfer or setting aside some other act or requiring positive action on the part of the trustee.

In severe cases, the breach may lead to additional damages in the form of removal of the trustee and perhaps denial of compensation in part or wholly. A related issue which often arises is the ability to offset gains made on one transaction against losses on another with the touchstone being that the court does not want to encourage further gambling by the trustee and therefore, the court will not allow "separate" transactions (an equitable conclusion) to be offset against each other.

However, trustees are not liable to pay damages to a beneficiary "for a loss or depreciation in the value of trust property or for not having made a profit," in absence of a breach of trust, according to Uniform Trust Code § 1003.

D. QUIZ ON TRUSTEE DUTIES

QUESTIONS

1. What approach is suggested by the text as an approach to problems involving potential breaches of trust duties?

2. What are the major trust duties described in this text?

3. What are the four methods of obtaining a defense to liability for an act which otherwise would be a breach of trust?

4. Which are the duties of a trustee that are least capable of being eliminated by the settlor?

5. Which duties are potentially breached by a banking corporation, as trustee, if the trust assets include a controlling block of the bank's shares and stock rights are issued by the banking corporation and exercised by it as trustee of the trust?

6. A corporate trustee acquires a mortgage in its own name for the purpose of holding various parts of the debt and mortgage in various trusts of which it is trustee. How many duties are potentially breached by this mortgage participation?

7. What potential trust problems are created by the existence of shares of (or certificates of beneficial interest in) a mutual fund as part of the trust assets?

ANSWERS

1. The elements of an unintentional tort problem—duty, breach, causation, defenses and damages.

2. Loyalty (Not to Self-Deal), Administer, Make Productive, Invest, Earmark (Not to Commingle), Account, Not to Delegate, Diversify and Be Impartial.

3. Exculpatory clause in trust instrument, statute, court permission to do the act, informed consent of all beneficiaries.

4. Account, Loyalty (except that some self-dealing may be specifically permitted by the trust instrument) and Administer (as to active trusts).

5. The duties of loyalty, diversification and due care in making investments. Other facts would be necessary to raise issues of impartiality or duty to make productive.

6. Loyalty, duty to earmark, propriety of investment (possibly including diversification).

7. Problems of allocation of capital gains distributions between the life tenant and the remainder person raise the issue of the trustee's duty of impartiality. In addition, the investment may not be on the statutory list of approved investments (or may not be an exercise of due care in investment) and may raise issues of delegation of the investment power and diversification of investments.

CHAPTER 12

TRUST ADMINISTRATION PROBLEMS

Trust administration problems may arise in several contexts. For example, they can occur when the trust has successive beneficiaries, when conflict arises between beneficiaries and trustees, when third parties claim rights, or when the trust is terminated or modified. All these potential conflicts are discussed herein.

A. SUCCESSIVE BENEFICIARIES (PRINCIPAL AND INCOME)

As indicated earlier, according to the Uniform Trust Code § 803, if a trust has two or more beneficiaries, the trustee must "act impartially in investing, managing, and distributing the trust property, giving due regard to the beneficiaries' respective interests." The most common division of beneficial ownership in testamentary trusts is into a life estate and a remainder. A life estate may be left to the settlor's surviving spouse, with the remainder to their issue.

If we assume that the purpose of the life estate is to ensure an orderly flow of income without bunching or accumulation in the hands of the beneficiary, the life estate is an imperfect device. First, there is generally no correlation between the net income paid by the trust and the needs of the beneficiary.

Second, in testamentary trusts composed of the residue of an estate, income accumulates during the administration of the estate, but is not given to the trustee or otherwise available for distribution until the estate administration is completed. Those dependent upon the decedent-settlor are usually entitled to probate family allowance, but it is unusual for probate family allowance to be charged against accumulated trust income.

Third, whenever there is a change among successive income beneficiaries, a portion of the income is usually in process in the sense that it has been received by the trustee but not yet distributed to the income beneficiary. Thus, the estate of a deceased life estate beneficiary is entitled to the income which was accumulated and unpaid at the time of the life tenant's death. The life tenant derived no benefit from the income, and administration of the life tenant's estate may be necessary for the accumulated income.

Generally a life estate is created by the settlor directing that the "net income" be paid to the life beneficiary and that the "principal" be paid to others at the death of the life tenant. In such an arrangement, we encounter all the problems of dividing principal and income.

1. PRINCIPAL AND INCOME GENERALLY

Principal is the property given to the trust by the settlor, and the amounts received in exchange for that property. Income is the return in money or property from the use of the principal. Typical examples of income are rent, interest, regular cash dividends and receipts from business.

"Receipts" and "disbursements" can be "allocated to" principal or income or "apportioned between" them. In resolving problems of apportionment or allocation, the following steps should be taken in the order presented.

First, the terms of the trust are controlling. The settlor could provide that all income and principal is to go to one beneficiary. This eliminates problems of allocation and apportionment of principal and income. The trust terms may also indicate that one beneficiary is to be favored over others by providing that income is to be paid to one beneficiary for the beneficiary's lifetime. The Uniform Principal and Income Act § 102 (last revised and amended in 2008) broadens "terms of the trust" beyond the trust instrument itself to "intent of a settler . . . expressed in a manner that admits of its proof in a judicial proceeding, whether by written or spoken words or by conduct."

Second, legislation has been enacted to resolve many questions concerning the allocation or apportionment of principal and income. The Uniform Principal and Income Act has had several different forms. It was originally promulgated in 1931 and revised in 1962, 1997, and 2008.

Third, if the trust instrument gives the trustee discretion to determine what is income or principal (or if the trust instrument and underlying law are silent or obscure), the trustee is required to make the allocation or apportionment in a prudent manner consistent with the duty of impartiality between beneficiaries.

2. TRADITIONAL PRINCIPAL AND INCOME ISSUES

The Principal and Income Act, which was last amended or revised in 2008, set forth distinctions by which income and expenses could be allocated to or apportioned between principal and income. Among the earlier issues were the following:

a. Expenses

Section 201 of the Uniform Principal and Income Act provides, "paying from income or principal, in the fiduciary's discretion, fees of attorneys, accountants, and fiduciaries; court costs and other expenses of administration; and interest on death taxes, but the fiduciary may pay those expenses from income of property passing to a trust for which the fiduciary claims an estate tax marital or charitable deduction only to the extent that the payment of those expenses from income will not cause the reduction or loss of the deduction. These expenses were characterized by their relationship to either principal or income. Another group of expenses can be allocated or apportioned based upon their recurring or nonrecurring nature.

Generally, periodic expenses such as utilities were allocated to income (or apportioned between different income beneficiaries) while nonrecurring expenses such as estate taxes of the settlor were allocated to principal. Some periodic expenses (e.g., the trustee commissions, attorneys' fees, court costs) are for the benefit of both the principal and the income. Extraordinary expenses, such as lawsuits to defend the title to assets, were generally charged to principal.

b. Probate Administration Income

A testamentary trust of the residue of the settlor's estate necessitated the allocation and apportionment of all of the receipts and disbursements during the probate administration of the settlor's estate. Generally, the principal of the trust is the net principal after the payment of administration expenses, death taxes, debts (including accrued expenses), funeral and burial expenses, family allowances, exempt property and the spouse's forced share. The income earned during the administration of the estate, if not payable to the specific devisees, was treated as income of the trust by the Uniform Principal and Income Act.

c. Interest, Bond Premium and Discount

The apportionment of interest on a daily basis presented practically no problems. At common law, interest was deemed to accrue on a daily basis.

In the absence of legislation, courts did not require amortization of bond premium or discount for bonds which were initial trust investments, but did often require amortization when the trustee purchased the bonds at a premium or discount.

d. Dividends and Other Corporate Distributions

Ordinary cash dividends were clearly income and a single liquidating distribution in exchange for the stock of a corporation was clearly principal. The difficulties come with the items in between those two poles. Additionally, there were problems of successive beneficiaries in deciding when cash dividends were earned or whether a liquidating distribution includes any income element.

The Uniform Principal and Income Act provisions allocate by type of dividend: Stock of the issuing corporation is principal; cash and other property (including stock of other corporations) is income, regardless of when earned by the corporation. This resulted in a windfall to an income beneficiary in a corporate "spinoff" by which the shares of one corporation are distributed by another. In such a case, there was an impairment of the value of the principal and the income beneficiary is unduly benefited.

Corporate distributions which are the results of mergers, consolidations, acquisitions, reorganizations or liquidations are almost always principal. It may be difficult to determine whether a particular distribution is a partial liquidation or an extraordinary dividend.

e. Rents, Depreciation Reserves

An initial problem with rental income stems from the common law concept that the entire rent accrued on the date that it was due, rather than being apportioned on a daily basis. Despite the existence of the rule for determining rights between landlord and tenant, proration among trust beneficiaries tends to produce fairer results than allocating the entire rental income to the beneficiary who was entitled to the income on the date that the rental was due or was paid.

It is clear that the net rental received for the use of trust property should be allocated to the income beneficiary. In arriving at the net income, it is also clear that expenses directly attributable to the rental property (utilities, maintenance, repairs, real property taxes etc.) should be deducted from the gross rental. It is not clear whether a "depreciation reserve" should be created.

Unless the trust instrument provides otherwise, the trustee is under a duty to establish a depreciation reserve in order to preserve the value of the principal. Alternatively, the trustee may sell the property and invest in a proper trust investment which does not require a depreciation reserve.

f. Wasting Assets, Depletion

At common law, realty was generally considered to be the singularly indestructible asset with all other assets being "wasting" assets in the sense that they are used up in the production of income. Livestock were considered to be typical personalty of the wasting type.

Leasehold interests in land and the mineral rights in the land were also capable of being consumed.

Amortization can be "depreciation" or "depletion." Depreciation is the method of amortizing tangible property. If the property is intangible, "Depletion" serves the same purpose. Among the wasting assets (i.e., assets which are subject to depreciation or depletion) are copyrights, patents and franchises.

Some states recognize the "open mine" doctrine by which the trustee may allocate to income all receipts from an existing asset of a wasting nature (e.g., the settlor put an "open mine" into the trust).

The Uniform Principal and Income Acts section 402 provides rules for timber and section 411 for "minerals, water, and other natural resources." The trustee must account for receipts from an interest in minerals or other natural resources, including all rents and production payments as income. By contrast, if an amount received as a royalty, shut-in-well payment, take-or-pay payment, bonus, or delay rental is more than nominal, 90 percent must be allocated to principal and the balance to income.

As for timber, the trustee must allocate to income to the extent that the amount of timber removed from the land does not exceed the rate of growth of the timber during the accounting periods in which a beneficiary has a mandatory income interest. The trustee must allocate timber receipts to principal when the amount of timber removed from the land exceeds the rate of growth of the timber or the net receipts are from the sale of standing timber. The difference between whether the receipts should be allocated to income or principal ultimately derives from whether the timber was permanently removed beyond a standard rate of growth.

g. Unproductive and Underproductive Assets

Amortization (Depreciation and Depletion) is required for assets which produce so much in the way of receipts that it is questionable whether all the receipts are income. On the other hand, there are some assets which produce little (or no) income. These assets tend to favor the remainder person (who ultimately receives the wealth) over the life tenant (who would have received greater income from another investment).

Although most authorities agreed that the income beneficiary was entitled to a portion of the proceeds upon the ultimate sale by the trustee of an unproductive asset, there was substantial disagreement among the Restatement of Trusts and the Uniform Principal and Income Act as to whether there was a duty to sell what constituted "unproductive property," whether the rule applied to sales at a loss, and what should be the formula for computing the delayed income. This includes what percentage return should be allocated to income and when the period should commence.

3. CHANGES MADE BY THE CURRENT PRINCIPAL AND INCOME ACT

The Uniform Prudent Investor Act and Restatement of Trusts, Third, view the trust portfolio as a whole rather than focus on individual investments. They also permit tailoring of the investments to beneficiary needs. For example, tax-exempt municipal bonds would be appropriate for a high-bracket taxpayer, but improper for a charitable (and therefore tax-exempt) trust. The tradeoff in all investing between risk and return ("modern portfolio theory") is the trustee's central consideration. The Uniform Principal and Income Act takes the process one step further.

Section 104 of this Act grants the trustee power to adjust between principal and income "to the extent the trustee considers necessary if the trustee invests and manages trust assets as a prudent investor, [and] the terms of the trust describe the amount that may or must be distributed to a beneficiary by referring to the trust's income." The trustee must also determine that he or she is unable to comply with the terms of the trust as specified.

Section 104(b) directs the trustee to consider all factors relevant and itemizes a large number of factors to be considered "to the extent they are relevant." Adjustments cannot be made which would have an adverse tax effect, such as the federal estate tax marital deduction requirement that certain trusts pay income for life to the surviving spouse.

In making the allocation, the trustee must use reasonable care, skill and caution. The standard of prudence requires both loyalty to and impartiality among beneficiaries.

The statute does not purport to be prospective only (the traditional limitation of statutes), but rather attempts to fit the changes to the law under prior definitions. The net effect is that an "income only" beneficiary from a pre-existing document may receive principal amounts if the trustee decides that is an impartial allocation. In non-tax situations, the income beneficiary might not receive all of the trust income because of trustee "adjustments."

4. LIABILITIES AMONG BENEFICIARIES

Normally trust duties are owed by the trustee to the beneficiaries and few duties are owed by the beneficiaries to the trustee or to each other. The interest of a beneficiary in the trust may be subject to an equitable lien or charge because of a debt to the trust, including a debt resulting from a breach of trust. The breach of trust may be by a beneficiary who is also trustee or because of profit from or participation in a breach of trust or because the beneficiary agreed to be liable for a loss. An agreement by a beneficiary to create a debt to the trust or a lien against the beneficiary's trust interest is valid if there was no improper advantage taken of the beneficiary, the beneficiary is not under a legal incapacity and the trust does not contain an effective spendthrift clause.

If a beneficiary owes money to the trust, the trustee is under a duty to withhold payment to the beneficiary until the debt is eliminated. The trustee, however, cannot withhold payment or assert a lien against the share of the beneficiary in order to satisfy a debt owed to the trustee personally.

B. BENEFICIARIES VS. TRUSTEES

1. REMEDIES FOR BENEFICIARIES

Any beneficiary (contingent or vested) or group of beneficiaries can maintain an action against the trustee to enforce the trust. Although a guardian ad litem can maintain an action on behalf of a trust beneficiary who is under a legal disability, no person (including the settlor) other than a beneficiary can seek the assistance of the court of equity to enforce the trust. Although the beneficiary may also use a court of law to obtain a fixed sum or specific item which the trustee is under an immediate duty to pay or deliver, all other actions to enforce the trust are instituted in a court with equitable powers.

The trustee is liable to the beneficiaries for all breaches of trust duties and for profits made by the trustee in the administration of the trust even if there is no breach. The beneficiaries generally can choose from one or more of the following remedies, set out in Uniform Trust Code § 1001(b):

- Specific enforcement to compel the trustee to perform his or her duties;
- An injunction prohibiting the trustee from violating his or her duties;
- Compel the trustee to redress a breach of trust by paying money damages, restoring property, or other means;
- Order a trustee to account;

- Appoint a special fiduciary to take possession of the trust property and administer the trust;
- Suspend the trustee;
- Remove the trustee;
- Reduce or deny compensation to the trustee; and
- Void an act of the trustee, impose a lien or constructive trust on trust property, or trace trust property wrongfully disposed of and recover the property or its proceeds.

Some of these remedies, such as removal and denial of compensation, are usually only used in egregious cases. A court may also order any other relief deemed appropriate. Since a number of alternatives are available and any one or more of the beneficiaries can sue to enforce the trust, the court will accept the choice of all beneficiaries if they all have capacity and agree. If not, the court will generally impose the remedy which is most beneficial to the trust as a whole.

Beneficiaries generally have their choice of approach to the measure of damages by charging the breaching trustee with any one of the following:

a. Any loss resulting from the breach; or

b. Any profit made by the trustee in the breach; or

c. Any profit which would have accrued had there been no breach by the trustee.

The goal is to "restore the value of the trust property and trust distributions to what they would have been had the breach not occurred," according to Uniform Trust Code § 1002(a)(1). When the trustee's breach involves specific property, the beneficiaries are permitted to trace the specific property to restore it to the trust unless it has been acquired by a bona fide purchaser for value without notice of the breach of trust. The trustee may breach a duty to sell or not to sell, to buy or not to buy. In any of those breaches, the beneficiaries may affirm the action taken or may insist upon the profits (or item) which would have been in the trust if the trustee had performed his duties without a breach.

As a general rule, a trustee is not allowed to set off the losses incurred in one breach of trust by the gains made in another breach of trust, but the trustee is liable for only the net loss if the breaches are not separate and distinct. There is some uncertainty in this area as to which breaches are separate or the same. Among the factors which are considered in determining whether separate breaches have occurred are whether the same trust property is involved, whether successive dealings with the same property are involved, the time elapsed, timing of breaches and accountings by the trustee, the good or bad faith of the trustee (e.g., intention to misappropriate, intentional breach or inadvertent breach) and how consistently the trustee has dealt with the trust property.

> EXAMPLE: In breach of trust, Trustee invests the entire $50,000 of a trust in certain securities

which are not a proper trust investment because purchased from himself. He sells these securities for $30,000 and makes a proper investment in other securities, which are sold for $35,000. The proceeds are invested in a non-diversified and therefore improper investment, but sold for $55,000, a gain of $20,000. Neither the $5,000 gain on the proper investment nor the $20,000 gain on the improper investment is offset against the $20,000 loss on the first improper investment. The transactions are separate because of the time interval, the intervening investment and the general policy of not wishing to encourage the trustee to take further risks with the trust property in an effort to "break even."

Generally a trustee is not liable for the acts of a co-trustee or predecessor trustee unless the trustee knew or should have known of the breach by the other trustee, participated in it, or failed to take steps to rectify it upon discovery. For example, in *Matter of Rothko's Estate*, 372 N.E.2d 291 (N.Y. 1977), two of the trustees were held jointly and severally liable with two art galleries for $9,252,000, the value at the time of the trial of the Rothko paintings that were inappropriately sold. A third trustee's joint and several liability was "limited" to $6,464,880, the value of the paintings when sold (no appreciation damages) since he was not acting in his own self-interest in the transactions. A trustee is also liable for the acts of a co-trustee or an agent if the trustee improperly delegates the power or fails to exercise reasonable care in the supervision or (in the case of agents) selection of the agent.

2. TRUSTEE EXPENSES AND FEES

Section 709 of the Uniform Trust Code permits trustees to be reimbursed for their expenses, with interest as appropriate, out of trust property. Such expenses include those that were properly incurred in the administration of the trust, and those that were not properly incurred in the administration of the trust if necessary to prevent unjust enrichment of the trust. Should the trustee advance money for the protection of the trust, the trustee receives a lien against trust property to secure reimbursement with reasonable interest.

Trustee fees may be fixed by agreement, trust provision, statutory schedule or by the court supervising the trust. Modern corporate trustees generally have fee schedules which are adhesion contracts for most trusts, but tend to be negotiable in the case of multi-million dollar trusts. The schedule may be set out in the trust instrument or not. Even when not set out in the trust agreement, the corporate fee schedule tends to be enforced. If the trust agreement provides a fee schedule, that schedule will be followed unless it was the product of overreaching by the trustee or there are reasons for deviation, such as a change in circumstances which makes trust administration far more difficult.

Almost all jurisdictions have statutes which permit trustees to be compensated; more than half of them merely state that the trustee shall be entitled to "reasonable compensation." About a fourth of the states set out fee schedules, usually based upon the principal value or the income of the trust. These fee schedules are sometimes phrased as maximums.

Charges for various functions of the trustee may be imposed. A "set-up" fee may be requested for initial services and a "termination" fee for partial or complete terminal services. The main charge is usually an annual fee expressed as a percentage of principal (.5% to 1.00% is the common range) or income (5% is a common figure). The method of phrasing the base for the annual fee should not be confused with the allocation or apportionment of the expense to the principal or income account.

The trust or statute may simply provide that the trustee is entitled to "reasonable compensation." As a practical matter the size of the trust (or its income) is often very determinative, but writers traditionally state that the court in setting or approving the reasonable fees will consider, in addition to trust wealth, the skill and diligence of the trustee and the results of the trust administration.

Most jurisdictions allow the trustee extra compensation for extra services such as complicated sales of major trust assets, tax work or legal work. The risk of self-dealing is present when the trustee employs himself, herself or itself to perform a service which an independent agent (e.g., a realtor, accountant or attorney) could also perform.

Except in New York, multiple trustees (whether co-trustees or trustee and successor trustee) traditionally share a fee fixed by trust agreement or statute. In the jurisdictions where "reasonable" compensation is allowed, the fees are generally required to be based upon the services performed by each trustee and therefore tend to be more, in total, than the reasonable fee of one trustee.

If a trustee has breached trust duties, the court may, in its discretion, deny some or all compensation or grant some or all compensation. In fixing "reasonable compensation," the court may take the fidelity of the trustee into account. The court does not deny compensation in all cases. Normally there must be a serious breach of trust such as misappropriation, repudiation of the trust, intentional commingling of trust and personal assets or intentional failure to keep records and render accounts.

When the breach has been less serious, such as errors in judgment, failure to use skill and care or failure to diversify, the court is less likely to deny compensation. In theory, denial or reduction of compensation is not a penalty for the breach, but rather reflects the poor quality of the services rendered.

A trustee can waive, expressly or impliedly, the right to compensation. An implied waiver has been found in instances where the trustee distributed the principal or income of the trust without reserving funds for trustee's fees and later sought such fees from the beneficiaries. A change in circumstances on the part of the beneficiaries (or the death of the life tenant) would strengthen the case against a retroactive allowance of trustee's compensation.

3. INDEMNITY OF TRUSTEE

Uniform Probate Code § 7–306 makes the trustee personally liable "for obligations arising from ownership or control of property of the trust estate or for torts committed in the course of administration of the trust estate only if he is personally at fault." However, "a trustee is not personally liable on contracts properly entered into in his fiduciary capacity in the course of administration of the trust estate unless he fails to reveal his representative capacity and identify the trust estate in the contract." In these situations, the trustee is entitled to indemnity from the trust assets. Section 816(17) of the Uniform Trust Code provides that the trustee may exercise "the right to indemnification for expenses and against liabilities, and take appropriate action to collect the proceeds." The indemnity may be in any of the following forms:

- Paying the claim from trust assets. (Exoneration)
- Reimbursement from the trust assets to the trustee who pays the claim from the trustee's personal assets.
- Retaining trust assets (i.e., an equitable lien) until the trustee is repaid amounts owed.
- Obtaining a declaratory judgment in equity that a judgment obtained or about to be obtained at law against the trustee is against the trustee in that capacity and not individually.

- A small minority of states follow the English rule of permitting the trustee to obtain reimbursement from a trust beneficiary when the assets are inadequate. In most of those cases, special factors such as one or more of the following existed: The trust was created for a business purpose; there was an agreement by the beneficiary to reimburse; the beneficiary was also the settlor; or there had been a prior distribution to the beneficiary who had not subsequently changed his or her position.

The ability of the trustee to pay from trust assets or seek reimbursement, if not at fault or in breach of trust, is itself not a breach of the duty of loyalty even though the trustee is given a lien and a claim which is hostile to that of the beneficiaries. The trustee is not allowed indemnity if there is no benefit to the trust and the liability arose as a result of a breach of trust duty. If the trustee, in mistaken good faith, exceeded his powers in incurring an expense and some benefit accrues to the trust, the trustee is entitled to indemnification to the extent of the lower of the benefit to the trust or the amount expended.

EXAMPLE: Trustee properly employs a servant who negligently injures a third person. The trustee is liable to the third person upon the principle of *respondeat superior*, but is entitled to reimbursement from the trust estate. If the trustee had improperly employed the third person (or had committed an intentional tort), the trustee would remain liable, but would not be entitled to indemnity from the trust assets.

In a few states there has been a recognition of the trustee as a legal entity, but the majority still require the two-step process by which the liability is first imposed upon the trustee as an individual and then his right to indemnification is separately determined on a basis of whether he was acting properly or whether the trust derived any benefit from his mistaken actions if he was acting improperly. See Uniform Probate Code § 7–306.

C. RIGHTS OF THIRD PARTIES

1. TRUSTEE LIABILITY TO THIRD PARTIES

a. Classic Approach

At common law the trust and the trustee were not juristic entities. An action could be maintained only against a trustee individually. If the trustee was not in breach of trust and if the trust was solvent, the trustee could be indemnified from the trust assets.

Many states maintain this archaic distinction. A creditor of the trustee cannot have legal (as opposed to equitable) enforcement of a judgment against trust assets; he must attach or levy execution upon the personal assets of the trustee. Naturally, a number of exceptions have developed. All of the exceptions require that the third-party creditor seek enforcement in the court of equity. The following are the clearest of the exceptions which are recognized:

- The trustee would be entitled to exoneration, but does not have personal assets which the creditor can reach: For example, the trustee is bankrupt, dead or out of the jurisdiction.
- Even though the trustee was not entitled to exoneration (usually because he acted in breach of trust), a (typically contract claim) creditor may be allowed to reach trust assets to the extent a benefit was conferred upon the trust, unless other factors prevent such equitable relief.
- The terms of the trust provide for liability of the trust estate directly (usually simultaneously providing that the trustee shall not be personally liable): This provision is usually found in Massachusetts business trusts, but is relatively rare otherwise.
- The trustee specifically contracts with the third person that the third person shall look to the trust and not to the trustee personally. Courts disregard the self-dealing aspect of such contracts in order to fashion another exit from the uncomfortable rule of trustee liability. Most of the questions in this area stem from attempts to interpret a contractual term to see if the liability has been shifted from the trustee, individually, to the trust.

Signature "as trustee" alone is probably not enough to effect such a change in liability, while a clear statement that the third party agrees to look to the trust and not to the trustee personally for payment or a signature "as trustee and not personally" does permit and require the third party to look only to the trust assets. This can be disadvantageous to the creditor in situations where the trustee is more solvent than the trust.

A provision of this type may be ignored by a court of equity if the trustee has, by an unrelated breach of trust, diminished the trust estate so that it cannot satisfy the obligation. If the trustee purports to execute a contract as trustee and not individually, but does not have the authority to execute such a contract, the trustee is liable individually to the creditor for breach of the implied warranty of authority (and not on the contract itself, although that contract provides the measure of damages).

b. Uniform Trust Code § 1010

There has been a trend to seek other means of allowing a creditor to impose liability directly upon the trust assets without the intervening personal liability of the trustee. Uniform Trust Code § 1010 provides that except "as otherwise provided in the contract, a trustee is not personally liable on a contract properly entered into in the trustee's fiduciary capacity in the course of administering the trust if the trustee in the contract disclosed the fiduciary capacity." However, section 1010(b) holds a trustee "personally liable for torts committed in the course of administering a trust, or for obligations arising from ownership or control of trust property, including liability for violation of environmental law, only if the trustee is personally at fault."

2. BENEFICIARY LIABILITY TO THIRD PARTIES

Since the trustee's individual liability remains a shield to the trust in most jurisdictions, it follows that liability of the trust beneficiary to creditors of the trust is rarely found. The general rule is that a trust beneficiary is not liable for a contract, tort or other debts imposed purely because of the ownership of the property. The few exceptions to this American rule of no personal liability for debts of the trust are as follows:

- Specific agreement by the beneficiary (with the creditor or the trustee) to be liable. Commercial lenders therefore seek the "co-signature" of the beneficiary.
- Receipt by the beneficiary of all or substantially all of the trust assets from the trustee. Tracing of the assets is permitted unless they are in the hands of a bona fide purchaser for value without notice or unless the beneficiary has so changed position that it would be inequitable to hold the beneficiary personally liable.

3. THIRD PARTY LIABILITY TO TRUST

Third party participation in a breach of trust could arise whenever the third party pays money to a trustee or acquires trust property. Formerly there existed a duty on the part of any person paying money to a trustee to see that the funds were properly applied to trust purposes. This rule has been rejected or severely limited in almost all jurisdictions today.

A third person can purchase property from a trustee and acquire it free of trust if the sale is not in breach of trust. No duty exists to inquire as to the power of the trustee to transfer negotiable property, but the transferee of non-negotiable property from a trust is under a duty to inquire as to the power of the trustee to transfer the property.

Similarly, one who accepts trust property in payment of the trustee's personal debt is guilty of participation in a breach of trust. Beneficiaries may sue a transferee who is chargeable with notice of the trust, its terms or the breach of the terms jointly with the trustee.

The recipient of trust property sold in breach of trust receives it "subject to the trust" unless the recipient is (or claims through) a bona fide purchaser for value without notice. A transferee with notice can be compelled to restore the property to the trust or pay its value or its proceeds if the transferee has disposed of it.

The transferee is entitled to credit to the extent the transferee paid for the property and the trust has received the benefit of the payment. A donee of the property also must restore it (or its proceeds) to the trust, but is not required to surrender any gain or make up any loss resulting from a sale of the property.

Defenses to liability of the third-party participant in a breach of trust (or recipient, without consideration or with knowledge of the breach, of trust property transferred in breach of trust) include the following:

- Informed consent (or release) by the adult competent beneficiaries who would otherwise be able to maintain an action. The consent may be given before or after the act which would otherwise be a breach of trust.
- Estoppel by reason of an active or passive misrepresentation of a fact (such as the existence of a trust or the non-existence of the power to transfer) made by the beneficiary upon which the third party justifiably relied, will prevent the beneficiary from asserting the breach of trust.
- The statute of limitations may apply or the matter may have been reported to, and approved by, the court in an accounting.
- Laches—an unreasonable delay on the part of the beneficiary, which makes it more difficult or impossible for the defendant to make an adequate defense—will bar the remedy of the beneficiaries.

Third parties who deal with the trustee in a situation in which there is no breach of trust should ordinarily be sued by the trustee and not by the beneficiaries. The trustee insulates the beneficiaries from the need to participate in legal actions. Even under statutes requiring that legal actions be maintained in the name of the real party in interest, a trustee of an express trust may sue without the need to join the beneficiaries in the lawsuit.

If the trustee is unwilling or unable to bring suit, the beneficiaries are required to bring a suit in equity to compel the trustee to do the trustee's duty; to avoid circuity, the third parties may be joined in the equitable action by the beneficiaries.

Moreover, the Uniform Trust Code protects third parties in certain situations in their dealings with trustees. Section 1012, for example, shields a third party "who in good faith assists a trustee, or who in good faith and for value deals with a trustee, without knowledge that the trustee is exceeding or improperly exercising the trustee's powers is protected from liability as if the trustee properly exercised the power."

Further, under section 1012(b), a third party who in good faith deals with a trustee is not required to inquire into the extent of the trustee's powers or the propriety of their exercise. If this third person, in good faith, delivers assets to a trustee, the third party does not need to ensure their proper application. Finally, a third party who in good faith assists a former trustee or who in good faith and for value deals with a former trustee, without knowledge that a trusteeship has been terminated, is protected from liability as if the former trustee were still a trustee.

D. TERMINATION OR MODIFICATION OF A TRUST

A trust can be terminated or modified by any of the following occurrences.

First, a settlor who possesses the power of revocation can revoke under certain circumstances. At common law, a trust was irrevocable unless the settlor reserved the power to revoke. Uniform Trust Code § 602 provides: "Unless the terms of a trust expressly provide that the trust is irrevocable, the settlor may revoke or amend the trust." A trust is thus revocable unless the instrument expressly states that it is irrevocable.

Second, rescission or reformation of the transfer of property into trust is available on the same bases as rescissions or reformations of transfers of property generally—fraud, duress, undue influence or mistake.

Third, termination in accordance with the terms of the trust. Some trusts are designed to last for a specified period (such as eleven years) or until the happening of some event (such as the death of the life beneficiary). Additionally, the settlor may grant the trustee or a third person the power to terminate the trust.

Fourth, subsequent impracticality, impossibility or illegality may lead to the termination of a trust which was initially practical and legal, but which encountered difficulties which were not provided for by the settlor.

Fifth, consent of all beneficiaries (or their representatives) if no material trust purpose is defeated by the termination. A spendthrift provision in the trust may prevent such a consensual termination. The additional consent of the settlor permits termination despite the defeat of a material trust purpose.

Sixth, merger which occurs when the trustee and the beneficiary are the same person either because of the terms of the trust or conveyance of the entire beneficial interest to the sole trustee. The spendthrift trust sole beneficiary who becomes the sole trustee possesses the merged estates, but is said to have the power to reinstitute the spendthrift trust within a reasonable time or to take the property free of trust.

Upon termination or partial termination of the trust, the trustee may send the beneficiaries a proposal for distribution, according to Uniform Trust Code § 817. Any beneficiary may object to the proposed distribution within 30 days. This right of objection terminates if the beneficiary does not exercise it within the specified time period, so long as the original proposal informed the beneficiary of the right to object and the time permitted to object. The trustee must expeditiously distribute the trust property to those entitled, although he or she may keep a reasonable reserve for payment of debts, expenses, and taxes.

CHAPTER 13

PROBATE ADMINISTRATION

A. JURISDICTION OVER WILLS AND TRUSTS

Probate administration varies in procedures among states. The administration of a decedent's estate involves a process of passing certain landmarks. The process may be "formal" use of a petition to the court, notice to the interested parties and a court hearing resulting from a hearing. This can take two years or more. Informal probate, the most common form can take less time to complete. The probate court's jurisdiction will be specific to cover certain types of estates. In some jurisdictions, such as New Mexico, the Probate Court has jurisdiction over estates exceeding $50,000. Anything less than $50,000 is considered a small estate and the assets can be distributed more expeditiously, usually within six to nine months. The process may contain part or all of the following, each of which is usually represented by a document:

1. LETTERS TESTIMONY

A Letter of Testamentary, a Letter of Administration, or Letter of Representation is a document granted by a local court to the legal executor or personal representative for a particular estate, stating the person has the ability to act as such. Executor and personal representative tend to be used interchangeably as either have to be appointed by a court to administer an estate.

Typically an executor has been pre-named in a will while a personal representative may be appointed to administer an intestate estate.

The letters of the personal representative are the identification card by which the decedent's name is linked with the personal representative of the estate. Unless there is an emergency or a procedure by which letters can be obtained "ex parte" (without a notice of a hearing being served upon interested parties), the petition for letters is usually the opening round. Those who desire to contest the will usually must take action in a short period. If bond is to be required of a personal representative, the first occasion for posting it is upon "qualification" and the issuance of letters testamentary or letters of administration.

2. INVENTORY AND APPRAISAL

The personal representative or executor is expected to take an inventory of the decedent's assets. This inventory may be combined with an appraisal of the estate assets. This document can be completed by either the estate personal representative or executor. In instances involving large estates, an IRS officer may become involved in the inventory or appraisal as part of the tax determination process.

After artist Georgia O'Keeffe decide her estate became tied up in a dispute with the IRS over the appraisal of her art work. For tax purposes, the IRS seeks the highest valuation possible so the estate can become subject to taxation. The executor sought the lowest valuation possible. Appraising art of a famous person can be particularly challenging as to whether you value the art based on prices currently charged in galleries or do you seek a discount. Dumping a huge volume of art on the market can lead to declining prices.

Following Rothko's death in 1970 his estate composed primarily of 798 paintings became embroiled in a long dispute between his children and his executors. His executors were later removed after selling his art work at steep discounts and being charged with self-dealing. The record for a Rothko painting was set in 2012 when "Orange, Red, Yellow" sold for $86.9 million at Christies in New York.

3. CLAIMS BY CREDITORS

With the opening of formal probate, the personal representative must print, post or serve notice to the decedent's creditors. Each creditor (with varying exceptions, such as secured creditors) must present a formal statement of the amount of the claim within a specified period of the notice. Failure to comply with the deadlines can lead to a barring of creditor claims.

4. DEATH TAX

The estate of a dead person will be exempt from paying taxes on the first $12,060,000 of assets in 2022. This amount is adjusted for inflation yearly. The person in charge of the estate must check to see whether some or all of the assets are exempt from taxation, such as spousal gifts. Decedents can avoid paying taxes on additional assets above $12.06 million in 2022 by giving anything above that amount to charity. According to Investopedia.com, "In 2020, for example, just under 3.4 million Americans died from all causes. Of those, only 3,441 estates, or about 0.1%, had to file a Form 706, United States Estate (and Generation-Skipping Transfer) Tax Return. Of that number, just 1,275, or just under 0.04%, actually paid an estate tax." The bottom line is that vast majority of Americans do not pay estate taxes.

Only the exceedingly wealthy usually have estates subject to taxation. In 2010, Congress eliminated the estate tax for the year. When George Steinbrenner expired from a massive heart attack in Tampa, Florida on 13 January 2010, his family saved an estimated $500,000,000 in estate taxes. Had Steinbrenner died in 2020, his estate assets above $12.06 million exemption would have ben subjected to a maximum 40% federal taxation rate. Some states also charge estate or inheritance tax.

The United Kingdom exempts its monarch from having to pay taxes on inherited personal wealth. When Queen Elizabeth II passed away in 2022, her personal estate was valued at approximately $500 million. Because she was the monarch, her estate avoided having to pay the 40% UK inheritance tax rate, for a savings of approximately $200 million.

In the United States, if the federal estate tax is an elephant trap, catching only the largest of the estates, then the state death tax is more the octopus—interested in small and large prey and active in reaching out and attaching the assets of a decedent. For example, state death tax procedures may require an inspection of safe deposit boxes, may impose requirements for transfers of bank accounts and securities, and may have a local death tax lien on real property. Any of these must be satisfied before particular property can be transferred.

These federal and state estate taxes encourage testators and settlors to lower the amount of their estate potentially subjected to taxation. As the value of real estate soared in 2021, for example, many a testator or settlor with substantial property holdings changed their estate documents to give even more to their designated charities to lessen the value of their private gifts below $12 million so their estates would not be subjected to substantial death taxes.

5. ACCOUNTING

The personal representative must provide an accounting of the assets in the estate to the court and potential beneficiaries. He or she reports the items initially received and their value in the inventory and appraisal. The personal representative reports receipts, disbursements, sales and other changes during the period of estate administration (except changes in value) and shows the balance on hand for distribution.

6. RECEIPTS AND DISCHARGE

Once the court has authorized distribution of the assets of the estate to the beneficiaries, each must provide a receipt. These receipts are filed with the court. The personal representative then traditionally seeks termination of his appointment and discharge of himself from any further liability.

Under Uniform Probate Code § 2–1003, estates may be closed with the sworn statement of the personal representative filed with the appropriate court.

B. PROBATE COURT JURISDICTION OVER INCAPACITATED PERSONS

Under some state laws, any person can petition a court to place someone under temporary guardianship. While some jurisdictions require the petitioner to immediately notify all next of kin of the petition, others do not. This can result in strangers being appointed to handle the personal and financial affairs of a person with devastating results to the person's overall well-being.

A court may declare a person legally incapacitated and deserving of protection due to a variety of circumstances. A minor person under the age of 18 lacks legal capacity. A sixteen or seventeen year old can obtain legal capacity by petitioning an appropriate court to become an emancipated adult and having the court grant the petition.

An adult may become incapacitated due to mental illness, mental deficiency, mental disorder, physical illness or disability, chronic use of drugs, chronic intoxication, confinement, detention by a foreign power, or disappearance. Any of these circumstances can trigger a need for the continuing care and supervision of a guardian.

An example of foreign detention occurred after W.N.B.A. star Brittney Griner was detained in Russia in February 2022 on charges of having vape cartridges containing hashish oil in her luggage, a charge that can come with up to 10 years in prison. Griner became essentially (although not legally) incapacitated to manage her affairs in the United States. Her wife, Cherelle, whom she married in 2018, began managing her affairs and actively calling for the United States government to bring her home.

Legally appointed guardians can be of the person, of the estate, or both. Guardians of the person make decisions as to residence, medical care, and so forth. Guardians of the estate manage the financial affairs of the ward. Corporate fiduciaries will only accept a guardianship of the estate.

When individuals are appointed as guardian of the person, they may also seek or have thrust upon them an additional appointment as a conservator. This title is necessary to enable an individual guardian to manage the property and financial affairs of the incapacitated person.

1. POWERS OF ATTORNEY CAN AVOID PROBATE COURT JURISDICTION

In cases where a person is considered legally incapacitated by reason of age, a disability, or other dire circumstance mentioned above, a probate or other court, depending on the jurisdiction, may appoint a guardian, or conservator, or both. An adult can avoid this jurisdiction by carefully drafting a power of attorney to become effective upon incapacity and terminate upon recovery from illness or upon death. This is usually revocable at any time prior to death. It can be set up to spring into action once the attorney-in-fact obtains notarized statements from two qualified health care professionals, one of whom is usually a physician, as to the principal's incapacity. This is often defined as the inability to effectively manage personal care, property or financial affairs.

In a power of attorney document, the person can specify a person, such as a husband, sibling or child, be appointed as guardian or conservator of the person or estate in the event it becomes necessary. During the principal's incapacity, the attorney-in-fact shall have the power to act in the principal's name.

Powers of attorney save time and money. The case of *Sarhan v. Rothenberg*, 2008 WL 2474645 (2008), presents an example of a situation that could have been avoided had there been a power of attorney. A son challenged a court's finding of incapacity for his elderly mother and appointing a guardian over her. The son also alleged that a probate judge acted unlawfully when he appointed the same attorney to represent his mother as to represent her guardian.

The son filed a petition that sought to rescind the guardianship over his mother, arguing that the appointment was based on fraud, and that all assets and property be returned to their rightful owner (his mother) prior to the guardianship appointment. In addition to this relief, the son sought $100,000,000 in punitive damages for the alleged fraud. The court dismissed his petition, finding that the son lacked standing to bring a petition on his mother's behalf because he was not her legal guardian. Had the mother established a power of attorney before her incapacity, her son would have had standing to protect her interests in court.

To obtain legal guardianship and conservatorship over a minor or disabled person through the court system can involve an extensive investment of time and cash in the legal system. As a guardian, a person becomes responsible for managing the ward's personal affairs, including dealing with doctors, nurses, case managers, and dietitians.

As the ward's conservator, a person will manage the ward's assets, including qualifying the ward for Social Security disability insurance and Medicaid if necessary and obtaining control over bank accounts and real estate. The conservator must also file, if appropriate, any tax forms with the IRS on behalf of the ward and is qualified to negotiate with the IRS on behalf of the ward for any late taxes.

The court costs and attorneys' fees can be expensive. If the attorney is not retained on a flat-fee basis, the prospective guardian may be billed in six-minute increments, meaning every time the attorney reads a two-lined email, a cryptic text message, or listens to a 30-second phone message, the prospective guardian will be charged for six minutes of the attorney's time.

In situations where the person is of means, several people may want to serve as guardian and conservator, perhaps triggering jurisdictional conflicts. If the potential ward is not of means, then he or she will be lucky if there is someone who loves him or her enough to take on this role. If there are no volunteers, the court may appoint a professional.

A guardianship case involving multiple individuals seeking guardianship concerned socialite Brooke Astor, an author who had married the son of John Jacob Astor IV, who was the richest person in the world when he perished on the Titanic in 1912. Around 2006, Astor's grandson Philip Cryan Marshall, a historic preservationist and associate professor at Roger Williams University, filed a lawsuit seeking to remove his father Anthony Dryden Marshall as Astor's guardian, and replace him with Annette de la Renta, a friend to Mrs. Astor and the wife of fashion designer Oscar de la Renta. Astor's grandson's suit alleged that Anthony D. Marshall was not providing for Astor, who suffered from Alzheimer's disease. The suit further alleged that Anthony Marshall was using the income from Astor's estate to support his lavish lifestyle.

Affidavits supporting a change in guardianship were written by Annette de la Renta, Henry Kissinger and David Rockefeller. The New York Supreme Court appointed de la Renta guardian and JP Morgan Chase & Co. in charge of her financial affairs. On July 29, 2006, Astor was moved from Lenox Hill Hospital to her estate Holly Hill in the village of Briarcliff Manor, New York.

Brooke Astor died at age 105 on August 13, 2007 at her home in Briarcliff Manor, New York. On November 27, 2007, Anthony Marshall and his attorney Francis X. Morrissey Jr. were indicted on charges of grand larceny, criminal possession of stolen property, forgery, scheming to defraud, falsifying business records, offering a false instrument for filing, and conspiracy to plunder Brooke Astor's $198 million estate. Anthony Marshall was convicted on October 9, 2009, of fourteen criminal counts, including fraud and one of two charges of grand larceny. Morrisey was convicted of forgery.

In *In re Astor*, 62 A.D.3d 867 (N.Y. 2009), Anthony Marshall sought to stay discovery related to the probate of several purported wills pending the resolution of related criminal proceeding against him, but the court denied his request. Brooke Astor executed more than 30 different wills and codicils over a period of 50 years. In the lower case of *In re Estate of Astor*, 18 Misc.3d 1124 (N.Y.Sur.2008), JP Morgan Chase N.A and Annette de la Renta filed a petition for the probate of the 1997 instruments, Anthony Marshall filed a petition for the probate of the 2002 instrument and its first two codicils only, and Philip Marshall filed a petition for the probate of the 1997 instruments.

The various petitions and the case resolved on March 28, 2012, when the parties reached a global settlement that was accepted by the Judge. As a result, Anthony Marshall had his inheritance cut to $14.5 million from about $31 million.

2. JURISDICTIONAL CONFLICTS OVER GUARDIANSHIP

The Uniform Adult Guardianship and Protective Proceedings Jurisdiction Act (Uniform Adult Guardianship Act) was drafted in 2007 by the Uniform Law Commission to address areas of guardianship and protective proceedings for both vulnerable minors and adults. As of 2022, 49 of 53 potential jurisdictions (including the District of Columbia and Puerto Rico) had adopted the Uniform Adult Guardianship Act. The four jurisdictions that had yet to adopt the Act included Florida, Kansas, Michigan, and Texas.

Guardianship is a state law issue. Because even after adopting the Act, states can vary its terms. Consequently there are more than 50 different guardianship systems in the United States. The Uniform Adult Guardianship Act attempts to provide uniformity in resolving guardianship and protective proceedings issues in three main areas. First, it provides a mechanism to resolve multi-jurisdictional disputes that arise when there is a question as to the state of the adult's domicile. This is accomplished by creating a standardized priority of domicile for jurisdiction. The order of priority begins with the home state, followed by a significant connection state. The Act clearly defines each.

Section 201(a)(2) defines "home state" as "the state which the individual was physically present, including any period of temporary absence, for at least six consecutive months immediately before the filing of a petition for a protective order or appointment of a guardian". Section 201(a)(3) considers a "significant-connection state" as the one in which the individual has a significant connection other than physical presence, and where significant evidence related to the individual may be located.

Four factors qualify a jurisdiction as a significant-connection state. These include the location of the individual's family, the length of time the individual was physically present in the state, the location of the individual's property, and the extent of other ties to the state such as voter registration, filing tax returns, driver's license, social relationships and receipt of services.

Second, it also seeks to resolve problems that exist without a dispute, such as an attempt to transfer a guardianship from one jurisdiction to another. This problem occurs when parties agree to transfer an existing guardianship or conservatorship, but there is no streamlined procedure for accepting such a transfer. As a result parties have to repeat all of the procedures for an original appointment in a new state, which is often time consuming and expensive.

For example, *Teresa L. v. Sauk County*, 514 N.W.2d 424 (Wis. Ct. App. 1993), involved a middle aged man who while temporarily working in Florida suffered an accident that rendered him totally incapacitated. Dade County appointed a stranger as his guardian ad litem. His ex-wife Teresa petitioned to be appointed guardian in Sauk County, Wisconsin, but the Wisconsin court refused because there was another guardian in Florida. The Dade County Court told the guardian he could petition for termination of the guardianship once Wisconsin had appointed a guardian. The court noted that Wisconsin did not lose its authority over Jimmie L merely because he was temporarily absent from the state.

One footnote pointed out that the Uniform Adult Guardianship Act § 203(1) could have resolved the matter by granting jurisdiction to the man's home state of Wisconsin had both states adopted the Act at the time. Wisconsin eventually adopted the Act in 2018, and Florida introduced the bill of adoption in 2022 but it died in the Rules Committee.

The third area the Uniform Adult Guardianship Act addresses is that of out of state recognition. Guardianship and protective proceedings are an exception to the full faith and credit clause in Article IV, Section I of the U.S. Constitution that requires court orders from one state be honored by another. Because of this exception, sometimes one state's registration of a guardianship or protective order is not recognized in a neighboring state, and proceedings must be repeated.

The Uniform Adult Guardianship Act is organized into five articles. Article one consists of definitions used throughout the Act, designed to be adopted by courts in different states, such as the previously mentioned definitions of "home state" and "significant connection states."

Article 2 establishes a three-level priority for guardianship jurisdiction among states. The highest priority for guardianship or conservatorship is given to the court in the individual's home state, followed by the court or courts in one or more significant connection states. If the court in the home state and in a significant connection state declines jurisdiction, than a court in any other state may claim jurisdiction.

Article 3 provides a procedure for transferring an existing guardianship or conservatorship to another state. To execute a transfer, the transferring court must determine that the incapacitated person is physically present or reasonably expected to soon move permanently to another state, and that adequate arrangements have been made for the incapacitated person's care in the other state.

In re the Guardianship of Jane E.P., 283 Wis.2d 258, 261, 700 N.W.2d 863, 865 (Wis. 2005), exemplifies a case that could have been more easily resolved if the two involved states had adopted the Uniform Adult Guardianship Act. It involved a woman who became incapacitated, leading to the appointment of her sister as her guardian in Illinois. Jane resided in an Illinois nursing home for five years. Almost all of her family, including her guardian, lived across the border in Wisconsin. Her family wanted to move her to a nursing home in Wisconsin. They initiated a new guardianship proceeding in Wisconsin, which was initially dismissed because Wisconsin law required Jane to be a resident of Wisconsin before the proceeding could continue. This situation created a difficult problem for the family and the courts. Jane could not become a resident of Wisconsin without first moving there, but she could not move to Wisconsin without the consent of a Wisconsin guardian.

Since the Uniform Guardianship Act provides for specific transfer procedures, its adoption could have remedied this situation without prolonged litigation. If both states were adopters, Jane's sister who was already appointed her guardian in Illinois would file a petition with an Illinois court to transfer the guardianship to Wisconsin under § 301(a). She would need to provide notice to all interested parties, and the Illinois court would be required to hold a hearing under § 301(b). The court must provisionally grant the transfer so long as the court finds the incapacitated person is reasonably expected to move to the other state. In this case, the court could have found Jane was going to become a permanent resident of Wisconsin. After Jane's sister received the provisional order granting transfer in Illinois, she would take it to a Wisconsin court and petition it to accept the transfer.

Article 4 authorizes a guardian or conservator to register protective orders in other states, which allow the exercise of all powers authorized by the orders except those expressly prohibited by law of the registration state. Article 5 consists of miscellaneous provisions, including sections that call for uniformity of application and construction, the use of electronic signatures, repeals, transitional provision, and the effective date of enactment.

The Adult Guardianship Act, along with the Uniform Probate Code, the Uniform Trust Act, and the Uniform Principal and Income Act are examples of attempts to unify laws in the wills and trusts area.

INDEX

References are to Pages

(This list is not exhaustive. Some references may have been listed only in passing in the text.)
